John Paul Jones

To my parents, who dreamed the life I've led.

Contents

Foreword

John Paul Jones! There's a name to conjure with. So much so, that writers have tried to co-opt his resounding achievements as a great American patriot and sea warrior to express their own views on "life, liberty and the pursuit of happiness." But Jones was a person with strong convictions on living up to these themes of the young American republic, and he was an important player in how those themes played out in a most improbable chapter of history. Admiral Callo makes this clear in this incisive and enlightening portrayal of the man in action, in which Jones speaks for himself, in word and deed.

Jones's message has been blurred by over-handling during the nineteenth century and the first half of the twentieth century, notwithstanding President Theodore Roosevelt's admonition, "Every officer should know by heart the deeds of John Paul Jones." In truth, Jones's earlier champions erected a plaster saint, and more recently, others have picked up on his very large ego, quick temper, and his sometimes callous treatment of female admirers to create the image of a bully and social eccentric.

Jones was admittedly a difficult man. Difficult to put up with, if you were his friend. Very difficult to understand, if you wanted to get close to him. And, fortunately for America, difficult—almost impossible—to beat if it was your fate to be his opponent in battle. In fact, few could accept Jones on his own terms, which were often outrageously demanding. As a result he was easily outmaneuvered by lesser men in the politics of advancement and recognition by which people make their careers.

In the crucial instances where he forced things to go his way, he did things that shook the world as people knew it. And if he had not done that, the world—or certainly America and not least the United States Navy—would not be what they are today.

One of the most moving letters in this book is from his supporter Benjamin Franklin, who quietly but firmly urged Jones to be less loud in his own praise and in disparaging of the poor performance of others, so that he'd have a better chance of getting his own views across. Fat chance. One wishes Jones could have had a stern but kindly father figure in his naval service, as Nelson had John Jervis, to chide him and advise him and then stand back and give his genius free rein.

One fault Jones has lately been accused of—financial greed—he absolutely did not have. A recent commentator condescendingly compared him to Jesse James, the famous Western bandit. The problem with this is that the commentator had his facts wrong. The fact is that Jones regularly refused the easy option of sailing as a privateer, which could have made him both rich and famous. He refused this option because he chose to serve in the Continental Navy. Navy service was not a well-paid job, and it had nothing in common with armed robbery. Jones's raids on British towns were, among other things, reprisals for actions by British forces burning American towns to bully the inhabitants into line, as even one British newspaper noted at the time. In his naval service Jones never deliberately killed a single civilian. That renders absurd the notion, recently suggested, that Jones had anything in common with today's terrorists.

The victories that earned Jones his recognition were hard fought. And it took Jones to win them—it's just not possible to imagine any other captain carrying off the feats he did. Imagine taking a worn-out French East Indiaman, the *Duc de Duras*, renaming her the *Bonhomme Richard*, arming her with cast-off guns, and taking her to sea with a polyglot pickup crew to overwhelm and capture a first-class British frigate of the heaviest class, just short of ship of the line status. This would seem more than a little unlikely, but it happened.

What made this near miracle possible? For starters, Jones had a freer hand than in the past to train the crew, and he trained them well and commanded their respect. But that crew couldn't have done it without the invincible resolve of Jones. To that resolve was added his unfailing ability to snatch every advantage possible in a rapidly changing devastating encounter in which his own ship suffered more casualties than his hard-fighting British opponent did. Joe Callo takes you through those fraught developments to show just how the incredible victory of *Bonhomme Richard* over HMS *Serapis* was won and what it meant.

The change of name from *Duc de Duras* to *Bonhomme Richard* is a vital part of the story and at the epicenter of Jones's stormy resolve. America's French allies, who provided the old ship and her armament, were intent on having her serve under French naval orders. Benjamin Franklin, one of the American commissioners to France living in Paris, had an international reputation and was made much of by the French court. He used his arts of persuasion and sweet reason to arrange freedom for the tempestuous Jones to act as representative of a free republic, rather than one subservient to the French crown. Franklin reminded Jones as he did so that the American bargaining position was weak, the nation having virtually no funds and little credit but what the French saw fit to grant them. So there was solid pragmatic reason behind Jones's choice of name for the *Bonhomme Richard*—she was named for Poor Richard, the pseudonymous author of Franklin's famed *Almanac.*

Look deeper and a more profound reason for the choice of name appears. I believe that Jones's choice was more significant than a mere thank you to Franklin for help in securing the frigate. Poor Richard, or Bonhomme Richard, was a uniquely American name, and a practical, serviceable one at that. A Poor Richard could speak for America—as she did eloquently at the battle off Flamborough Head—as no *Duc of Duras* ever could. Poor Richard was an expression of the American ethos.

Jones's feats in carrying the war to the shores of the greatest naval power in the world played a vital role in winning the American Revolution. The British losses in ships and men, and their forced diversion of ships and men to catch Jones, were costly to the enemy. But far more important was the impact on public opinion, above all among Americans themselves—still divided in the 1770s, still unsure of their ability to defeat an enemy all-powerful at sea. And the effect on British public opinion was monumental. Edmund Burke in Parliament had been leading the charge that Americans were fighting for British rights. Admiral Lord Richard Howe, leader of the large invasion force assigned to conquer New York, proceeding cautiously from the outset, had resigned when he saw that Americans were determined to fight for their freedom. He returned to London to use his considerable influence to end the war. Jones's victories underlined the truth of Howe's findings, as nothing else could. While much of the British press reviled Jones as a pirate, other newspapers spoke up in his defense. So the strategic effect of Jones's victories had a compelling ultimate role in encouraging Britain to opt out of the war after Washington's army, with French support and naval intervention, brought about the strategic victory at the battle of Yorktown in 1781.

Jones never commanded large squadrons or fleets in the Continental Navy. The one good-sized squadron he did command—the one formed around the *Bonhomme Richard*—fragmented when the strongest ship in it, the new frigate *Alliance*, under the command of a strange character named Pierre Landais, stood out of the battle between *Bonhomme Richard* and *Serapis*, except to fire broadsides into both combatants, killing more Americans than Britons.

Jones, however, achieved the remarkable feat of using his single ships to strategic effect! His lone taking of a British sloop in the *Ranger* and his lone overcoming of HMS *Serapis* in *Bonhomme Richard* put heart in the pro-American forces in Britain. These were rude shocks that, combined with Washington's victory at Yorktown, helped to force Lord North's resignation as prime minister and brought to power a British ministry resolved on peace. This was an unparalleled achievement on the world stage, carried out by a few hundred men carrying the fight to the enemy's doorstep under a captain who achieved his results by his leadership, tactical skill, and unmatched will to win.

When at length Jones returned to America, he failed for various reasons to get a ship to sea under his command. He later got himself assigned to a French battle fleet to learn fleet maneuvers. He believed that America would have in the not-too-distant future the strongest "marine" in the world—a word that encompasses both naval and merchant ships.

His one experience with fleet command was as rear admiral in command of a Russian fleet fighting to clear the Turks from the north shore of the Black Sea. In a way this experience epitomized his career of stunning achievement at sea and dismal failure ashore. Jones's adventure as rear admiral in Catherine the Great's navy was a picaresque political saga. He inspired previously poorly led Russian sailors to new heights, and from one of them, who rowed Jones in a small boat to reconnoiter the opposing Turkish fleet, we learn that Jones chalked on the stern of a major enemy ship a bold and defiant message. This message, as Callo points out, had a serious purpose: to instill in Russian hearts the conviction that the Turks, who had for centuries defeated all Russian attempts to gain the north shore of the Black Sea, did not stand ten feet tall and could be defeated.

For war was serious business to Jones. He was well aware of its cost in human life and suffering, and he always took the lead in exposing himself to danger, never asking his crews to do anything he did not do himself. His battles with bureaucrats on his crews' behalf show his concern with the well-being of the men who served under him. With rare exceptions, Jones's problems stemmed from people he had to report to (or sometimes people who wanted his job), and from his manifest inability to follow the precepts in the letter his friend and protector Ben Franklin wrote him on his dealings with others.

But enough passing of judgments on a person who contributed so much to the cause of freedom to America, a nation he never ceased to hold first in his affections. In the book before you, Admiral Callo takes us to sea with Jones, with the perspective of a naval leader with more than thirty years of experience as a reserve officer and a seaman with far-ranging experience under sail, including three hurricanes at sea. And above all is his strong devotion to seeking out the factual basis of history. Callo singles out the points of decision that defined Jones's life and career, and beyond that, I believe he gets to Jones's core purpose.

So let's single up our lines and then cast off to follow the course of the man who was never humble but in service to his cause. I can think of no more fitting message for the voyage than the one Jones himself inscribed to his high-spirited friend the Marquis de Lafayette, written aboard the *Bonhomme Richard* as she was about to leave Lorient on the voyage that ended with her immortal fight with *Serapis*.

"I expect to leave this evening," wrote John Paul Jones, "and you will perhaps hear of me soon."

Peter Stanford
President Emeritus
National Maritime Historical Society

Acknowledgments

I thank Tom Cutler for his encouragement and wise counsel on this project. I am also indebted to those who believed that the time had come to view John Paul Jones primarily as a professional naval officer, including: Mark Gatlin, Fred Rainbow, and Tom Wilkerson.

The professional input of Jim Cheevers and John Reilly at key points in this project had a lot to do with keeping things on track. Janelle Rohr's superb copyediting brought order, and Linda O'Doughda, managing editor at Naval Institute Press, guided production skillfully.

And finally, I thank my wife, Sally, for providing innumerable sanity checks and constant encouragement along the way.

Chronology

1747	
6 July	Born as John Paul at Arbigland, Scotland.
1761(?)	Apprenticed to the merchant ship *Friendship*, an armed brig of approximately 180 tons.
1766	Appointed first mate in 30-ton brigantine *Two Friends*, a merchantman out of Kingston, Jamaica, engaged in the slave trade.
1768	Returned to Scotland in the 60-ton brigantine *John*, merchantman from Liverpool; took over command of that ship when the master and chief mate died of natural causes; appointed master and supercargo of that ship.
1769	Departed for the West Indies as captain of *John*.
1771	
April	Ended assignment as master of merchant ship *John*. Took up local trading between Whitehaven and the Isle of Man.
1772	
October	Appointed master of the full-rigged ship *Betsy*, out of London.
1773	
October	Left the merchant ship *Betsy* after killing a seaman in an altercation while in Tobago. Fled to Virginia.
1775	
Late November–early December	Assigned to lead the fitting out in Philadelphia of the former merchantman *Black Prince* to become the Continental ship *Alfred*.
3 December	Raised one of the versions of the new American flag (thirteen stripes with the crosses of St. George and St. Andrews in the upper left corner) in the ship *Alfred*. It was the first time an American flag was flown in a Continental Navy vessel.

7 December	Secured preliminary appointment as a lieutenant in the Continental Navy.
22 December	Appointment of Jones as a lieutenant in the Continental Navy confirmed by the Continental Congress.

1776

3 March	Participated in the attack on New Providence (now Nassau) in the Bahamas (first combined navy-marine amphibious assault in American history).
10 May	Appointed to command the ten-gun sloop of war *Providence*.
21 August	Deployed from Philadelphia as captain of *Providence*, on independent mission against British merchant shipping off the coasts of the thirteen American colonies and Canada.
8 October	Successfully completed independent mission in *Providence* and returned to Narragansett Bay.
10 October	Appointed to the permanent rank of captain in the Continental Navy.
1 November	Deployed from Providence, Rhode Island, in *Alfred*, accompanied by *Providence*, on independent mission to raid Cape Breton, Nova Scotia, and to attack British shipping off the Canadian coast.
15 December	Successfully completed mission in *Alfred* and returned to Boston harbor.

1777

14 June	Ordered to command of the Continental ship *Ranger*.
1 November	Departed from Portsmouth, New Hampshire, for France in *Ranger*.
22 December	Arrived in Nantes, France.
December	Traveled to Paris to meet American Commissioner Benjamin Franklin, and learned that he had lost the opportunity to comand the new frigate *L'Indien*.

1778

28 January	Returned to Nantes.
14 February	Entered Quiberon Bay, France, in *Ranger* and exchanged official salutes with the French ship *Robuste*, marking the first official foreign salute of the American Stars and Stripes.
10 April	Began his first cruise against British commerce in British home waters.

22–23 April	Raided the port of Whitehaven on the west coast of England while commanding the Continental ship *Ranger*.
23 April	Raided the home of the Earl of Selkirk on St. Mary's Isle, failing to abduct the earl. Allowed the raiding party to loot the family silver from the manor.
24 April	Defeated and captured HMS *Drake* in one-on-one battle.
8 May	Returned to Brest, France, with his prize, HMS *Drake*.

1779

February	Secured command of the former French East Indiaman, *Duc de Duras*, and renamed her *Bonhomme Richard*.
19 June	Departed from Brest, France, in *Bonhomme Richard* for duty escorting French merchant ships in the Bay of Biscay.
1 July	Returned to Lorient.
14 August	Departed from Lorient's outer anchorage in *Bonhomme Richard*, accompanied by two small frigates, a corvette, and a cutter. The French had placed the squadron under Jones's command and the American flag for commerce raiding off the coasts of the British Isles and raids on ports along those coasts.
23 August	Arrived off Dingle Bay at the southwest corner of Ireland and began a cruise up the west coast of Ireland, around the north of Scotland, and down the east coast of Scotland and England, taking British merchant ships and creating alarms all along the coastlines.
23 September	Fought and won a single-ship action against HMS *Serapis* off Flamborough Head, England.
25 September	The Continental ship *Bonhomme Richard* sank as a result of battle damage during the Battle off Flamborough Head. Jones tranferred his commodore's flag to the captured *Serapis*.
3 October	Arrived in the Texel, Holland, in the badly crippled *Serapis* and with the ships of his squadron, *Alliance, Pallas*, and *Vengeance* in company.
November	Shifted commodore's flag to *Alliance*, as French retake control of French ships that had been placed under Jones's command and the American flag the previous August.
27 December	Escaped from the blockading British squadron off Texel in the Continental ship *Alliance* and sailed southwest, directly down the English Channel and into the Bay of Biscay to hunt for British merchantmen.

1780

16 January	Put into La Coruña, Spain, for resupply and repairs.
27 January	Departed from La Coruña for Lorient.
19 February	Anchored in Lorient.
17 April	Arrived in Paris.
May	Informed that Louis XVI would award the French Cross of Military Merit (with the title of Chevalier) and gold-hilt ceremonial sword to him.
1 June	Ordered back to Lorient to get the Continental frigate *Alliance* under way for America as soon as possible.
Early June	Lost command of *Alliance* to her former commanding officer, Captain Pierre Landais, and subsequently placed in command of the Continental sloop of war *Ariel*.
7 October	Departed from Lorient for America in command of *Ariel*. Struck immediately by a major storm.
12 October	Returned to Lorient with dismasted *Ariel*.
18 December	Departed from Lorient for America in command of repaired *Ariel*.

1781

18 February	Arrived at Philadelphia in *Ariel*.
14 April	Commended by Congress for his deployments in *Ranger*, *Bonhomme Richard*, *Alliance*, and *Ariel*.

1782

26 June	Appointed to command of the Continental Navy ship of the line *America* and designated to complete construction of that ship at Portsmouth, New Hampshire.
4 September	Notified that Congress would present *America* to the French Navy as a gift.
30 November	Signing in Paris of provisional articles ending the American Revolution.
4 December	Assigned to the fleet of the French admiral, the Marquis de Vaudreuil, as a pilot and active observer of fleet operations.

1783

18 May	Arrived in Philadelphia in ill health.
August	Health restored.
3 September	American Revolution ended officially with the signing of the Treaty of Paris of 1783.

10 October	Summarized his accomplishments in a letter to Agent of Marine and civilian head of the Continental Navy in Congress, Robert Morris.
13 October	Applied for position as agent in Europe for prizes taken during his deployments.
1 November	Appointed prize agent in Europe.
10 November	Departed for France in the merchant packet *General Washington.*
6 December	Arrived in Paris after detour through London.
17 December	Authorized by Ambassador Franklin to receive prize money due to officers and men of his squadrons during deployments from France.

1785

3 June	Continental Navy ended with Congress's authorization of the sale of *Alliance,* America's only remaining naval ship.
15 July	All prize monies due Jones, his officers, and men from his deployments from France ordered to be paid to Jones.
September	Partial payment of prize money to Jones.

1787

Spring	Departed from Paris for Copenhagen; trip was cut short, departed for America.
July	Arrived in New York City.
11 October	Congress approved payment of prize money by America.
16 October	Received a special gold medal from the U.S. Congress.
11 November	Departed from New York for Europe.
December	Arrived in Dover, traveled to London then to Paris. Resumed efforts to secure prize money from Danish government for three captured ships sent into Bergen in 1779. Learned of Russian interest in having him command their Black Sea Fleet.

1788

24 January	Received credentials as agent to Denmark to negotiate prize money.
4 March	Arrived in Copenhagen.
18 April	Assignment in Denmark terminated.
Spring	Offered commission in Russian military.
April	Arrived in Saint Petersburg.
25 April	Met with Russian Empress Catherine II.
19 May	Ordered to command a Russian fleet in the Liman of the Dnieper River.

26 May	Hoisted his personal flag as a rear admiral in the Russian ship of the line *Vladimir*.
June	Led Russian fleet during the Battles of the Liman at the mouth of the Dnieper River.
October	Relieved of command of Russian squadron.
31 December	Arrived in Saint Petersburg.

1789

April	Arrived in England on private business.
May	Returned to Paris.
September	Left Saint Petersburg for Warsaw, traveled through Europe.

1791

November	Published Treatise on the Existing State of the French Navy.

1792

1 June	Appointed U.S. commissioner to negotiate release of U.S. prisoners with the Dey of Algiers.
18 July	Died in Paris.
20 July	Buried in St. Louis Cemetery, outside Paris.

1794

2 January	United States Navy established by Congressional legislation to protect U.S. merchant ships and sailors.

1905

31 March	Casket that possibly contains Jones's body discovered after years of searching.
7 April	The body of Jones preliminarily identified and removed for scientific verification that the remains are Jones's.
6 July	A celebratory service held at American Church of the Holy Trinity in Paris for the recovery of Jones's remains.
8 July	The cruiser USS *Brooklyn* with Jones's remains departed from Cherbourg, France, for the United States.
23 July	The remains of John Paul Jones arrived at Annapolis, Maryland.
24 July	The remains body of Jones placed in a brick vault on the grounds of the U.S. Naval Academy.

1906

24 April — Commemorative ceremonies at U.S. Naval Academy mark the return of Jones's remains to the United States.

1913

26 January — Body of John Paul Jones interred in a place of honor in the U.S. Naval Academy Chapel.

John Paul Jones

Introduction

John Paul Jones captured the essential idea of the American Revolution before he captured a single British ship. His naval service, unlike that of most officers of the leading navies of his time, was not a matter of family tradition or of seeking a respectable career. And unlike that of many of the American privateers of the War of Independence, it was not a matter of money. It was mostly a matter of fighting for liberty.

Unfortunately, that principal aspect of Jones's naval exploits and other underappreciated circumstances of his astonishing career are being lost. One recent biography of Jones says, for example, that "ambition—ever present, all-consuming, and limitless—was his most defining characteristic." That characterization is simply wrong. No person driven primarily by personal ambition could have achieved what Jones accomplished. There had to be something more powerful at the core of his personality, something that drove him through life-threatening combat and career-threatening political crosscurrents in both America and Europe.

Jones had embraced the proposition articulated by Lord Acton: "Liberty is not a means to a higher political end. It is itself the highest political end."[1] And when he went into battle to fulfill what he and many of his colonial American contemporaries considered a transcending mission, he had an urgency that was closely tied to his basic motivation. In October 1776, Jones described those feelings with verbal economy in a letter to Robert Morris, a member of the Continental Congress: "The situation of America is new in the annals of mankind, her affairs cry haste, and speed must answer them."[2]

Jones's letter, written from the cramped captain's cabin in the converted merchantman he had sailed aggressively against Britain's maritime power, recorded an impressive score: "I have taken sixteen sail—manned and sent in eight prizes, and sunk, burnt, or destroyed the rest." He then went on to list the ships captured and destroyed. The tally was remarkable in light of the conditions of his deployment in the 67-foot, ten-gun *Providence.* But it was only an early suggestion of the crucial and even more important strategic accomplishments that would be the result of his core motivation.

In introducing a more complete assessment of the career of the man many consider to be the Continental Navy's most significant hero, it is also important to better understand some of the external factors that shaped his behavior. Among those was the fact that he was a self-taught naval officer in a nascent navy that began with no purpose-built warships. It is also important to understand that he served in a new navy with none of the unifying traditions of an established military service, and the navy he fought was the epitome of those unifying traditions. And related to those two circumstances was the special challenge of serving in the navy of a country that was struggling for recognition of its national existence in the world community.

With the Declaration of Independence in July 1776, the Continental Congress defined the cause of the American colonies in language that was emotionally charged. The King was accused of much more than misguided political policies. Among the writers' grievances: "He has plundered our seas, ravaged our Coasts, burnt our towns, and destroyed the lives of our people. He is at this time transporting large Armies of foreign Mercenaries to compleat the works of death, desolation and tyranny, already begun with circumstances of Cruelty and perfidy scarcely paralleled in the most barbarous ages, and totally unworthy of the Head of a civilized nation."[3]

In summation, the shapers of the Declaration wrote, "And for the support of the Declaration, with a firm reliance on the protection of divine Providence, we mutually pledge to each other our Lives, our Fortunes and our sacred Honor."[4] Those words and other dramatic statements from Continental politicians and pamphleteers set the general tone for the times and specifically for Jones's career. They would have fixed the concept of liberty as both the intellectual and emotional center of his naval service.

The circumstances of Jones's career confirmed his commitment to something more profound than personal aggrandizement. For example, he never accumulated wealth from his combat successes, notwithstanding the system of prize money for captures at sea that could make a navy captain in the age of sail a significant commercial enterprise. And during Jones's lifetime, despite his powerful drive for recognition, he never received the level of public or official approbation that was clearly merited by the importance of his military contributions to the colonies' struggle against Britain. That level of approbation would require more than one hundred years of post-American Revolutionary War history to crystallize.

Two deeply embedded elements of Jones's persona worked in tandem with his commitment to the American cause: Scottish ties with the sea and the Scottish traditions of rebellion. A strong case can be made that the basic script for Jones's career as an exceptional fighting captain had been written and rewritten in Scottish ships and on Scottish battlefields for centuries before he was born. Tales of the legendary fifteenth-century Leith Sea-Dogs and the fiery thirteenth-century Scottish insurgent William Wallace almost surely would have been spun into his earliest childhood. It was not at all surprising then that Jones chose to fight in the underdog Continental Navy (at least in terms of operational assets), pitted against a monarch and government in London.

Added to the profound influence of Jones's Scottish blood was the imprint on his character made by his early experience at sea. At thirteen years of age, Jones went to the nearby English port of Whitehaven. There, he signed on for a seven-year apprenticeship with a local trader and embarked in a merchant brig sailing for Barbados and the American colonies. For a boy entering his teen years, there was only one choice for survival in a merchant ship of the eighteenth century—become a man, fast. Clearly that is what young Jones did, and his journey to learn the ways of the sea and seamen began.

Jones's youthful and abrupt introduction to the make-or-break environment of shipboard life began his professional relationship with the sea. It was at sea where he proved himself and where he shaped his identity as a young man. And although he navigated reasonably well socially when ashore, he was basically a loner. Thus, he never found a female life partner. His true soul mate was the sea, and combat was their ultimate intimacy.

Although Jones's shipboard apprenticeship was not in naval service, his early experience in the merchant service made him physically hard, professionally competent as a seaman, and mentally tough. And it started his career with the view from the lower decks up. That view was different from that of an officer who began his career as a naval midshipman. It made him a seaman warrior, not a warrior seaman. As a result, Jones devoted a considerable amount of his professional energy trying to make up for his lack of the more traditional naval officer's credentials.

The intense challenges of his early life at sea tempered Jones's character and gave him a steeliness that was resilient enough to stand up in the most desperate combat situations he eventually faced as a naval officer. In addition, the ability to overcome long military odds was particularly important for Jones, since he was matched at sea against an enemy that was more numerous, more heavily armed, and better trained militarily. In fact, when Jones was commissioned in the Continental Navy in 1775, Britain had a navy that was more than a third larger than either of its two closest competitors, France and

Spain, and comparisons with the Continental Navy would have been considered ridiculous by Royal Navy professionals and the British Admiralty. There simply was no comparison, and that was the environment in which Jones would go on to pursue his naval career.

Just as important as his ability to survive in a war against a massively overwhelming navy was Jones's ability to survive the risky political crosscurrents of the American voyage to independence. And as history has demonstrated, many militarily brilliant leaders, individuals who clearly had the ability to win in combat, foundered in the dangerous political waters of their time. But just as his personal toughness filled gaps in his naval training, it also helped him succeed in the uniquely difficult political circumstances of America's birth, circumstances involving, among other momentous issues, the new nation's leaders groping toward the concept of effective civilian control of its military.

What these and the many more subtle elements of Jones's career added up to was much more than a one-dimensional naval hero. He was a complex and multifaceted personality with imperfections. He made mistakes, for example, in dealing with his civilian leadership, his Continental Navy peers, his subordinates, and his country's allies. And he was not a charismatic leader who was loved by those he led. In fact, at times only the patience of political leaders who focused on his combat abilities—men like George Washington, Benjamin Franklin, and Thomas Jefferson—prevented that negative personal side from ending his naval career prematurely.

In comparison with the overwhelmingly heroic image of the naval leader that emerged during the late-nineteenth and early-twentieth centuries and the opposing negative image portrayed in recent years, Jones's life was actually more than either of those extremes. He was among the shapers of our nation. But notwithstanding that role, he also had an Everyman quality that invites us to look to him for principles of leadership applicable to our own lives and times. He experienced success and failure, joy and grief, conviction and doubt. He felt the unique pleasure of a well-sailed ship in perfect equilibrium with the wind and the sea, and he clung to whatever was within reach when threatened by the sea's terrible violence. He knew the special fatigue of long periods of sleep deprivation while under way, but he also soaked in the renewing warmth of a sunrise at sea. Walking his quarterdeck he had to bear the crushing weight of taking fellow human beings into deadly combat, but he also experienced the profound elation of survival and victory in what he embraced as a transcending cause.

Jones also loved women and was loved in return, but his affairs of the heart never seemed to get beyond the recreational stage; there was no stabilizing marriage, no epic romance. Jones's affairs were interesting sidebars to his life story, and in some instances, they had an impact on a specific aspect of his career that is worth noting. But, to make more of the romances than that, entertaining as they may be, distorts the true picture of one of the least understood players in the drama of the American Revolution.

Jones was an essential factor in arguably the most liberal revolution in history, and it is the sum of all the facets of his character that helps take us past the flat image portrayed on the pages of our history books and the deconstructed image of modern observers. He has been enthusiastically characterized by writers as a "knight of the seas," "one chosen by fate," "the sailor whom England feared," "a genius prone to adventure," "the lover of a princess," "America's greatest captain," and, inaccurately, "the father of the American navy."

He has also been labeled recently as "too suspicious and self-defeating to be a gifted leader" and "a violent-tempered, self-dramatizing paranoiac."

While those overheated characterizations are wildly wide of the mark, one label *does* emerge as a beginning point for understanding his persona: America's *first sea warrior.* He was the first American naval hero to achieve significant public acclaim beyond his country's borders, and he was America's first serving naval officer to demonstrate an understanding of how profoundly naval power would play in the history of the United Sates.

Above all, he was a naval officer whose war-fighting qualities could fashion stunning combat victories under unlikely circumstances. He was—in the words used to describe him in April 1906 at the official ceremony marking his interment at Annapolis—"that man who gave our Navy its earliest traditions of heroism and victory."[5]

As the events leading to the American Revolution were accelerating, John Adams wrote to his wife, Abigail, "Great things are wanted to be done." John Paul Jones was one who answered that call on the quarterdecks of Continental Navy ships.

I
Beginnings

"There are few more impressive sights in the world than a Scotsman on the make."

Sir James Matthew Barrie

The hero known in history as John Paul Jones was born John Paul, and his first breath was laced with the salt air that rolls off southern Scotland's Solway Firth. That primal introduction of John Paul to the sea took place on 6 July 1747 at Arbigland, the estate of Robert Craik, a local squire and member of the British Parliament. Craik's estate was located in the Scottish parish of Kirkbean and the ancient lordship of Galloway. In contrast to so much of the rugged landscape of Scotland, Arbigland was set on a fertile plateau, where the scent of flowers and grain took the cutting edge off the salt air. That contrast between the gentler climate of Kirkbean's plateau and the violent coasts of so much of Scotland was an earthy metaphor for the contrasts in the personality of the Continental Navy's hero-to-be.

Some early biographers contended that John Paul was born in poverty, but there was nothing lowly about the multiroom, whitewashed cottage of his parents, John and Jeannie Paul. His father was the skilled and respected landscape gardener for the Arbigland estate, and his mother was a member of a family of long-standing landholders in the area. Jones's parents were representative of the hard-working social strata that soon would emerge as the British middle class. The younger John Paul was the fourth of the family's seven children, two of whom died at childbirth. Some biographers suggest that he was actually the bastard son of Robert Craik, but there is no substantive evidence of that.

Although young John Paul's family connections could have led him into a relatively secure trade in the Kirkbean area, it was the nearby sand flats and coves of Solway Firth to which he was drawn. There, he explored and began his first experiences of the sea. He can be visualized as a toddler, poking along the water's edge with a stick, perhaps in the charge of an older sister. Then later, as a young boy, alone in his own small boat, he would have enjoyed the only truly unburdened sea command of his career.

As John Paul grew, he watched and listened to the sailors from the merchant ships and the local fishermen in the nearby port of Carsethorn, at the mouth of the River Nith. The sailors' tales of what lay beyond his view from the shore's edge were, no doubt, magnified by young John's imagination, even beyond the sailors' traditional exaggerations. Most provocative of all for the boy would have been the ships working their way out of the Firth and heading into the Irish Sea and beyond, toward people and places unknown. As he stood with his back to Scotland's Southern Uplands and his face toward the shore of England on the distant southern horizon, the bows cutting Solway Firth's choppy waters were etching a path for John Paul. They were marking the way to someplace else, a place where people would debate and then decide to fight to secure a new way to govern themselves, a way to "form a more perfect union."

Those ships working their way out of Solway Firth were also something else. In a broader and more immediate sense, they were signs of Jones's times. In Great Britain at the middle of the eighteenth century, powerful economic, social, political, and technological forces were stirring. Central to those forces was the early development of the means of machine production and national and global distribution of products, which was accompanied by the beginnings of a consumer society in Britain. Coffee, tea, fine fabrics, sugar, and tobacco—all imported—were among the products in this nascent British consumer culture. With maritime trade as the catalyst, those economic and technological forces would soon explode into the Industrial Revolution, a phenomenon that would radically change Britain's social and political landscape.

With Britain's growing maritime commerce, there was a symbiotic need for naval power, and both Britain's trade and its accompanying naval activity continually collided with France, Spain, and other European nations. As the eighteenth century advanced, the previous century's emphasis on colonies for the sake of extracted wealth was rapidly evolving into a fierce competition for colonies as captive trading partners and providers of raw materials and basic commodities. The result of this ongoing competition for colonies was an early version of a world war, an on-again, off-again military struggle between France and Great Britain for empires and global dominance. The ongoing conflict would last through the beginning of the nineteenth century. And it was in the context of that prototypical world war that the career of the American colonies' best-known naval hero played out.

It accurately has been said of the time that British influence reached to the six-fathom curve of any shoreline in the world. And the tough, industrious, and sharp Scots were well suited to taking advantage of the increasing global commercial activity connected to that maritime reach. For example, the British East India Company of the time, one of the major manifestations of the rising tide of world trade, was 50 percent Scottish in its personnel.

The lives of John Paul's siblings were an expression of Britain's geographically expansive attitude. His older brother, William, immigrated to Fredericksburg, Virginia, where he started his own business as a tailor. His sister Mary Ann, who married a Whitehaven shopkeeper, immigrated to Charleston, South Carolina, and one of his cousins immigrated to Charleston as well.

After primary education in the local Presbyterian parish school, John Paul experienced the first defining event of his career. Although the records are not clear about the exact date, it probably was 1761 when he was apprenticed at the age of thirteen to John Younger, owner of the merchant ship *Friendship*. The 85-foot brig was typical of the sturdy, two-masted trading ships that were the workhorses of the age of sail. And although she was a merchantman, *Friendship* was armed with eighteen cannons mounted on her main deck. In an era of privateers, pirates, and navy commerce raiders, she no doubt could give a decent account of herself if attacked.

In that compressed seagoing world within a world that was the *Friendship* and her crew, the boy in his early teen years lived and learned. His duties would have been menial at first, but he was expected to take on a man's work quickly. Sail handling and repairing, line handling, helmsmanship, simple carpentry, the rudiments of celestial navigation, basic coastal piloting, serving the guns, and much more would have been among the skills that he began to master. In that intricate society, which was manned and maintained around the clock and operated in a potentially dangerous environment, he carried out his duties in seemingly never-ending cycles. There was no such thing as routine sleep, and the food was marginal in quality and monotonous. A merchantman offered no formal training program, and in contrast to naval midshipmen—his age counterparts in the British Navy—he had no rank. He was at the bottom of the skills chain and no powerful sponsor sustained him in his new career. In a crew that probably numbered fewer than thirty, he worked very hard physically, learned fast, and carried his own weight—or else.

In addition to the skills of seamanship, there were larger lessons to be learned. Such discoveries as the importance of standing up to a bully, the generally high rate of return for helping a shipmate, the dangerous implications of carelessness at sea, the potentially lethal cascading of a ship's small weaknesses in nasty weather, the absolute authority of a ship's captain, and the satisfaction of being part of a skilled team were, no doubt, among the more interesting elements of

John Paul's broader seagoing education. His was not a gentle transition from childhood.

The *Friendship* was part of the busy triangle trade of the era, generally making one complete circuit from Whitehaven, England, to Barbados in the West Indies, to the American colonies and back to Whitehaven in a year.[1] Because of the prevailing winds of the Atlantic Ocean, the departures from British ports generally took place from November through January. From Whitehaven *Friendship* carried finished products manufactured in Britain, such as high-quality tools, tableware, furniture, and fashionable clothing. In Barbados those finished goods would be sold or bartered, primarily for rum and sugar. In addition, the cargo loaded in the West Indies also might include such exotic commodities as pimento, indigo, and mahogany. In the American colonies, the rum, sugar, and other West Indian products were sold or bartered for barrel staves, tobacco, and commodities or finished products of the colonies that would later be sold in Britain. The cargo for the return to Britain might also include pine masts and spars, particularly important strategic materials for Britain's navy and merchant marine.

One of the positive aspects of this cycle for John Paul was that it provided an opportunity for him to visit his older brother, William, who had become a successful tailor in Virginia. Those visits were John Paul's initial introduction to America, with its stripped-down ethic based on hard work and self-reliance and a social structure that featured pragmatic politics, future orientation, and personal freedom. Those early visits to the American colonies would also have provided a view of daily life relatively unencumbered by the heredity-based class structures of "the old world" in general and Great Britain in particular. Later in life he would describe the American colonies in a letter to Benjamin Franklin as "my favorite Country from the age of thirteen, when I first saw it."[2]

In 1764, after John Paul had served just three years of his seven-year apprenticeship, the owners of *Friendship* sold the ship, and he was released from his obligation. His next two berths at sea were as third mate and then first mate in the blackbirders *King George,* out of Whitehaven, and *Two Friends,* which he signed on board in Kingston, Jamaica. He later indicated that the two slavers repulsed him, describing their work as "that abominable trade." He left *Two Friends* in Kingston after one round-trip voyage.

In Kingston in July 1768 he met the Scottish captain of the merchant brig *John,* registered in Liverpool, England, and based in Kirkcudbright, a small port close to the Paul home on the north shore of Solway Firth. The shipmaster, Samuel McAdam, agreed to carry John Paul home as a passenger, and that

Atlantic transit had an unanticipated and pivotal effect on his future. During the voyage both the captain and the only other ship's officer died. Despite his youth—he was barely twenty-one—John Paul took command of the ship and managed to navigate her safely back to her owners in Kirkcudbright. It was an accomplishment requiring a significant level of mariner's skills and a high degree of self-confidence. The ability to take command of a ship and crew with which he was not familiar was an early indication of his unusual abilities as a leader.

As a result of his saving *John* and her cargo, John Paul was made master of the ship. Thus in his new role as a merchant ship captain, he had reached his first position of significant leadership. In 1769 he departed in *John* for Kingston, and for the next two years he made two round trips between Kirkcudbright and Jamaica. It was the time for his self-confidence to be affirmed, and based on anecdotal accounts, it was.

Although at approximately five feet, five inches tall John Paul was slightly below average height, he was physically strong. And he had an overall manner that broadcast that physical strength. He was neat in his dress, poised in social situations, and articulate. His body and facial features were well proportioned, and he was exceptionally courteous with women. Women, for their part, were attracted by his strong good looks and often intrigued by his mannerly attitude toward them. John Adams's wife, Abigail, once commented that the fearsome American naval officer seemed, to her, more suited to the boudoir than to a rough life at sea.

At sea the young merchant shipmaster had an entirely different aspect; he was a no-nonsense captain, frequently showing a hard edge to his crew and others around him. As a result, he was respected by his crews for his seamanship but not beloved by any means. In fact Captain Paul's hard edge with his crews led to the first serious untoward incident of his career as a merchant ship captain.

In early 1770, after unloading cargo in Tobago, John Paul punished the ship's carpenter, Mungo Maxwell, by flogging. Maxwell appeared to survive the flogging without lingering physical effects, and he left the crew of *John* and set out to return to England in a Spanish packet. Based on first-hand testimony, Maxwell was apparently in good health when he began that voyage, but he died en route to England. Maxwell's relations accused his captain of causing Maxwell's death, and with some difficulty Captain Paul established that his crewman had died of other causes.

Maxwell's family was from the same region as John Paul's family, and their accusations were the source of considerable ill will toward John Paul in and around Kirkbean. In fact after he returned to Kirkcudbright in *John,* Captain Paul apparently was jailed briefly on the basis of the accusations made by his crewman's family. Eventually, however, the court in Tobago and the master of the ship in which Maxwell died provided statements clearing Captain Paul. The incident was a forerunner of an incident in which John Paul's toughness would cause an even bigger problem, a situation that would radically change the direction of his life.

In October 1772, after briefly commanding a local packet, John Paul was appointed captain of the three-masted ship *Betsy* out of London. It is likely that he also purchased a share in the ownership of the British merchantman. With a larger ship and considerably more cargo capacity than *John, Betsy* was a means for John Paul to advance both his qualifications as a merchant captain and his business success. Captain Paul's new command traded among ports in England, Ireland, the Madeira Islands, and Tobago.

Two additional aspects of Captain Paul's character began to emerge during this brief period. Correspondence later in his life suggests that he thoroughly enjoyed his opportunities for female company during his time in London. In addition, it is clear that he was successful in the business aspects of his trade in *Betsy.* Perhaps the best demonstrations of the latter were his partnership with a local plantation owner in Tobago and the profits he compounded by selling, buying, and bartering as *Betsy* transited from port to port.

In January 1773 Captain Paul departed from Plymouth for the West Indies, but major structural problems with his ship's hull forced him into Cork, Ireland, for extensive repairs. After a long delay in Cork and a stop in the Madeira Islands, he arrived in the port of Scarborough, Tobago, in the fall of that year. In a dispute over back wages, Captain Paul was involved in an altercation with a member of his crew, which ended with that crew member attacking the captain, and John Paul running him through with a sword. Captain Paul immediately left his command and fled to Virginia. The slain crewman was a native of Tobago and perhaps the previous legal entanglements precipitated by relatives of Mungo Maxwell influenced John Paul's reaction. It also is possible that he actually feared for his life at the hands of the dead crewman's relatives and friends in Tobago—it was not Kirkcudbright, after all.

The details of John Paul's flight from Tobago, presumably at the end of 1773, and his initial years in America are a matter of considerable conjecture. His route out of Tobago to America would not have been simple, and it is possible that he had to make several separate transits before finally arriving in a port in the American colonies. One theory had John Paul taking command of a sloop out of Tobago and sailing her to Virginia. The sloop in question had been commanded by a James Jones, facilitating—perhaps precipitating—Captain Paul's brief use of the name John Jones. Documents show that he signed "J. Jones" on official documents, presumably to best match the previous signatures on the ship's papers. In any event, it is apparent that John Jones was the initial alias used by Captain Paul while a fugitive in the American colonies.

The only known written account of the killing's immediate aftermath appears in a letter from Captain Paul, by then known as John Paul Jones, to Franklin, dated 6 March 1779. The reference by Jones was sketchy: "It was the advice of my friends, Gov. Young among many others, when that great Misfortune of my Life happened, that I should retire Incog to the continent of America, and remain there until an Admiralty Commission should arrive in the Island."[3] In the same letter, Jones pointed out that the advent of the American Revolution intervened: "I had waited that event Eighteen Months before Swords were drawn and the Ports of the Continent were Shut." The timing of the convening of the Admiralty Commission in Tobago and the rising tide of revolution in the American colonies raises one of the more intriguing "what if" questions in U.S. naval history.

Unfortunately the letter to Franklin provides none of the details of how he got from Tobago to the American colonies. In any event his hasty departure from Tobago was an uncharacteristic action for the physically and mentally tough John Paul. His unwillingness to defend his actions through legal means ended his promising career as a successful merchant captain, but it soon set him on a course toward a unique role in the birth of a nation.

Once in the American colonies, Jones spent time in Virginia and North Carolina, and he also visited Philadelphia. He began to make friends, often through his Masonic lodge membership.[4] Joseph Hewes, a successful merchant and politician from North Carolina, was among those first American friends. Hewes was a representative from North Carolina to the First Continental Congress, and as a member of its Naval Committee, he became the first civilian leader of the Continental Navy. He also became one of the most important influences on Jones's commissioning in the Continental Navy. Among other notables of the time who Jones is believed to have met during this period was Thomas Jefferson.

Jones's political contacts, although helpful, were not overwhelming. And of particular significance, the fact that he was not strongly associated with any one American colony limited his political leverage. His early political contacts, however, were of some importance as his naval career unfolded, and significantly, they were an indication that he understood that influence was a pervasive fact of life.

Another career fact of life that Jones fully understood by this time was that being in command at sea was a position of limited, not limitless, power. Notwithstanding the popular wisdom that the authority of a ship's captain is total, he had come to understand that no position of authority is truly absolute. The affairs with Mungo Maxwell and the crewman he had killed in Tobago etched that lesson in his mind. And although he had prospered on the basis of his abilities and hard work, he had also come to know that, at times, one's past performance is not the only key to one's future.

Clearly, in addition to being physically strong and mentally tough, Jones was highly intelligent to have reached such astute conclusions while still a young man. Jones understood that along with the unique authority of a captain at sea there are nuanced aspects of that position that must be addressed if a naval career is to be successful.

During this early period in America, Jones also found time for at least one noteworthy relationship with a woman. Early biographers indicate that the relationship between Jones and Dorothea Dandridge, daughter of prominent Virginia plantation owner Nathaniel West Dandridge, was based on sincere and mutual attraction. We know very little of Dorothea as a person, but no doubt Jones's good looks, combined with his courteous approach to women, would have accounted for his half of the romantic equation. As it turned out, however, Dorothea eventually married the colonial lawyer and political leader Patrick Henry. Henry, who became one of the notables of the American Revolution, clearly was a more suitable husband for the daughter of a prominent Virginia landholder than a fugitive ship captain, even one as attractive and astute as Jones.

The courtship of Dorothea appears to be the last time Jones seriously contemplated marriage. It definitely was not, however, Jones's last relationship with a woman.

During this period from 1773 to the start of the American Revolutionary War, Jones apparently hoped to give up his seagoing career for a quiet life as a landowner, as he referred to it, a life of "calm contemplation and Poetic ease." Two realities were working against him in that ambition. For one thing, the profits he had accumulated as the captain of *Betsy* were tied up in Tobago. He simply did not have money available for a significant land purchase. For another thing, and arguably as important, it was far from a quiet time in the

American colonies. It would have been difficult for Jones, who was not placid by temperament, to remain detached from the dynamic cultural, commercial, and political movements that were coursing through life in the American colonies during the 1770s. Undoubtedly, the rising tide of rebellion would have stirred his Scottish blood, notwithstanding his protestations about seeking a quiet life.

A basic dynamic of the time was the population explosion in the colonies. In the period from 1700 to 1777 the population of the American colonies soared from approximately 250,000 to 2.5 million. Instead of there being 20 people in Britain for every 1 in the American colonies, there were only 3 people in Britain for every 1 in America by 1777. The American population also was more varied than that of England. Proportions of voluntary immigrants from Scotland, Ireland, and the European continent in the population were rapidly increasing, as were the numbers of slaves transported from Africa mostly to the southern colonies. In the latter case, the number of African slaves imported to America was roughly three times the number of voluntary immigrants during the second half of the eighteenth century.

In commerce, burgeoning trade was a source of prosperity—and anxiety. As major ports such as Boston, New York, Philadelphia, Baltimore, Charleston, and Savannah developed, so did the industrial infrastructure for an American merchant fleet. But as an American shipbuilding industry and homegrown trading houses grew, they increasingly found themselves in direct competition with Britain's mercantilist policies and the businessmen in Britain who were protected by those policies.[5] Those protectionist national principles, formalized in Britain's Navigation Acts passed in the mid-seventeenth century, positioned colonies to generate wealth for Britain and to serve as bases for military power projection for the mother country.

In the American colonies the wealth was primarily in the form of commodities and semi-finished products. These included lumber, barrel staves, and tobacco that would be sold, with the proceeds being used to purchase finished products in Britain. The finished products were then exported back to the American continent and the West Indies, as well as other colonial markets, for sale at a profit. There also was the matter of strategic naval material, such as pine masts.

The American colonies experienced Britain's power projection in the provocative form of permanently deployed British troops, ostensibly based in America to protect the colonies from the French and the indigenous Indians.

Along with the army troops, there was the ubiquitous British Navy, ever present in major ports and off the thirteen colonies' Atlantic Coast. The positive—for Britain—commercial results of the process were known as a favorable balance of trade. And as a corollary to the above, the ocean commerce involved was to be carried in British ships, excluding ships owned by foreign countries and to some extent, those of the American colonies. Given the circumstances in the mid-eighteenth century, it was more than coincidence that the earliest spirit of rebellion in America was centered in its major seaports, particularly Boston.

In addition to the merchant class, a growing class of small business owners and craftsmen also were finding the rising level of trade in the American colonies to be a mixed blessing. There was a general increase in business activity for them, but one of the other elements of Britain's mercantilist policies of the era required that finished goods from England must be exported to the burgeoning American market. And the value of those exports was supposed to exceed the value of the commodities and basic products flowing in the opposite direction. As a result the American colonies' growing class of small business proprietors and skilled craftsmen was increasingly fearful of losing both its sources of income and the basis of its socially independent status. For members of this group, the prospective benefits of liberty were rapidly becoming the key to their future.

Exacerbating that situation was the tendency among some British politicians, business leaders, and King George III to patronize the obstreperous colonials to their west. In 1763, at the end of the Seven Years' War between Britain and France—carried on in America as the French and Indian War—the British colonists in America believed that they had played a major military role in the defeat of France in North America. What they expected from the mother country was economic and political gratitude; what they got was an increase in duties and taxes levied against them from London. The theory in London, where the American colonies competed for attention with India, the West Indies, and other commodity-rich colonies, was that the colonies should bear more of the burden for their protection by the British Army and Navy. The colonists' reaction was that, in effect, they were being forced to pay for the means of arbitrarily limiting their commercial and personal freedoms.

The situation could be described as an impending collision between two powerfully expansionist movements. The colonists, with an aggressive we're-as-good-as-anyone attitude, were carving out a potentially freestanding national entity on a rich but underdeveloped continent. Author and history professor John Ferling described the American colonists' important sense of equality:

"While most colonists in 1763 were the descendants of those who had left the British homeland for America, they nevertheless happily thought of themselves as British who by happenstance lived in America."[6] John Adams, however, put a real edge on it: "I say we are as handsome as old English folks, and so should be as free."[7]

The London-centered British empire builders, some with an imperious, you-upstarts-are-fouling-up-a-good-thing attitude, were shaping an unparalleled global trade and military structure with Great Britain at its hub. And although there were many in Parliament who did not share the domineering attitude of some of their colleagues, the legislation that body enacted in the face of unrest in America was clear-cut. The laws were, according to naval historian Peter Padfield, "seeking to not only remove the trading irregularities which had become traditional and even vital to their [the colonists'] economy, but to assert the principle of taxation by Parliament."[8]

The American colonists eventually synthesized their resentment of the attitudes and actions emanating from London into the American cause for liberty. That creation of a political force, something that could be articulated so precisely and emotionally, was arguably the most powerful event that carried the merchant captain John Paul into the Continental Navy as John Paul Jones and then on to fame.

As tensions with Britain heightened in 1774 and 1775, the thirteen American colonies were far from united. Each had its own legislature, and there was no reliable funding for a central government. In addition, the economic interests among them differed, particularly between the colonies in the North and those in the South. Among the colonies of the South, maritime issues merely were a corollary to their agrarian—particularly plantation—economy. In the New England colonies, however, maritime matters were at the core of their economic life, which to a significant degree revolved around shipbuilding, fishing, and maritime trade. This difference in regional self-interest would carry over to the difficult birth of the Continental Navy and the subsequent development of the U.S. Navy, which was later established by Congressional legislation in 1794. The First Continental Congress in Philadelphia in 1776 was, however, a clear sign that unity was developing and accelerating.

Despite the regionalism and economic factionalism, there was one powerful common denominator among the colonies: the growing dissatisfaction with what was perceived to be heavy-handed control by Britain. And as that dissatisfaction grew, so too did talk of independence and the inherent rights of man.

Patrick Henry epitomized the time and demonstrated the high emotional content of the political concept of liberty. In a passionate speech in March 1775 to the Virginia Convention, the second in a series of five meetings devoted to opposition to Britain's colonial policies, he focused on the presence in the American colonies of the British Navy and Army. "Has Great Britain an enemy, in this quarter of the world, to call for all this accumulation of navies and armies? No, sir, she has none. They are meant for us; they can be meant for no other. They are sent over to bind and rivet upon us those chains which the British ministry have been so long forging." He continued, "If we wish to be free—if we mean to preserve inviolate those inestimable privileges for which we have so long been contending—if we mean not basely to abandon the noble struggle in which we have been so long engaged . . . we must fight! An appeal to arms and to the God of hosts is all that is left us!"[9]

In the same speech, Henry referred to "the great and arduous struggle for liberty" and "the holy cause of liberty." He ended his oration with the provocative challenge: "I know not what course others may take; but as for me, give me liberty or give me death!"[10] These were the same kinds of exhortations that had echoed through the Scottish hills of Jones's forebears. And as his own subsequent writing showed, they stirred Jones's commitment to the concepts of political liberty and individual freedom.

It must also be noted that in the run-up to the American Revolution, many remained committed to "King and Country" and were increasingly uncomfortable with what Henry characterized as the "holy cause of liberty." In fact, there are estimates that the number of Loyalists was roughly equal to the number of those who eventually opted to commit for American independence, and many of the Loyalists actually fought against colonial militia forces.

Not unexpectedly, what could accurately be labeled as America's first civil war created splits in colonial families. Those emotional divisions were personal metaphors for the split between the colonies and their mother country. George Washington's mother, for example, was a Loyalist who refused to talk to him after he committed to the independence of the colonies. Similarly, Benjamin Franklin's son, William, at one point governor of the colony of New Jersey, was adamantly opposed to armed rebellion, and the father and son remained estranged after the war ended.

The inflamed rhetoric in the colonies during Jones's first two years in America was no more provocative than the increasingly violent events taking place. In 1770—only a few years prior to Jones's flight to America—a confrontation between townspeople and British troops quartered in Boston escalated into the Boston Massacre. On 5 March, while British troops were involved in controlling threatening demonstrations against taxes on imports, they were peppered with snowballs, clamshells, and rocks. They eventually responded by firing into the crowd of colonials, killing five men.

Not surprisingly, accounts of the actual circumstances differed depending on one's loyalties, and the trial of eight of the soldiers and their commanding officer resulted in the conviction of two of the soldiers for manslaughter. John Adams, who was among those Americans who combined reason with their passion for liberty, skillfully defended the British officer and soldiers. The killings and what seemed to be lenient judicial action to some provided volatile ammunition for the colonial pamphleteers and political firebrands. Samuel Adams, John Adams's cousin and a future signer of the Declaration of Independence, was among those who most vigorously exploited what had happened, describing the events of 5 March in Boston in a report to Franklin as "the horrid massacre."

The Boston Tea Party on 16 December 1773 coincided closely with Jones's arrival in America and was another of the dramatic events moving the American colonies toward revolution. It signaled the collision between Britain's determination to reinforce Parliament's right to tax its colonies with a duty on imported tea and the colonists' determination to resist what they believed to be tyrannical behavior by officialdom in London. The actual economics of the situation arguably had become less important than the principles being defended, with mounting emotion on each side.

First the local inhabitants of Boston prevented the unloading of three British ships laden with 342 chests of tea. Then the royal governor of the colony refused to allow the ships to sail back to Britain until the duty had been paid. Next a raiding party of Bostonians, disguised as Indians and apparently led by Samuel Adams, threw the tea into the harbor. The British then closed the port, practically shutting down the local economy. Anger among many in the colonies rolled south from New England like waves driven by gale winds.

In April 1775, the storm of rebellion broke at Lexington, Massachusetts, and nearby Concord, and the first shots of the American Revolution—or the American War of Independence, as many called it—were fired. At Lexington on 19 April, a British column of nearly one thousand men easily dispersed a militia formation in Lexington, killing eight of the militiamen in the process. When the British troops then advanced to nearby Concord, the results were different. Militiamen fighting unconventionally in small, dispersed units routed the British, who suffered approximately two hundred casualties by the time they returned to Boston. The battles of Lexington and Concord were followed on 17 June by the battle of Bunker Hill, which resulted in the deaths of four hundred colonial militiamen and approximately one thousand British soldiers.

By this point musket and cannon fire had replaced the heated verbal exchanges that had been passing between British political leaders in London and their counterparts in the thirteen American colonies. The tipping point in the relationship between Great Britain and its American colonies had passed. Men who never would have put their lives at risk to achieve a tax reduction were willing to risk their careers and fortunes and were even willing to die for liberty. Action-oriented men like Patrick Henry and more reflective thinkers like John Adams understood the importance of that transition. But to an unfortunate extent, the centers of power in London did not.

As blood began to spill, attention shifted to military issues. For example, in June the legislature of Rhode Island colony commissioned several small ships to harass the British Navy in Narragansett Bay. In May 1775 the Second Continental Congress convened, and soon there would be unified and more far-reaching actions by all thirteen of the American colonies. Within months, the maritime Goliath of Great Britain would face its David, and thus the stage was set for the naval career of twenty-eight-year-old John Paul Jones.

2
The Miracle Birth of a Navy

"A decisive naval superiority is to be considered as a fundamental principle, and the basis on which every hope of success must ultimately depend."

General George Washington

On 15 June 1775 the Second Continental Congress voted unanimously to appoint George Washington to "command all of the continental forces raised, or to be raised, for the defense of American liberty."[1] And in September Washington demonstrated his awareness of the naval component of the coming struggle when he began chartering and arming schooners on his own initiative. Then the Continental Congress authorized the commissioning in October of two schooners to attack British supply ships, and the Continental Navy was born.

Washington's early military experience had been as an officer in the Virginia militia, serving the British cause during the French and Indian War. Following that war, he served as an aide-de-camp in the British Army in the American colonies. Despite his army and southern plantation background, however, Washington clearly recognized that there was a crucial naval element to his assignment as commander in chief of America's first all-volunteer military force. He further understood that it was not a matter of symmetrically matching the British Navy's power; that was simply impossible. The 108 ships of the line—the capital ships of the day—that the British had in commission in 1775 were the credible evidence of that reality.[2] The most visible sign of the overwhelming British naval power Washington faced was the approximately ninety warships—including ten to twelve ships of the line and scores of frigates and smaller ships—maintained in the American theater during the initial years of the American Revolution.[3] And even after its formal alliance with America on 6 February 1778, France's navy was, at least initially, little more than a distraction for the British Navy in the American theater.

For Washington and America at the beginning of the revolution three components made up the asymmetrical, narrowly focused naval strategy that would be pursued:

1. Interdict Britain's supplies to its army in America and, to the extent possible, capture British military matériel for the Continental Army.
2. Project naval power against the British Isles for economic and psychological impact.
3. Selectively establish decisive naval superiority in crucial, short-term situations.

The requirement for interdiction and capture of military matériel was most pressing and was among Washington's earliest efforts as commander in chief. The attacks against the British Isles and their surrounding waters took somewhat longer to mount, and it was in this second power-projection phase that John Paul Jones made his greatest contribution to the American colonies' cause of liberty. In terms of establishing localized sea control in a crucial situation, that would not become a major factor until the battle of Yorktown, when the French accomplished the colonies' final strategic naval objective at the battle of Chesapeake Bay. There, a fleet under Vice Admiral Comte de Grasse denied support from the sea for the beleaguered army of General Charles Cornwallis and became the enabler for Washington's final victory on the ground. At that crucial point, it was the French Navy alone that turned back the British fleet attempting to relieve General Cornwallis's army. It was a momentary—and momentous—tilt in the local balance of naval power in the Virginia Capes area, an event that, from the British point of view, "brought the disaster at Yorktown."[4]

Recognizing the importance of facing first things first, General Washington took action on his own authority, and within weeks of his appointment as commander in chief, he immediately began commissioning and arming local New England schooners to intercept British supply ships. The first of those makeshift raiders was *Hannah,* a sturdy fishing schooner out of Beverly, Massachusetts. *Hannah* set sail on 5 September, under the command of Nicholas Broughton from Marblehead, Massachusetts. Washington's hopes for much needed equipment for his army were high, as were the hopes of Captain Broughton and his crew for prize money.

Hannah's cruise accomplished neither objective, but it helped Washington begin to learn the complexities of raising a naval force shaped to the strategic needs of the thirteen American colonies. Washington's naval learning curve remained high as seven more schooners were fitted out and deployed, again with very modest results. Notwithstanding the modest beginnings, however, Washington's schooners captured more than fifty British prizes in late 1775, 1776, and early 1777. It wasn't much, but it was *something.*

On 3 October 1775, as broad political support for a navy had begun to coalesce, the Rhode Island General Assembly put a naval resolution before the Continental Congress. It proposed the construction and fitting out of a Continental fleet. The resolution also stated the rationale for their action: "The building and equipping of an American fleet . . . would greatly and essentially conduce to the preservation of the lives, liberty and property of the good people of these Colonies." The Rhode Island legislature's resolution had been precipitated by the British Navy's closing of the harbors in Narragansett Bay.

Not surprisingly, representatives to the Continental Congress from the South vigorously opposed the resolution, saying in effect that Rhode Island's problem was not their problem. At that point, Congress took no immediate action on the establishment of a single naval force for the American colonies.

Ten days later, however, the Continental Congress did act, authorizing the fitting out of two former merchant ships of unknown lineage to seek out British supply ships. They were the fourteen-gun brig *Andrea Doria,* named by the Continental Congress for the Genoese statesman and admiral, and the fourteen-gun brig *Cabot,* named for the Venetian navigator who is acknowledged as the European discoverer of North America. The date of the authorization, 13 October 1775, is recognized as the official beginning of the Continental Navy. Within weeks, the fitting out of two more ships was approved. One was the three-masted, twenty-four-gun former merchant ship *Alfred,* named for the ninth-century Saxon king credited with beginning the English navy. *Alfred* was the former *Black Prince* out of Philadelphia. The other ship authorized for fitting out was the three-masted, twenty-four-gun *Columbus,* named for the European discoverer of the Americas. *Columbus,* the former merchantman *Sally* out of Philadelphia, was the first Continental Navy ship to capture a British warship. *Alfred* and *Columbus* were roughly comparable in size to a small frigate of the time, but definitely not comparable to a frigate in fighting characteristics.

The practice of taking up merchant ships and fitting them out for naval service, although a practical necessity at the beginning of the American Revolution, was a poor substitute for having purpose-built navy ships. And the reduced operational capability of Continental Navy ships not only shaped the three-part naval strategy of General Washington and Congress but also the tactics of captains like John Paul Jones in deployments and engagements to come.

In a logical next step on 22 December 1775, the Continental Congress confirmed the commissioning of the first officers of the Continental Navy with the following legislative action:

Resolved, That the following naval officers be appointed:
Esek Hopkins, Esq., Commander-in-Chief of the fleet.
Dudley Saltonstall, Captain of the *Alfred.*
Abraham Whipple, " " " *Columbus.*
Nicholas Biddle, " " " *Andrew Doria.*
John B. Hopkins, " " " *Cabot.*
1st *Lieutenants,* John Paul Jones, Rhodes Arnold, —— Stansbury, Hersted Hacker, Jonathan Pitcher.
2nd *Lieutenants,* Benjamin Seabury, Joseph Olney, Elisha Warner, Thomas Weaver, —— McDougall.[5]

The initial commissionings of Continental Navy officers were hardly auspicious. One of the first lieutenants and one of the second lieutenants were only known by their last names, and politics were very much involved in the process. The influence of Rhode Island member of the Continental Congress Stephen Hopkins, for example, was instrumental in the selection of his brother Esek as commander in chief of the new Continental Navy. And Jones himself admitted that his appointment was largely due to the influence of Joseph Hewes, chairman of the Marine Committee of the Continental Congress at the time.

Politics on a broader scale were also heavily involved in the events leading up to the commissioning of those first fourteen Continental Navy officers under the Commander-in-Chief, and the authorization of the American colonies' first four ships. Those wider ranging politics focused on the basic debate over whether the colonies should even have a navy. As noted, delegates to the Continental Congress from the South strongly opposed the original Rhode Island resolution, claiming that a navy was not needed by the colonies and, if one were established, it primarily would benefit the New England and Middle Atlantic colonies. This regional division on naval matters persisted beyond the conclusion of the American Revolution and, in fact, into the twenty-first century.

In early December 1775, before the confirmation of his appointment as a lieutenant in the Continental Navy, Jones was assigned to oversee the naval fitting out of *Alfred* in Philadelphia. His willingness to go to work before confirmation of his commission as a lieutenant is among the evidence of his enthusiasm for the cause of liberty. As a result of his quick start, on 3 December he became the first person to raise an American flag on board a navy ship.

The event was staged on a clear, crisp day and crowds stood along the waterfront at the foot of Walnut Street. Ships in the harbor had decorated their masts, spars, and rigging, and their crews gathered at their ships' rails to view the ceremony on board *Alfred.* Commodore Hopkins was rowed smartly from shore to the ship, and as he climbed the side of *Alfred,* the Continental Navy's first flag officer was ceremoniously piped aboard by the ship's boatswain and welcomed by her prospective captain, Dudley Saltonstall. As one of the first actions of the unique ceremony, the quartermaster hoisted a flag—with the combative motto "Don't Tread on Me"—on a mizzenmast signal halyard. It was a variation of one of the earliest flags of the American Revolution, known as the Gadsden flag, and it would serve as the personal battle flag of Commodore Hopkins. The "Don't Tread on Me" flag would also evolve into the first navy jack, which is still used on U.S. Navy ships during special periods.

Next, Jones, as the ship's executive officer and second in command, hoisted the Grand Union flag—with thirteen alternating red and white stripes and the British flag in the upper left corner—probably to the mizzenmast gaff peak. With the hoisting of the colonies' first naval ensign, the harbor and waterfront reverberated with cheers and cannon salutes. The commodore's commissioning pennant then quickly went aloft and appropriate Congressional resolutions were read. The Continental Navy's first operational squadron was officially in commission. On board the *Alfred,* Jones's hoisting of the colonies' Grand Union flag—one of the many Continental precursors of the American Stars and Stripes—marked the first time that Jones made history in a navy ship. It definitely would not be the last.

On 23 December Saltonstall officially took command of *Alfred,* and, as might be expected, the relationship between the captain and his second in command was not warm. Without direct supervision, Jones had led the arduous work involved in bringing *Alfred* to life as a navy ship, and he had commanded his own merchant ships prior to entering navy service. What he had achieved in his career was based on hard work and his own abilities. And there was no family influence to leverage his career. Saltonstall, in contrast, was a haughty New Englander from New London, Connecticut, with politically powerful family connections. This situation early in Jones's naval career illuminated what would be the very real drawbacks over the coming years of his limited education and modest social standing.

On 4 January 1776, *Alfred,* with Commodore Hopkins embarked and in company with *Columbus, Cabot,* and *Andrea Doria,* set sail from Philadelphia, along with the ten-gun sloops *Providence* and *Hornet* and the two eight-gun schooners *Wasp* and *Fly.* As it started down the Delaware River toward the sea, the tiny Continental Navy squadron wasn't much by the standards of the major navies of the world at the time. And it could very quickly have been dispatched by any one of scores of British Navy squadrons operating around the globe. Years later, Jones would ask if it was "madness in the first corps of sea officers" that led to the squadron's taking to sea.

It should be noted, however, that the ships of the newborn Continental Navy had at least one significant advantage: much of the British Navy was occupied elsewhere around the globe. Despite the developing British control of the world's oceans in general, the British Navy never had quite the number of ships needed to apply the level of naval power against the American colonies that could have ended the war in Britain's favor. For Britain, the American Revolution was overshadowed by the ongoing struggle between Britain and France and the naval requirements of that conflict elsewhere around the globe.

Notwithstanding its lack of ship size or numbers, America's first naval mission was clearly offensive in nature. The destination of the squadron was New Providence Island—now called Nassau—in the Bahamas, where there was known to be a store of British munitions. The objective was to seize crucial military supplies for the Continental Army and harass British bases and supply routes in the American theater. The New Providence mission was, in its implausibly brash way, an example of how an inferior naval power could exert pressure on a vastly superior naval force that was stretched thin around the globe. It also was an early sign of a navy that would increasingly place a strategic premium on projecting naval power and a tactical premium on seizing and holding the initiative.

The attack on New Providence established a precedent, unrecognized at the time, which would build during Jones's career and then, haltingly at times, mature through all of America's naval history. That mission in 1776 to confront the enemy offshore was a small but important first step toward a naval doctrine—that union of overriding beliefs that determines in broad terms how a navy will fight—of taking the fight *to* the enemy. That relatively short-range and modestly successful offshore projection of naval force to New Providence in the earliest stages of the American Revolution was the antecedent of the forward-deployed U.S. naval strategies of the twentieth and twenty-first centuries.

As in most wartime operations, unforeseen circumstances affected actual events at New Providence. To begin with, during a storm *Hornet* and *Fly* collided and were lost to the squadron. In addition, after an unopposed landing on 3 March—the first American navy-marine amphibious assault—it was discovered that the anticipated store of powder was gone. Apparently British intelligence was better than the Americans' ability to keep their mission a secret. The operation did net 88 cannon, 15 mortars, and 11,077 cannonballs, however, along with substantial amounts of other military munitions. Three prisoners of some consequence were captured: the lieutenant governor, a Tory councilor from South Carolina, and the governor's secretary.

On the return voyage there was an embarrassing brush with the twenty-four-gun small frigate HMS *Glasgow* near Block Island, an action that exposed the serious American shortcomings in naval tactics and gunnery. *Glasgow*'s captain, Tyringham Howe, was both aggressive and skillful. Despite the significant numerical strength of the American squadron he had encountered, Captain Howe employed boldness and superior ship handling to inflict serious damage to *Cabot* and *Alfred* and then escape from the squadron. The Continental Navy squadron performed more like an agglomeration of privateers than a disciplined naval unit. Congress censured Hopkins for his failure to press home an attack on *Glasgow,* and he was eventually dismissed from the service in January 1778.

The action with *Glasgow* demonstrated that the freelancing tactics of privateers, regardless how courageous or daring, would not do in combat against the experienced and skilled units of the British Navy. In the long run, that negative learning lesson was perhaps more important to Washington, Congress, and the infant Continental Navy than the modest military success at New Providence. The event also pointed out the danger of appointing naval leaders on the basis of political connections.

Despite the unsatisfactory action with *Glasgow,* however, the desperately needed artillery and munitions finally were delivered to General Washington in early April, and Jones's first naval operation was completed. Although the attack on New Providence was only a limited success, and Lieutenant Jones's participation was in a subordinate role, the mission gave Jones important initial military experience in naval raiding against shore facilities and single-ship combat. He had begun the transition from a merchant ship captain to a naval leader, and he was beginning to understand just how different those two worlds were.

After the New Providence attack, Jones wrote to Hewes about the mission. It was a mixed review for the small squadron that represented virtually the entire Continental Navy of the moment. He went on at some length, without naming names, to criticize the "rude ungentle treatment" of the junior officers and men by some of the captains. In all probability, the problem he was focusing on was one that could be expected from captains with no military training acting the way they thought naval captains acted. In contrast, Jones briefly praised Commodore Hopkins as a leader whose men "would go to any length to execute his orders." His criticism and his praise again touched on an extremely important issue: establishing good order and military discipline in the Continental Navy. It was an issue that Jones would continuously address during his career, with noteworthy failures and successes.

The final important lesson that the New Providence expedition taught General Washington and the Continental Congress was that the prospect of modest shares of prize money from captured British ships was not enough to shape crews that could stand up to the disciplined and trained British Navy. Beginning with Washington's cobbling together of his initial group of hastily armed sloops and then the official formation of the first Continental Navy squadron in 1775, it was becoming clear that establishing naval power wouldn't come easily or cheaply.

Jones's favorable official impression of his commodore based on the New Providence mission apparently was reciprocated, and on 10 May Commodore Hopkins placed him in command of the twelve-gun armed sloop *Providence.* Demonstrating how truly informal the organization of the new navy was, Jones's temporary appointment was written on the back of his appointment as a first lieutenant. *Providence,* like *Alfred,* had been a merchant ship, the former *Katy* out of Providence, Rhode Island, before conversion for naval use, again a reflection of the improvisational status of the Continental Navy.

Since the rank of captain in the Continental Navy was a temporary appointment for Jones, he quickly set out to convert it to a permanent promotion. He began with another letter to Hewes, this one written on 19 May. The letter tells us a lot about Jones, as well as about the navy and nation that simultaneously were taking shape. The first major issue he addressed was related to personnel.

Up to that time, many of those serving in the crews of Continental ships were soldiers, loaned to the navy by General Washington. Some of those soldiers had experience in merchant ships or fishing vessels prior to volunteering for the Continental Army; some were driven by patriotism, some by the hope for prize money; most by varying degrees of both motivations. Many were good seamen, but virtually none were familiar with the particular skills and discipline of naval service. Jones reported how he had "landed Gen. Washington's soldiers" and would seek "shipping men, if any can be obtained."[6] Jones surely had learned during the New Providence attack that training a military crew would go much faster with a crew that at least had some basic seamen's skills to begin with.

Despite the insecurity of being only a temporary captain, Jones did not hesitate to lecture Hewes on the subject of how to select officers of that rank: "A Captain of the Navy ought to be a man of strong and well connected sense, with a tolerable good education, a gentleman, as well as a seaman, both in theory and practice."[7] As political influence continued to shape the list of the new navy's captains, Jones was reflecting a justifiable concern about his own seniority. He had proposed a job description to Hewes that fit what he perceived to be his own qualifications, including a "tolerable good" education. And he was aiming high as he again wrote to Hewes somewhat later, "I should esteem myself happy in being sent for to Philadelphia to act under the more immediate direction of Congress, especially in one of the new ships. I must rely on your interest herein."[8]

The new ships to which he referred were a series of proposed frigates to be the first purpose-built significant naval ships of the Continental Navy. In hindsight, Jones's confidence in the general support of Hewes was reasonably well placed. His anticipation of commanding a frigate, on the other hand, was considerably ahead of events.

On 4 July 1776 the thirteen colonies took the pivotal step in their rebellion against Great Britain with final approval of the Declaration of Independence. The colonies were no longer fighting for their rights as British citizens; they were staking all on securing "Life, Liberty and the pursuit of Happiness" as citizens of a new nation. And in the late summer of the year, Jones began to come into his own as a naval commander. On 6 August he received orders from the Marine Committee of the Continental Congress to complete the provisioning of *Providence* and "Cruize against our enemies." He had opted to stay with that compact 70-foot, twelve-gun sloop, when given the choice of commanding her or another ship that was larger but was a poor sailer. Now, with a lively and well-found ship and a crew that he knew and that knew him, he was given what every ambitious naval officer wanted: an independent command. Since independent operations provide a special and unforgiving proving ground for naval command, Jones was demonstrating that he was not risk-averse. That quality would reemerge to his and his country's benefit many times in his later career.

When he sailed from Philadelphia on 21 August, his crew consisted of two first lieutenants, a ship's sailing master, one midshipman, and a reasonably experienced crew of seventy-plus.[9] He also had an amphibious capability with a Continental

Marine contingent and a brigade of Rhode Island infantry embarked. Jones and *Providence* constituted a serious naval unit, notwithstanding the relatively small size of the ship. And during his deployment of slightly less than two months in late summer–early fall of 1776, Jones put a significant dent in Britain's maritime activity along the American colonies' coasts. He was effectively contributing to the first strategic objective of Washington's naval strategy, that of interdicting enemy supplies bound for America.

Jones ranged from Bermuda to Nova Scotia, capturing several commercial ships and destroying numerous others, including virtually the entire British fishing fleet of Canso, Nova Scotia. When he returned to Narragansett Bay and Newport, Rhode Island, on 8 October, he had carried out a significant naval deployment in a professional manner. His written report to Chairman of the Naval Committee, Robert Morris, on 17 October listed his impressive accomplishments without embellishment.

The mission represented another positive step for the Continental Navy, just as the attack on New Providence had. And although this achievement lacked the geographic reach, drama, and public acclaim of Jones's later naval exploits, it must be recognized as a particularly significant step in the American cause of liberty and in Jones's own career. British, French, and Spanish naval power overwhelmingly dominated the world's oceans in the fall of 1776, but a tiny naval force, seemingly inconsequential in London, Paris, and Madrid, was coming to life along America's Atlantic coast, and Jones in *Providence* was a significant contributor to that process.

On 10 October 1776 Congress had confirmed a permanent appointment for Jones, not as captain of a particular ship, but in the rank of captain in "the Navy of the United States of North-America, fitted out for the Defence of American Liberty, and for repelling every hostile Invasion thereof." His official commissioning certificate contained previously written references to command of a specific ship crossed out and replaced with a reference to a generic navy rank. Even in its official administration, the makeshift status of the Continental Navy was evident.

Jones was justifiably unhappy about his relative ranking on the Continental Navy's captain's list, but he had achieved a degree of permanence as a senior commissioned officer in the navy representing all thirteen colonies, listed on the commissioning certificate as "New-Hampshire, Massachusetts-Bay, Rhode-Island, Connecticut, New-York, New-Jersey, Pennsylvania, Delaware, Maryland, Virginia, North-Carolina, South-Carolina and Georgia." John Hancock signed the certificate of appointment as president of the Continental Congress.

One of the by-products of Jones's new sense of job security was a continuing willingness (perhaps *eagerness* is more accurate) to speak out on naval matters to key members of the Continental Congress. In the same 17 October letter to Morris reporting the success of his deployment in *Providence,* he returned to personnel issues: "It is to the last degree distressing to contemplate the state and establishment of our navy . . . unless the private emolument of individuals in our navy is made superior to that in privateers, it never can become respectable; it never will become formidable. And without a respectable navy—alas! America!"[10]

The issue of recruiting carried over to his next mission: attacking the colliers supplying coal to the British Army in New York City and rescuing captured American seamen who were held prisoner and forced to labor in the coal pits of Cape Breton, Canada. To carry out the assignment along the coast of Nova Scotia, Jones was placed in command of *Alfred,* a step up from *Providence* in terms of size, and provided with the Continental ship *Hampton,* a fourteen-gun brigantine, to accompany him on the mission.

His first problem was adequately manning *Alfred.* When he went on board, there was a nucleus crew of thirty men, and with considerable effort, that number was doubled. Unfortunately, he was losing crew members to privateers almost as fast as he recruited them. Since the sharing of the proceeds from the sale of captured ships was a common practice among navy crews, the solution Jones proposed was to increase the share of prize money that went to the crews of Continental Navy ships. But he warned that the Continental Navy was pitted against "the best established and most formidable navy in the universe," and he assumed that "I need no arguments to convince you of the necessity of making the emoluments of our navy equal, if not superior, to theirs."[11] In addition, Jones proposed in this letter that he undertake an audacious naval expedition against British commercial interests on Africa's west coast, which he said would "carry all before them; and give a blow to the English African trade, which would not soon be recovered, by not leaving them a mast standing on that coast." He was beginning to look ahead to the second objective of Washington's naval strategy: the aggressive projection of naval power far beyond America's shores.

At the end of October the Continental Congress did address the issue of prize money, but that did not resolve the problem of manning *Alfred* for deployment before the winter months set in. And the expedition to Africa's west coast was never authorized. As a result, Jones departed from Providence, Rhode

Island, in *Alfred* and with *Hampton* on 27 October. *Hampton* ran aground before clearing the harbor, however, and the sloop *Providence* replaced her. The two-ship squadron then departed from Providence on 1 November.

This second deployment by Jones was another success. It began modestly with the taking of Continental Navy deserters off the Continental privateer *Eagle* at Tarpaulin Cove on Cape Cod, Massachusetts. Jones then captured a number of prizes, the most important of which was the British armed transport *Mellish,* whose cargo contained a large number of British Army winter uniforms. That portion of the cargo, which quickly found its way to General Washington's army, alone would have made the operation a success. Other ships, including British colliers, were captured, although the British Navy recaptured some of the prizes before they could make it to a safe American port with their prize crews. Jones also attacked Canso for a second time and destroyed a supply ship and a warehouse.

The final event of the deployment involved Jones's successful evasion of the twenty-eight-gun Royal Navy frigate HMS *Milford.* In the action Jones succeeded in getting *Alfred* and three of the four prizes he was escorting safely to Boston. The British recapture of the fourth prize, the armed merchant ship *John,* turned out to be a persistent thorn in Jones's side. Midshipman Robert Sanders, who was the prize captain placed aboard by Jones after the *John*'s capture, claimed that Jones should have come to his aid when *John* was attacked by *Milford.* Sanders, while a prisoner in Halifax, succeeded in getting a complaint to that effect to Commodore Hopkins. In addition, the owners of the privateer *Eagle,* from which Jones had removed navy deserters, filed a suit against Jones. As it turned out, Sanders could not support his charges and Commodore Hopkins took an active role in blocking the legal action initiated by *Eagle*'s owners.

Unfortunately, however, the charges made by Sanders and the owners of *Eagle* did undercut the success of Jones's second deployment to some degree. The two charges also signaled more professional irritations over the horizon. For the present, however, Jones took up lodging in Boston and again began making contacts and writing letters to members of the Continental Congress.

One of those letters, written to Robert Morris on 10 February 1777, addressed two significant issues, one new and one ongoing for Jones. The industrial base supporting the Continental Navy was Jones's first subject, showing his ability to see naval power in more than a tactical perspective. He wrote, "There are no officers more immediately wanted in the marine department, than commissioners of the dockyards, to superintend the building and outfit of all ships of war . . . and have in constant readiness, sufficient quantities of provision, stores, slops, &c., so that the small number of ships we have may be constantly employed . . . had such men been appointed in the first place, the new ships might have been at sea long ago."[12] It should be noted that having well-managed shipyards would not only have been a force multiplier for the Continental Navy, it also would have multiplied the career-enhancing opportunities for Jones, who still had his sights set on a new frigate.

The second subject addressed was the recruiting and retention of navy seamen, by then a frequently recurring theme for Jones, who advised Morris, "I must repeat what I asserted formerly, that unless some happy expedient can be fallen upon to induce the seamen to enter into the service for a longer term than twelve months, it will never be possible to bring them under proper subordination; and subordination is as necessary, nay, far more so in the fleet, than in the army."[13]

Jones was learning the hard way that not even patriotic merchant seamen and fishermen were immediately convertible to naval personnel. The issues concerned not only such naval skills as achieving rapid fire with gun crews, but also how much of a time commitment could be expected from naval personnel. No less a naval authority than British admiral Horatio Nelson recognized the latter problem when he was in charge of organizing a naval militia, called "Sea Fencibles," in August 1801 as England faced the threat of an invasion by Napoléon:

> Of the 2,600 Sea Fencibles enrolled between Orfordness and Beachy Head, only 385 have offered themselves to go on board a Ship, and serve at the Sand-heads, &c.; the Sea Fencibles of Margate, for instance, consist of 118 men, their occupation is pier-men belonging to the Margate hoys, and some few who assist Ships up and down the River. These men say, 'our employment will not allow us to go from our homes beyond a day or two for actual service:' but they profess their readiness to fly on board, or on any other duty ordered, when the Enemy are announced as actually coming on the sea.[14]

Nelson's letter to his leadership points out that problems with recruiting and retention go beyond financial rewards. And in the case of the Continental Navy, at least two other problems hindered recruiting and retention of sailors. On board a privateer, the discipline was more relaxed, and the chances of being killed, wounded, or captured were significantly reduced. And there was no chance that Congress would attempt to inhibit the navy's competition from privateers, since privateers had become a very effective naval weapon against British commerce.

Despite Jones's highly successful deployments in *Providence* and *Alfred* during 1776, he faced two major disappointments and a near court-martial at the beginning of 1777. The first problem was his seniority in the Continental Navy captain's list approved in October 1776 by the Continental Congress. Jones learned that he was eighteenth on the list of twenty-four. He believed that his experience, performance at sea, and combat record should have placed him fifth on the list. Some of those ahead of him on the seniority list lacked his operational successes. He also pointed out that he was chronologically senior as a commissioned officer in the Continental Navy to some of those placed ahead of him on the list.

Almost every captain on the seniority list was assigned a ship, and, not surprisingly, the assignments continued to be heavily influenced by regionalism. The frigates under construction were assigned to captains from the region where they were being built. There was more than political bias involved in that approach, however, since the captain usually was directly responsible for the final construction and fitting out of his ship. If he were from the area, he would doubtless be in a better position to deal with the shipyard involved.

That advantage of a captain being from the area in which a ship was fitting out would be driven home to Jones later, when he was placed in command of *Ranger.* But for the short term, presumably because he had no strong ties with any one of the individual colonies, Jones was assigned back to *Providence.* He not only wasn't advanced on the basis of his two successful deployments, he clearly was facing a demotion from the larger *Alfred.*

It was a heavy blow. Jones had been particularly effective in delivering significant successes for the American colonies during the confused and improvisational earliest stages of the Continental Navy, and now that the navy would have some *real* ships, he was being bypassed. He believed he had been ill-used and made it known to members of the Marine Committee and Commodore Hopkins. His relationship with Hopkins became particularly acrimonious and nearly resulted in his court-martial.

These events of early 1777 did not enhance Jones's reputation within the navy and the Continental Congress. Like some particularly effective combat leaders in other navies and in other times, Jones was establishing a reputation as someone who would win in combat but who was also politically difficult to handle. And he was, whether fairly or not, becoming known as an officer devoted to aggressively advancing his own career at the expense of fellow officers.

In February there was an aborted plan for Jones to command a squadron to attack British ships and installations in the West Indies, Gulf of Mexico, and possibly the west coast of Africa. Then in March there was a truly bizarre proposal by the Marine Committee that Jones cross the Atlantic in the French armed merchantman *Amphitrite,* "acting on suitable occasions as commander," which also came to naught. And it was a good thing that plan was never executed, since only a group of deskbound politicians could think that two captains from different nations on board the same ship could agree on "suitable occasions" when they would switch command.

Finally in June 1777, Jones was ordered to take command of a three-masted, eighteen-gun sloop of war *Ranger,* built in Portsmouth, New Hampshire. *Ranger* initially was intended for a different captain, a Portsmouth man named John Roche, who turned out to be of highly dubious character. The Continental Congress resolved the situation with refreshingly straightforward legislative language: "*Resolved,* that Captain Roach [sic] be suspended. *Resolved,* that Captain John Paul Jones be appointed to command the said ship *Ranger.*"

Ranger wasn't as powerful as any of the frigates Jones hoped to command, but she was new, had good lines, and was named for a noted New England fighting unit of the French and Indian War, Rogers' Rangers. Her figurehead was a Ranger rifleman, and given the superstitious nature of sailors in the age of sail, an association with a successful fighting unit, even by name only, would have been considered a good omen.

In fact, the Rogers' Rangers unit was a particularly appropriate role model for the commerce-raiding and coastal-raiding techniques Jones would soon launch from French ports in *Ranger* and her successor, *Bonhomme Richard.* Rogers and his men were a tough specialized scouting and raiding force that used intimate knowledge of their rugged environment and hit-and-run tactics to harass French army units during the French and Indian War. In addition, Jones was linked to the Rangers' leader, Robert Rogers, with a fascinating coincidence.

In 1757, Rogers and his Rangers were mauled and then pinned down by a superior French and Indian force in a wooded, snow-covered ravine, located in the Adirondack Mountains near Lake Champlain. During what became known as the battle of LaBarbue Creek, when there appeared to be no hope for the Rangers to survive, the French commander shouted for Rogers to surrender. Rogers replied, "Go to hell!" Then he and his men redoubled their efforts and fought their way out of a seemingly hopeless situation. Many years later, in a very different environment off the English coast, Jones would reprise the essential elements of the action at LaBarbue Creek—even Rogers' response to the invitation to surrender—in the Continental ship *Bonhomme Richard.*

When Jones was named to command *Ranger* at the beginning of 1777, the naval aspects of the American Revolution had taken on a discernable shape. The picture was deceptively ominous, and the most visible aspect of the naval war was the disturbing and regular loss of Continental Navy ships. In a steady stream of combat losses and weather mishaps, the sparse assets of the Continental Navy were being eliminated as fast as they were commissioned. Typical of those discouraging losses were the twenty-four-gun small frigate *Montgomery* and the larger thirty-six-gun frigate *Congress,* two brand new ships that had to be burned on the Hudson River to prevent their capture.

Even more serious strategic naval setbacks involved British blockades or actual occupation of the American colonies' major seaports. In September 1777, for example, a British force under Major General Sir William Howe defeated General Washington at the battle of Brandywine and occupied Philadelphia, then the Continental capital. The naval portion of that particular British campaign involved gaining control of the Delaware River from Philadelphia to the sea. This was largely the responsibility of naval units commanded by Admiral Richard Howe, General Sir William Howe's brother. Admiral Howe not only established the sea lines of communication for the British Army units occupying Philadelphia, he also forced the Americans to burn five ships of the Continental Navy to avoid their capture. Those ships included *Alfred,* the ship in which Jones started his naval career.[15]

The loss of Philadelphia to the British involved more than the key military ground of the city itself and the five ships. It also involved the loss of the lower Delaware River as a refuge for Continental ships seeking protection from the powerful British Navy units patrolling off the Atlantic Coast and the loss of the rope walks, piers, and chandleries of Philadelphia's harbor. Also lost were the shipyards along the Delaware, where some of the earliest purpose-built Continental Navy frigates were constructed and other American ships found first-class repair facilities.

The Penobscot Bay expedition in July 1779 continued the string of Continental Navy disasters. In June, the British had occupied and fortified a peninsula in Penobscot Bay that is now the town of Castine, Maine. Their objective was to secure the supply of timber that had been moving from the area south to the British Navy in New York. With Newport occupied by the British to the south and then Penobscot Bay under British military control to the north, the city of Boston was in a military vice.

To dislodge the British in Penobscot Bay a significant force consisting of both Continental and Massachusetts navy units was assembled. The combined naval expedition of twenty-two ships and three thousand embarked militiamen was the largest naval operation of the Revolutionary War. Captain Saltonstall, Jones's former captain in *Alfred,* was the commodore leading the force north on 19 July. After weeks of indecision on the part of Saltonstall and a total breakdown of army-navy cooperation, a powerful British squadron of ten ships, led by the sixty-four-gun ship of the line HMS *Raisonable,* arrived on 13 August to settle the issue. When the smoke cleared the Continental Navy expedition was all but wiped out, including the thirty-two-gun frigate *Warren,* one of the precious few purpose-built frigates the Continental Navy had. The naval disaster at Penobscot Bay was another highly visible demonstration that the outgunned, marginally trained, and inconsistently led Continental Navy was generally no match in main force confrontations with the British Navy.

Obscured by the more dramatic and visible losses of naval units and facilities, however, was a less dramatic but arguably more important strategic accomplishment of the Continental Navy. During 1777, it captured scores of British merchant ships to supplement the many others captured by American privateers. As a result, the portion of Washington's naval strategy involving attacks on the British sea lines of communication was markedly inhibiting British logistical support to its ground forces in America.

Those under-appreciated successes of the Continental Navy in commerce raiding, plus occasional victories against British Navy ships, would turn out to be more important in the long run than they appeared to be on the surface.

Particularly important, the relatively few but strategically significant Continental Navy's successes during the middle stages of the American Revolution were accomplished at a time when Britain was locked in a global life-and-death struggle with France. And very soon Jones and *Ranger* would become a dramatically significant military element in the projection of the American colonies' naval power against its enemy's home island.

3
The Cutting Edge of Strategy

"War, once declared, must be waged offensively, aggressively."
Rear Admiral A. T. Mahan

The Continental Congress's orders assigning Jones to his new command reached him in Boston, and by 12 July 1777 he was in Portsmouth, getting involved in the fitting out of his new sloop of war. *Ranger,* also classified as a corvette among eighteenth-century naval ships, was a bit heavier than comparably gunned British Navy ships. She was 116 feet long, had a crew of roughly 140, was designed with clean lines, and showed a potential for speed. Jones was understandably enthusiastic about her.

A recruiting poster for *Ranger,* believed to be one of the first Continental Navy recruiting handbills, was handed out in the New England towns of Portsmouth, Providence, and Boston. It painted an appealing picture of *Ranger*'s forthcoming deployment.

> ALL GENTLEMEN SEAMEN and able-bodied LANDSMEN who have a Mind to distinguish themselves in the GLORIOUS CAUSE of their Country, and make their Fortune, an Opportunity now offers on board the Ship RANGER. . . . The Ship Ranger, in the Opinion of every Person who has seen her is looked upon to be one of the best Cruizers in America—She will always be able to Fight her Guns under a most excellent Cover; and no vessel yet built was ever calculated for sailing faster and making good Weather.

Jones also ran a recruitment ad in *The Freeman's Journal* of Portsmouth on 26 July.[1] His message painted much too rosy a picture of *Ranger*'s coming deployment, presaging an inclination of future navy recruiters to occasionally overemphasize the positive. Reflecting a naïveté based on his lack of naval training, Jones also invited future challenges to his leadership by promising in print that he would be "answerable to every person . . . under my command, for the punctual and regular payment of wages."

Concerning prize money, he said that he would "seek the consent and approbation of officers and men" on the appointment of prize agents and make "punctual, just and regular payments to every person concern'd." Those two public promises were totally inconsistent with his very undemocratic role as commanding officer of *Ranger* and the reality that he would be in no position to guarantee wages or prize money to his officers and crew. In his enthusiasm, Jones may have convinced himself that he could really pay off on his promises. Reality set in quickly, however, and Jones's problems soon also included disputes with his crew over pay.

In the same recruiting handbills that had described the opportunities for both the seamen and landsmen "to make their Fortune," specific sign-on bonuses were promised to the crew. When the bonuses were not forthcoming, the crew complained. Jones claimed that the bonuses were for signing on for at least a year, and since the crew members insisted that they were signing on only for a single cruise, they were not entitled to the bonuses. The compromise Jones offered—half of a month's pay provided to the dependents of crew members—left a simmering discontent in *Ranger* that would reemerge after *Ranger* arrived in France.

In addition to recruiting, other major challenges confronted Jones before he could get to sea. For example, it was clear that his new ship was over-rigged. Her masts and yards were too large and too heavy, and as designed, she would carry too much sail. With such a top-heavy rig, *Ranger* would tend to roll excessively, and this would make her less seaworthy, even in normal sea conditions. In the seamen's term of her time, she was crank. Of particular importance in a warship, the excessive rolling would make her a significantly less stable platform for her guns. To make matters worse, the ship's builder had provided sails to *Ranger* that were cut of extremely poor material, further compromising her capabilities.

Jones knew the solutions to these shortcomings, and he complained bitterly about being held up by the lack of decent canvass for his sails and the other materials he needed for refitting *Ranger.* He was only moderately successful, however, in resolving the problems in the New Hampshire shipyard, where he had the disadvantage of not being a local captain.

In addition to the immediate problems with which Jones was wrestling were incipient problems that Jones mostly neglected as he pressed to get under way for France. The major problem was that all of the officers and about two-thirds of the 140 men recruited were from the Portsmouth area. That tended to make them a cohesive group within their ranks, but that circumstance also made the captain an outsider in his own ship. It was a command weakness that would plague Jones during his coming deployment.

Perhaps the most negative aspect of the situation involved *Ranger*'s officers, who had little loyalty to Jones and who, under other circumstances, would have been a bridge between Jones and his crew. Jones's first lieutenant was Thomas Simpson, brother-in-law to the local navy agent and a merchant seaman nine years older than his captain. *Ranger*'s second lieutenant was Elijah Hall, five years older than Jones and a local merchant seaman and shipbuilder. Lieutenant of Marines Samuel Wallingford and the ship's surgeon Doctor Ezra Green were both from Portsmouth. And *Ranger*'s midshipman David Wendell was from a Portsmouth family involved in shipping.

Compounding Jones's personnel problems was the fact that he was, as far as his shipmates were concerned, an immigrant. In colonial New England at the time, ethnic Scots were rare and the objects of serious prejudice. Jones would have been considered to be even worse than an outsider from Virginia—his officers and crew looked on him as a foreigner.

As he prepared his ship for deployment, however, Jones was apparently not concerned about incipient personnel problems. Toward the end of a letter to Robert Morris on 30 October, in which he complains at length about his seniority ranking among the navy's captains, he briefly mentions his crew: "I have an Orderly well disciplined and spirited Crew consisting of an hundred and forty odd." Also on 30 October, Jones wrote to Joseph Hewes. Again, there is a brief, positive mention of his crew. This time it is in the context of his complaints with the shipyard's lack of responsiveness.

It is possible that, in his anxiety to get to sea, Jones simply chose to ignore his personnel problems. It is more likely, however, that he truly did not recognize the hazards of a situation that an officer with more traditional naval training would have spotted. In any event, it is clear that with a crew that was accustomed to operating on consensus and officers who identified closely with their men and only remotely with their captain, Jones was heading for significant personnel trouble in his new ship. It was only a matter of time before critical discipline problems with both officers and crew arose, and Jones's failure to recognize and address this situation was a major flaw in his leadership.

Jones's focus was clearly on getting to sea. In a letter to Hewes, also on the 30th, his frustration is evident.

> You will no doubt be Surprised to find that the Ranger is still in port—but the wonder must cease when you understand that with all my own and my Officers Application and Industry I have not been able to complete a Single Suite of Sails till within these few days past—and other materials have been equally Backward. . . . I never before had so disagreeable a service to perform as this which have now accomplished, and of which Another will claim the Credit as well as the profit.

> I have been fully manned for near two months past—so you may imagine what I must have felt on being thus detained by a heavy Gale from the N.E.—when it clears up I propose to embrace the first Wind that will carry me thro' the *Enemies lines* and off the Coast.[2]

Finally on 1 November, the wind was favorable, and Jones was on his way out of Portsmouth. He had more potential problems than a captain taking a new ship to sea should have had, but he was predictably anxious to get to sea and into action. It was neither the first nor the last time a navy captain with a new command and an array of problems would seek escape by getting to sea. *Ranger*'s course was set for France, where Jones was ordered to deliver important dispatches, including news of the crucial American victory at Saratoga. Jones anticipated that, once in France, he would give up command of *Ranger* and then receive orders to another, presumably larger, ship. The winds continued to favor *Ranger* and, after a transit of thirty-one days, she arrived in Nantes, France, on 2 December 1777, with two small prizes in hand.

The transit bore out Jones's fears about *Ranger*'s performance shortcomings, and once in Nantes, he immediately set out to make the needed adjustments to his ship by installing more appropriately sized spars, relocating the masts, and securing better quality sails. He also showed that he practiced what he preached to the Continental Congress about attending to the financial incentives for navy sailors. Jones promptly advanced his crew pay from his own pocket. In late December, with the immediate needs of his crew and ship being attended to, Jones traveled to Paris and reported to the senior American diplomat assigned there, Benjamin Franklin. The meeting began a relationship that helped weave the concept of civilian control of the military into America's earliest military-political structure.

Despite the differences in age between the thirty-year-old navy captain and the diplomat who was his senior by forty years, there was a solid basis for friendship. Jones needed political support to get important assignments and a better ship, and Franklin knew that America needed warfighters who would produce combat victories. Those victories were not only militarily important, they were also politically important at home and among potential allies, including powerful France.

As Jones entered the slippery world of foreign diplomacy, a world his British Navy counterparts normally became familiar with as junior officers, Franklin became his political "anchor to windward." That support was something that the young and politically inexperienced naval captain needed, particularly in

Paris, a capital with heavy political intrigue even among the resident American commissioners.

A prominent player in that intrigue, the second-ranking American commissioner in Paris, Arthur Lee, was part of a faction in America driven by strong enmity towards Franklin. Based on Jones's developing friendship with Franklin, Lee saw him as a political enemy and began working against his interests. In addition, both of the confidential secretaries to Franklin and Lee were British spies. Edward Bancroft, Franklin's secretary, was to become a particular friend of Jones.

Beyond the inner circle of American diplomats in Paris was the French king, Louis XVI, his court, the French naval administration, and an assortment of commercial agents and advisers. Each of those individuals had an agenda, creating political crosscurrents that affected Jones's attempts to secure his next ship and significant assignments to advance the Continental naval strategy and Jones's career.

Once in Paris, the most important and clearly the worst news that Jones received was that the frigate that had been intended for him, *L'Indien,* would not be his. The ship was being built in a private shipyard in Holland for the Paris-based American commissioners, but funding problems derailed the deal. Jones's immediate hopes for a new purpose-built naval ship were dashed.

At this point, according to many contemporary accounts, Jones launched into one of his serial romances, this time with a French woman, Madame Le Ray de Chaumont. Sophisticated Parisians suggested that Jones was simply learning to speak French with what was referred to—with a knowing smirk—as a "sleeping dictionary." The romance eventually led to repercussions, since Madame Chaumont's husband, Jacques Donatien Le Ray de Chaumont, was a wealthy merchant fleet owner and a member of the King's Privy Council. In that position of influence, Chaumont had dealings with the French government and navy on matters relating to the American War of Independence and, coincidentally, with Jones's efforts to secure a new ship.

Neither Jones's correspondence nor Madame de Chaumont's correspondence, including that which passed between them, provides unequivocal evidence of a romantic relationship between them. Thus the question of whether they actually had an affair is at least a little doubtful. Hints of a romantic relationship do appear, however, between the lines of a letter from Jones to Madame de Chaumont written from Lorient in June 1779, when Jones claimed that he "never had more to say nor less power to express myself." In any event, the purported romance has contributed to Jones's reputation as a sailor who moved from woman to woman almost as frequently as he sailed from port to port.

Jones returned to *Ranger* and the reality of shipboard matters on 28 January 1778. He had adjusted to the disappointment of losing *L'Indien* and begun to think about alternative means of getting a new command. Stubborn determination in the face of adversity was, at that point, becoming as much a part of his career ashore as afloat.

Unfortunately the situation he found in *Ranger* had deteriorated significantly since he had left Nantes for Paris. His crew, with the encouragement of his officers, was focused on the disparity between the recruiting posters touting prize money and "an agreeable Voyage in this pleasant Season of the Year" and the hard refitting work being carried out far from home and in harsh winter weather.

Despite having advanced his crew pay from his own pocket, Jones was dealing with sullen sailors on the verge of outright mutiny. His first lieutenant had been capitalizing on the anticipation that Jones would leave *Ranger* for another command once they were in France, and he was using that probability to enhance his own opportunity to command *Ranger.* When Jones arrived back in Nantes, Simpson informed him that the men were refusing to work. They weren't interested in talk of honor and glory; they wanted to get home and presumably pick off a few valuable prizes along the way. Even the appearance of the American commercial agent in Nantes to pay off the prize money from one of the captures taken on the way to France did not substantially change the attitude of *Ranger*'s men. Jones had lost the prospect of commanding *L'Indien,* and now he was faced with the possible loss of the ship he still had.

There was, however, a bright spot in the dark picture. When the plans for *L'Indien* disappeared in the fog of diplomacy, two of the three American commissioners in Paris, Franklin and Silas Deane, wrote new orders for Jones. The orders were the best kind for an eager young naval captain—a virtual carte blanche. The orders began with an apology for failing to secure a new ship for Jones and then established wide latitude for his continued operations in *Ranger:* "As it is not in our Power to procure you such a Ship as you expected, we advise you after equipping the *Ranger* in the best manner, for the Cruise you propose, that you proceed with her in the manner you shall judge best, for distressing the Enemies of the United States, by Sea, or otherwise, consistent with the Laws of War, and the Terms of your Commission."[3]

Next the orders described the ports to which Jones would send the prizes he presumably would take, plus an admonition to avoid doing anything that would precipitate complaints from France, Spain, or other neutral countries. Since France and Spain were technically neutrals, the latter provided the political cover for the American commissioners in Paris that civilian officials are traditionally careful to secure for themselves when initiating military missions.

The final part of Jones's new orders instructed him to tell his crew, "Tho' it was not in our power to be particular as the rewards they should be entitled to, yet they must safely Rely on the Justice of the Congress." One can visualize Jones rolling his eyes at that last part of his orders and muttering at least one colorful expletive he had learned as an apprentice in *Friendship*. Only someone who never faced a Continental Navy crew at muster would propose telling them that they can "rely on the justice of the Congress" for their just due.

Notwithstanding the volatile situation with his alienated crew, Jones was determined to strike at Britain, and his new orders gave him the latitude he needed. His plan fit the part of the American naval strategy that called for the projection of naval power against the British Isles. He intended to raid British commerce off the coasts of Ireland, Scotland, and England and to attack weakly defended British ports. In the process, Jones also intended to create consternation among the British populace, throw its political leadership off balance, and divert its naval forces from the American theater. Jones had shaped his mission on a concept now very familiar in the twenty-first century: asymmetrical warfare.[4]

On 13 February, only days after America and France signed a secret alliance, Jones sailed northwest along the coast of the Bay of Biscay and anchored in Quiberon Bay. He was in one of the principal Atlantic anchorages of the French Navy. On entering the anchorage, Jones negotiated an exchange of salutes with the senior French admiral there, not so much as recognition of his status as a Continental Navy ship captain but more as a validation of America as a nation. Despite the fact that the imperious French officer returned only a nine-gun salute for the thirteen guns fired by *Ranger*, the event is considered to be another major milestone in U.S. history. It is believed to be the first such naval salute to the newborn nation, represented by the Stars and Stripes flag that had been adopted by the Continental Congress on 14 June 1777. In the broad sweep of global affairs, that local exchange of naval courtesies was a nonevent. To a new nation struggling to survive its war of independence, however, it took on highly significant psychological importance. The salute was the second time Jones was connected with a psychologically important first during the American Revolution.

During the following weeks, Jones remained in the general operating area along the northern coast of the Bay of Biscay. He continued to test and improve *Ranger*'s sailing qualities, and he began an important friendship with one of

France's senior naval officers, Admiral Comte d'Orvilliers. For Jones, operating from France, the importance of the admiral's friendship would be second only to that with Franklin, and a close second at that.

Admiral d'Orvilliers encouraged Jones in his bold plans and promised to provide specific support. This personal contact with the highly professional French naval leader, a senior officer in command of a significant fleet, was particularly valuable to Jones who, like the other Continental Navy captains, had no American military mentors. Jones and his Revolutionary counterparts were basically self-taught naval captains with little in the way of a military culture to support their careers. This significant gap in Jones's development is easy for historians and biographers to miss, and this fact explains much of Jones's behavior. The fact that Jones did not have the benefit of structured military training and support also provides insight to why this skillful captain was sometimes unable to inspire a high degree of personal loyalty from those he commanded in *Ranger.*

Finally Jones was ready, and after being driven back into port once by heavy weather, *Ranger* sailed for the Irish Sea on 10 April. Jones's ambitious plan of attack had three objectives:

1. Disrupt British maritime commerce by attacking a port and destroying the ships and port facilities he found there and thus cause panic in the local countryside. The raids would also be retaliation for British raids on American coastal cities.
2. Take a noteworthy hostage to trade for American sailors being held prisoner by the British.
3. Continue to attack merchant shipping along the coasts of the British Isles and, when possible, take prizes.

As he moved into the Irish Sea, Jones sank one small British cargo carrier of little value and captured another that was valuable enough to send back to Brest with a prize crew. It was a modestly encouraging beginning.

Then on 18 April off the northern tip of the Isle of Man, Jones and his crew confronted a British revenue cutter. Jones tried to pass *Ranger* off as a merchantman out of Glasgow. When that deception failed, *Ranger*'s gun ports flew open, and Jones maneuvered to deliver a broadside against the cutter. The British captain, however, took advantage of his fore-and-aft-rigged cutter's greater agility and escaped the clutches of the larger, square-rigged, less nimble American raider. The cutter's captain used tactics that Jones himself had employed in *Providence* when outgunned by a larger adversary.

Two days later, after sinking a sloop out of Dublin, Jones turned his attention to HMS *Drake,* a twenty-gun British sloop of war moored in Carrickfergus, a port town along the inlet leading to Dublin. Jones was for an immediate attempt to capture the British ship, which was roughly the same size as *Ranger.* His crew refused, however—an astonishing act on the face of it, but perhaps not so surprising in light of Jones's relationship with his crew and their lack of significant naval training. The crew finally agreed to a night attack, but foul weather eliminated any chance to pursue that course.

Next Jones turned to the centerpiece of his plan, an attack on an English port. The target was Whitehaven, where he had begun his apprenticeship in *Friendship.* It was an obvious choice, since he knew the sea approaches and the layout of the town well. The audacity of Jones's intentions was underscored by the fact that there had not been a serious enemy attack against an English port in many, many years. One Jones biographer established the date of the last raid on an English port as 1667.[5]

Once again, *Ranger*'s crew did not share the enthusiasm of its captain for an aggressive plan. Perhaps a fear of being out of their fighting element at sea and ashore in enemy territory held them back. Their situation, in fact, would have been the naval equivalent of being behind enemy lines in a land battle. In addition, from his crew's point of view, the proposed attack on Whitehaven not only was high risk, but also offered almost no prospect of lucrative prizes.

Jones had to put down an incipient mutiny before moving ahead with his plan. Then incredibly both ship's officers declined to join other volunteers for the landing. To make matters even worse, Jones lost the crucial element of surprise when the wind dropped and delayed his arrival in Whitehaven harbor. Jones pressed on, however, and after dividing a small amphibious assault force of thirty Continental Marine volunteers and ten seamen into two boats, he set out for shore. Jones commanded one boat, and Marine Lieutenant Wallingford took command of the second.

The landing party left *Ranger* at midnight on 22 April. After three hours of hard rowing against the tidal current, they reached the inner harbor. It was daylight by then, and the tactical benefit of surprise was gone. In fact, hundreds of townspeople were by now aware of Jones's presence and were starting to congregate on the waterfront. An audience for an amphibious raid is not a good thing, but Jones's one last advantage—the lack of significant enemy army or navy units in the immediate area—prevented a disaster.

Jones and his crew spiked the guns of the batteries flanking the harbor entrance and started a large fire on board a collier moored on the crowded waterfront.

This was accomplished despite the fact that one of the American raiders, a crewman who had enlisted in Portsmouth simply to get home to Ireland, bolted from the landing party and ran through the town giving an alarm. By 6 AM the raiders were back on board *Ranger,* which had moved shoreward to pick up the raiding party. Given the lack of training in the complexities of amphibious operations and the number of things that could go wrong under the best of circumstances, it is close to miraculous that the raid on Whitehaven was completed with no casualties.

At first glance, the raid on Whitehaven was of limited military importance. The townspeople extinguished the waterfront fire, and the harbor batteries were quickly reestablished. The shock to the general sense of security Britons felt, however, was immense, and that shock reverberated among the political and naval leadership in London. It could be compared, without overstatement, to a German destroyer sailing into Boston harbor during World War II, sending a landing party ashore to blow up shore batteries and set fire to an oil tanker on the waterfront, and then leaving unscathed. Despite the limited importance of the raid tactically, strategically it was a political and media bombshell for the American colonies, Great Britain, and France.

The London newspaper *Gazetteer and New Daily Advertiser* reported about a letter it had received from Whitehaven on 1 May: "We are all in a bustle here, from the late insolent attack of the provincial privateer's men. I hope it will rouse us from our lethargy."[6] The *Morning Chronical and London Advertiser,* dated 1–4 May 1778, reported, "Four companies of the Militia are now here. . . . Sunday last a company of gentlemen volunteers were formed for the protection of the town, exclusive of the ten companies of seamen, etc."[7] An early twentieth-century British biographer of Jones, despite some fabrications in his work, did manage to accurately describe the impact of Jones's raids in *Ranger* in more vivid, and even more perceptive, language:

> It taught the English that the fancied securities of their coasts was a myth, and thereby compelled their government to take expensive measures for the defence of numerous ports hitherto relying for protection wholly on the vigilance and supposed omnipotence of their navy. . . . The excitement along the coast was intense. The stout burghers, thoroughly aroused at the thoughts of being seized and carried off by pirates and desperadoes as they sat in the—once—safe shelter of their homes, formed themselves into companies of militia. . . . Never in the memory of man had they been so shocked and surprised out of their after-dinner meditations; but, most terrible warning of what might happen to them

> was the alarming fact: *that it doubled or more the rates of insurance,* which . . . as Jones wrote, *"in the long run proved the most grievous damage of all."*[8]

On a personal level, Jones had accelerated the momentum of his career. In six hours, with a crew that was under-motivated and marginally trained militarily, he had combined dramatic initiative and iron determination to incite a simultaneous awareness of his accomplishments in America, France, Britain, and elsewhere in Europe. He had graduated from a modest recognition of his achievements in his own country to international recognition of his boldness.

The next stage of Jones's plan was to take an important hostage, someone who could be used to negotiate the release of American seamen held by the British. It was a mission that harked back to his unsuccessful attempt, while captain of *Alfred,* to rescue American seamen imprisoned in Nova Scotia. Jones's decision to take a noteworthy hostage, an act characterized by many in Britain as no more than piracy, should be judged in the perspective of his own times, when the practice of swapping prisoners was part of warfare in the age of sail.

The target was the Earl of Selkirk, a British lord known to Jones from his early days in Kirkbean. The earl's manor was located on St. Mary's Isle, located in Kirkcudbright Bay in Solway Firth, a site also familiar to Jones from childhood. At 10 AM on 23 April, *Ranger* entered the Bay, and by 11 AM her cutter was ashore with Jones leading a dozen sailors, plus *Ranger*'s sailing master and his marine lieutenant. By cleverly claiming that he was leading a press-gang, Jones ensured that all of the able-bodied men on the island would give him and his party a wide berth.

Before even reaching the manor house, Jones learned that the earl was absent, and he decided to return to the ship. The sailing master and the marine lieutenant objected, however, arguing that the crew was entitled to loot the manor. After all, they claimed, there would be no prize money from the Whitehaven raid and the British frequently looted and burned private homes along the American coast. Clearly abdicating his responsibility as a leader, Jones reversed his own decision and assented. His later claim that he insisted that the looting be limited to the Lord's silver tableware didn't change the shabbiness of the event. He returned to the cutter and left matters at the manor to the sailing master and marine lieutenant. Jones's lack of a firm grip on his crew, notwithstanding the extenuating circumstances, was a notable leadership failure. Fortunately, what resulted was more of a farce than an atrocity.

The St. Mary's Isle raid degenerated to the level of a comic opera, with the master and lieutenant seeking out Lady Selkirk and demanding the family silver.

On the promise that no one would be harmed and that there would be no additional looting, the silverware was produced and the raiding party returned to *Ranger.* The countess, who had maintained her composure during the proceedings, later described the looters as "horrid-looking wretches" with more of a look of pirates than a disciplined navy unit. Her description and the looting event on St. Mary's Isle further contributed to Jones's growing reputation along the coastlines of the British Isles as a fearsome brigand. In the long run, it also put a blot on his reputation as a professional naval officer.

To his credit, the unmilitary and ungentlemanly aspects of the Selkirk estate looting bothered Jones. As a result, Jones initiated a series of letters among the countess, the earl, and himself. Jones was anxious to justify his actions, and in a long letter on 8 May, his first to the countess, he tried hard to put his behavior in a positive light. "It cannot be too much lamented that in the profession of arms, the officer of fine feeling and real sensibility should be under the necessity of winking at any action of persons under his command which his heart cannot approve; but the reflection is doubly severe, when he finds himself obliged, in appearance, to countenance such actions by his authority. This hard case was mine when, on the 23rd of April last, I landed on St. Mary's Isle."[9]

Not surprisingly, the countess did not respond to Jones's letter nor to a second one. It was the earl who finally responded on 9 June, in great detail and with considerable restraint and a certain amount of disdain. The earl attacked Jones's rationalization quickly. "I own I do not understand how a man of *Sensibility and fine feelings* could reconcile this [Jones's intention to abduct the earl] to what his heart approved. . . . You must, therefore, be sensible on reflection, Sir, that you have proceeded on a very improper and mistaken notion, and that had your attempt succeeded, its only effect would have been to distress a family that never injured any person, and whose wishes have certainly been very friendly to the Constitutions and Just Liberties of America."[10]

Unfortunately, the earl's letter never reached Jones. One can assume, however, based on Jones's continued attempts to return the silver to its owners that he had already realized that allowing sailors under his command to take the Selkirk family silver was beyond the exigencies of war. Although the incident had a humorous side, it also illuminated Jones's hypersensitivity to his reputation as a professional naval officer.

After the St. Mary's raid, events were moving quickly and Jones had not forgotten about HMS *Drake,* the British sloop of war at Carrickfergus. By first light on 24 April he was back at the inlet leading into Belfast harbor, and his timing was perfect. *Drake* was under way and heading out into the North Channel between the Irish Sea and the Atlantic. Combat was inevitable, and it was a fairly even match. The two ships were about equal in size—*Drake* mounted twenty 6-pound guns and *Ranger* had eighteen 9-pounders. The larger guns would have given *Ranger* an edge in firepower, but *Drake* had a larger crew, which would have given her an advantage if the ships were grappled together and it came to hand-to-hand struggle.

The two captains, on the other hand, were very different. Jones had spent most of his brief career preying on merchantmen and carefully avoiding larger ships and squadrons of the British Navy. His adversary, Commander George Burdon, was a very senior British naval officer, who was in fact nearing retirement. On that basis, it was a mismatch: an experienced naval officer with a disciplined crew, against a young captain still learning the ways of naval warfare with an under-motivated and under-trained crew.

Jones had the initiative, however. He had no doubt about the identity of *Drake,* and that was important. In contrast, Burdon, despite warnings about Jones's presence off the coasts of the British Isles, could not be sure of *Ranger*'s identity, which Jones had taken steps to mask while *Ranger* was still in France. Was she a harmless merchantman heading for Belfast? Was she the dreaded Continental Navy raider known to be in the area? Burdon sent a junior lieutenant in a ship's boat to identify the unknown ship. Maneuvering *Ranger* to present a stern view and keep the British from viewing her gun ports, Jones allowed the lieutenant to board and promptly took him prisoner. By this time it was becoming clear to Burdon that the unidentified ship was *Ranger,* and it was increasingly clear to the sightseers in the small boats gathering at the site that indeed there would be a battle.

The two ships worked their way seaward to allow more room for maneuver. First *Drake* hoisted her colors, then *Ranger* quickly followed suit with the Stars and Stripes. Jones succeeded in crossing the British ship's bow quickly, firing a devastating broadside of grapeshot along the full length of *Drake*'s decks. It was a telling first blow. After an hour's slugging match, Burdon was fatally wounded by one of the Marine marksmen in *Ranger*'s tops, and, at virtually the same time, *Drake*'s first lieutenant was seriously wounded. At that point the ship's sailing master was suddenly in command and, realizing that *Drake* was no longer manageable and that the outcome was inevitable, he surrendered to end the killing. Seizing the initiative and capitalizing on skilled ship handling had negated whatever disadvantages in personnel numbers or crew training that Jones might have had going into the battle. He and *Ranger* carried the day.

Jones sent a prize crew to take over *Drake.* They boarded a ship whose sails were cut to ribbons and whose rigging and hull were badly damaged. Four of *Drake*'s crew were killed and nineteen were wounded. *Ranger,* in comparison, had suffered three killed and five wounded, and, although she had suffered considerable damage, she was still maneuverable. It was stunning and a significant Revolutionary War achievement for a Continental Navy ship to emerge the clear victor after head-to-head single-ship combat against a roughly equal British Navy sloop of war.

In most navies of the time, however, it would not have been considered a huge victory. After all, the two ships were not even large enough to be rated as frigates. But for the American representatives in Paris, the Continental Congress, and the supporters of American independence in the thirteen American colonies, however, it was momentous. The Continental Navy was not only surviving, incredibly, it was beginning to establish itself against the greatest empire and greatest navy in the world. That was an accomplishment of inestimable psychological importance to the American colonies as they continued to coalesce into a viable nation. If Jones had established significant momentum for his career with the raid at Whitehaven, his victory over the captain and crew of *Drake* increased that momentum exponentially.

Among the after-action reports was one in the *Morning Chronical and London Advertiser* of 9 May 1778. The article pointed out a number of possible reasons for *Drake*'s drubbing, but one comment at the end of the piece stood out. After the discussions of supposed advantages of *Ranger,* the paper opined: "In our engagements with the French and Spanish such a superiority would have been laughed at; but the case is widely different when we engage with our own country-men; men who have the same spirit and bravery with ourselves."[11] That was a sobering admission, a conclusion Jones would soon reinforce even more dramatically off a different coast of the British homeland.

Repairs to *Drake* and *Ranger* were begun on the 25th, the day after the battle. The *Ranger*'s crew interrupted their repair work briefly to capture a brigantine out of Whitehaven and, at some point, Jones released two fishermen he had captured several weeks before the battle. He sent them ashore with a small amount of money, adding to a reputation among a few of the local populace as a raider with a heart. By 28 April, Jones had passed through North Channel between Scotland and Ireland and was heading down the western coast of Ireland, neatly avoiding the British ships hunting for him in the Irish Sea and the North Channel. Lieutenant Simpson had been put aboard *Drake*—now marginally seaworthy—as prize master, with orders to remain close to *Ranger* during the return to France.

There were no untoward events until 4 May, when the two ships were off the coast of France, almost in sight of the island of Ushant and the port of Brest. At that point, *Ranger* was towing the marginally seaworthy *Drake,* and Jones ordered the towline cast off, as he headed off for a potential prize that had appeared. As he cleared away to race off after the unknown contact, Jones shouted an order for Simpson to follow him. Simpson continued on toward Ushant and Brest, however, claiming later that he had misunderstood Jones's shouted order. The potential prize turned out to be a neutral ship, and when Jones caught up with Simpson in *Drake,* he relieved him as prize master and accused him of disobeying his order. It was not clear whether Simpson had deliberately disobeyed his commander's order or had simply misunderstood it. Perhaps Jones's frustration with his first lieutenant's lack of enthusiastic support finally boiled over. In any event, the confrontation was a negative ending to an otherwise successful deployment.

On 8 May 1778 Jones and his prize sailed into Brest. With the exception of Admiral d'Orvilliers, almost no one acknowledged the accomplishments of Jones and *Ranger,* despite the fact that word of Jones's successes would have reached Paris before his return to Brest. For an ambitious captain, it would have been a disappointing, even enraging, return. Jones's resentment was palpable when he reported icily to the American commissioners in Paris on 9 May that he had returned with the British Navy ship *Drake* as a prize, and that he would follow up with the particulars of his cruise. Jones went on to suggest that, in the meantime, the commissioners could refer to the account of his mission provided by Admiral Comte d'Orvilliers to the French minister of marine.

Jones's report mentioned the two hundred prisoners he had taken during his deployment and then ended brusquely, "I have suspended and confined Lieutenant Simpson for disobedience of orders. I have only time at present to add that I have the honor to be, with much esteem and respect, Gentlemen, Your very obliged, very obedient, very humble, servant, John Paul Jones."[12] Between the lines was a warfighter's suggestion for his political leaders: "Go to hell."

4
Beached

"No good deed shall go unpunished."
Anonymous

The months in France after Jones's return to Brest in May 1778 were nearly as personally testing as his combat actions. He had risked his life and his ship by attacking a British Navy vessel comparable in combat capability to his own ship and commanded by a captain much more experienced than he was. And he had achieved an important psychological victory for his country in that one-on-one battle. Jones had exercised initiative in carrying out raids against the enemy's homeland. In contemporary terms, he had gotten "inside the enemy's decision cycle" by forcing the British to react to his offensive actions against their homeland. At a strategic level, the latter accomplishment was the most significant result of his deployment in the Irish Sea.

His immediate reward, however, was to be conspicuously ignored by his civilian leadership in Paris, which at that time consisted of Benjamin Franklin, Arthur Lee, and John Adams. (Adams arrived in France only a few months before Jones's return to Brest in *Ranger.*) Particularly galling to Jones was the fact that French naval personnel in Brest could plainly see the commissioners' failure to publicly recognize his accomplishments. For an officer with Jones's drive for international recognition for his newly independent country, as well as his need for personal recognition, that had to be hard to take.

Beyond coping with the public slight by the American commissioners in Paris, Jones faced many other problems during the nine months he would spend "on the beach" in France in 1778, and they were the kind of administrative entanglements that frustrate operationally oriented military leaders. One of the most serious of these distractions was dealing with Lieutenant Thomas Simpson, who had disobeyed his verbal order—at least in Jones's opinion—off Brest. When Jones relieved Simpson of command of the prize HMS *Drake* and placed Second Lieutenant Elijah Hall in command, Jones's blunt written order to Hall reflected how serious he considered the incident and what he expected from Hall in the performance of his duty: "You are to put Lieut. Simpson under arrest for disobedience of orders. You are to keep company with me, and pay punctual attention to the signals delivered herewith for your government."[1]

Unfortunately for Jones, however, the circumstances involving Simpson's performance of duty off Brest were not clear-cut. Jones's order had been shouted across open water, from one quarterdeck to another, and could reasonably have been misunderstood by *Ranger*'s first lieutenant. Another complicating factor was that Simpson was more popular with the crew than Jones was. In fact, he had been undercutting Jones's command authority since *Ranger* left Portsmouth by constantly making it clear that he would soon take command of the ship. That raised the question of whether Jones's arrest of Simpson was based on his first lieutenant's willful disobedience to an order that could have been misunderstood or on Jones's pent-up anger over Simpson's long-standing disloyalty.

Jones had confined Simpson to *Drake* as soon as they were back in Brest. In different circumstances, he would have charged his first lieutenant immediately with specific violations of Continental Navy regulations, and a court-martial would have been convened. Then both Jones and Simpson would have presented their witnesses and evidence to a court composed of impartial officers. It would have been a time-consuming process to be sure, but there would have been an official end to the matter, one way or another.

Unfortunately, not enough Continental Navy and Marine officers were available to initiate the court-martial. As a result, Simpson was confined to *Drake* while Jones tried to figure out what to do. In that circumstance, Simpson was in a position to continue undercutting his commanding officer's authority, and he took full advantage of the situation.

Jones next arranged for his first lieutenant to be transferred to a cabin in a French prison ship in Brest. His hope—that the Simpson problem would be easier to control, at least temporarily if the lieutenant was in French custody—was wrong. Simpson continued to foment trouble, and Admiral d'Orvilliers eventually had him transferred to a French prison ashore. While in prison ashore, Simpson was able to maintain regular contact with *Ranger*'s crew, and the result was a petition sent to Franklin in Paris, defending Simpson and signed by seventy-seven crew members. A similar document sent to Franklin was signed by twenty-eight warrant and petty officers, plus Lieutenant Hall, the ship's sailing master, and the ship's doctor.

Now inconvenienced and annoyed, the commissioners in Paris pressured Jones to relent in his charges against Simpson. In a conciliatory move, Jones had Simpson released on his own parole. The American commissioners' lack of support for Jones in this difficult situation was palpable in an astonishing letter from Lee, who continued to obstruct Jones's career ambitions. The letter, dated 23 May, was apparently the first official communication to Jones after his return in *Ranger.* Lee's letter contained no recognition of Jones's achievements in *Ranger.* It sounded more like a reprimand, focusing at the end on the problem with Jones's first lieutenant:

> We have heard of your arrival at Brest with a prize, and are surprised that you have not given us an account of that, and your other proceedings. We desire that you will not take any measures relative to the prize and prisoners, you may have made, except in securing them, nor incur any considerable expense without our orders.
>
> Upon receipt of this, you will immediately send us an account of what you have done upon your cruise; of what your prizes consist of; what repairs you want; and what further measures you propose to pursue. Upon all these subjects you will await our directions. Lieutenant Simpson has stated to us your having put him under arrest for disobeying orders. As a Court Martial must by order of Congress consist of three Captains, three Lieutenants, and three captains of Marines, and these cannot be had here, it is our desire that he may have passage procured for him by the first opportunity to America, allowing him whatever may be necessary for his defence. As the consequences of an arrest in foreign countries are thus extremely troublesome, they should be well considered before they are made.[2]

Lee's letter was a verbal thrashing of a senior naval officer by his civilian leadership and to characterize it as demotivating would be a gross understatement. Focusing on administrative convenience, Lee all but dismissed the very serious charges of disobedience to an operational order, and Lee demanded that Simpson be returned home in command of a ship. Jones, being in France, would thus find it impractical to pursue the matter in a court-martial in America. Lee then ended his letter with a thinly veiled rebuke. If Jones's terse 9 May report on *Ranger*'s deployment could be equated to firing a verbal shot across the bow of the American commissioners in Paris, then Lee's 23 May letter was a double-shotted verbal broadside that made a direct hit.

Jones's problem with his civilian leadership in Paris in the spring of 1778 was likely fed by his unresolved resentment at being placed eighteenth on the Continental Navy promotion list in October 1776. That ranking had to do with more than ego; it was the keystone for his career, and it would influence the quality of his assignments and the possibility of promotion to rear admiral.

In his correspondence with Joseph Hewes before his departure for France in *Ranger,* Jones had tried to make it clear how important the matter of his seniority was. On 30 October 1777, he had written emotionally to Hewes, even intimating that he was tempted to leave the service because individuals less qualified than he was superseded him on the Continental Navy's captains list:

> Why alas! Should my Honor and my Duty seem incompatible?—tho this may appear a Solecism yet its reality affects me more than all the former misfortune of my Life—some of them were perhaps br'ot about by my own misconduct—this I am sure was not,—I cannot think of quitting the Service especially while the liberties of America are Unconfirmed—I therefore must look up to you as my Patron and Protector—Shall I take the liberty to add, as my kind Friend and benefactor—with full dependence that you will do your Utmost to set me right so as to enable me to continue in the Service.[3]

There can be no doubt that Lee's letter would have rubbed those raw emotions in Jones, and one can also presume that it was his dedication to the cause of liberty that got him past the rebuke from one of his civilian leaders.

The heavy-handedness of Lee's letter and omission of any recognition of Jones's achievements in *Ranger* brought the issue of civilian control of the military to the fore for Jones. It was a severe test of his willingness to accept the principle, a test that he was able to pass. Thus while Jones is justly honored for establishing the U.S. Navy's "earliest traditions of heroism and victory," it should also be noted that with his decision to persevere in the service despite the actions of the American commissioners, Jones also helped secure the Navy's tradition of subordination to civilian leadership.

As ordered by Lee, Simpson was freed, placed in command of *Ranger,* and returned to America. Lee loomed larger as an ongoing political obstacle to Jones's aspirations to play an aggressive role in America's war with Britain. *Ranger* departed Brest for Portsmouth on 21 August 1778, with her crew finally able to look forward to getting home. Upon Simpson's return to America, the charges against him were dropped. Congress promoted him to captain, notwithstanding the highly questionable performance of his duty as Jones's first lieutenant. He then took *Ranger* back to sea with modest success, until the British captured him in 1780. He ultimately returned to the merchant service and was lost at sea.

Ranger was eventually sold by the British Navy to the merchant service. It was an ignominious turn for a ship that performed well for the Continental Navy. Simpson probably deserved his undistinguished ending, but the sturdy little *Ranger* deserved better. She may not have been a ship of the line or even a frigate, but she had served Jones and her country well in the severest of all environments—combat.

The Simpson affair was clearly not Jones's finest hour. He had failed to gain full control of his officers and crew, a basic responsibility of naval command. Today that responsibility is laid down unequivocally in Article 0702.1 of U.S. Navy Regulations: "The responsibility of the commanding officer for his command is *absolute,* except when, and to the extent, relieved there from by competent authority."

His status as an outsider among a crew from the Portsmouth area had given Jones a daunting challenge in regard to the motivation of his officers and men, but certainly not one unique in naval history. And, in fact, it was a particularly prevalent problem in the Continental Navy, where there was no tradition of military discipline among the officers and men within that new organization. Jones and his fellow officers were mostly merchant captains, men who had reached their positions of naval authority based on merchant marine experience, where the ground rules for almost every aspect of shipboard life were different from those of naval service. In addition, the crew members of the Continental Navy ships were a particularly independent sort. They were quick to respond to patriotic appeals to serve their emerging nation in the war against Britain, but they often were not prepared to accept the military discipline attached to those responses. Jones emphasized the Continental Navy's discipline problems with a florid pronouncement to the commissioners in Paris: "When gain is the ruling principle of Officers and an Infant Navy—it is no wonder that they do not cultivate by their precepts nor enforce by their Example the principles of *Dutiful Subordination, cheerful unrepining* Obedience in those who are under their command, nor is it strange that this principle should weaken the sacred bonds of order and Discipline, and introduce the Mistaken and baneful Idea of Licentiousness and Free Agency under the specious name of 'Liberty.'"[4]

It is worth marking that Jones, despite his overheated prose, was pointing at a very real recruiting and retention challenge that still exists in democratic societies today: how to convince individuals who are inured with concepts of personal liberty to submit to the discipline demanded by military service. That challenge is further complicated by the reality that individual initiative, even at the lowest levels of rank, has been a factor in the most crucial military engagements in U.S. history for more than two centuries.

Despite the Simpson affair, Jones managed to reestablish a proactive relationship with the commissioners. True to his style, however, he did not shrink from the contest. On 27 May he responded to Lee's letter of 23 May, and reported in detail his commerce raiding, the attack on Whitehaven, and his capture of *Drake.* Not surprisingly, his account painted a highly favorable picture of his performance. The letter ended with Jones on the offensive with the commissioners, who had refused to honor Jones's credit draft for 24,000 livres. The victor over HMS *Drake* was not only not to be lionized, he was, in his own words, being placed in the untenable position of being unable to feed his men.

> Could this indignity be kept secret I should disregard it; and, although it is already public in Brest and the fleet, as it affects only my private credit, I will not complain. I cannot, however, be silent when I find the public credit involved in the same disgrace. I conceive this might have been prevented. To make me completely wretched, Monsieur Bersolle (a French commercial agent) has told me that he now stops his hand, not only of the necessary articles to refit the ship, but also of the *daily provisions.* I know not where to find tomorrow's dinner for the great number of mouths that depend on me for dinner. Are then the continental ships-of-war to depend on the sale of their prizes for a daily dinner for their men? . . . I will ask you, gentlemen, if I have deserved all of this? Whoever calls himself an American ought to be protected here. I am unwilling to think that you have intentionally involved me in this sad dilemma, at a time when I ought to expect some enjoyment.[5]

In fairness to Franklin, Lee, and Adams, however, the problem was much more one of severely limited financial resources, rather than one of administrative incompetence or a deliberate effort to frustrate Jones (although the latter was increasingly a factor in the case of Lee). Rich in motivation and potential, the newly united American colonies were poor in financial resources. There was no national treasury to support military needs, and only the individual colonies had the right to tax their citizens. During those early years the government had not reached any real financial equilibrium. Financing by individuals, foreign loans, the issuing of nearly worthless paper money, and outright gifts, particularly from France, combined to form the shaky financial underpinning of the American Revolution. And in regard to the daily problem of providing for his officers and men—as much of a factor in his day-to-day activities in France in 1788 as the winds and tides—Jones was no more exempt from the difficulty than was his commander in chief in America, General Washington.

Jones was forced to turn to Admiral d'Orvilliers and other French contacts willing to advance funds to him as personal loans. At that point, Jones was personally subsidizing the maintenance not only of the crew of *Ranger* but the British prisoners he had captured as well. Jones vented, not with the commissioners, but with others. On 27 May he wrote to Franklin's secretary, Edward Bancroft, "That America should suffer this damned disgrace, in the presence of the French fleet, and the knowledge of every officer and person here, covers me with shame. None of my prizes can be sold, and my officers and men want the withal to cover their nakedness."[6]

Beyond Lieutenant Simpson and day-to-day funding, still more problems plagued Jones during the summer and fall of 1778. There was, for example, the complicated and related matter of securing his and his crew's prize money. Jones had been instructed to return his prizes to French ports, which he did. The smaller prizes from the early part of his deployment were sent into Bordeaux, and *Drake* had been taken into Brest with Jones and *Ranger.* At that point, however, Jones and his crew were at the mercy of appointed prize agents who were authorized to sell the ships and cargoes. It was a process that could go on for years and often wound up in extended legal tangles. The system invited a tremendous amount of dishonesty among the agents. As it turned out, the prizes Jones had captured were sold below their actual value, to his and his crew's financial detriment.

Jones eventually succeeded in getting a meager advance in the crew's prize money and also succeeded in getting the commissioners in Paris to petition Congress for a special bonus for the men who went ashore with Jones for the Whitehaven raid. Ironically, despite all his efforts, which included borrowing money on his own credit to pay his crew, the officers and crew of *Ranger* blamed him for the delays in their pay and prize money.

Even with the departure of Simpson and *Ranger*'s crew in August, Jones had yet another administrative problem: the prisoners that had been taken during *Ranger*'s operations as a raider in British waters. Jones's correspondence makes it clear that the matter of prisoners was particularly difficult for him.

Since the British did not recognize the American colonies as a nation, their Continental Navy prisoners were considered rebels and pirates, not military prisoners of war. And one of Jones's objectives during the raids against shipping off British shores was to take prisoners who could be bartered for the freedom of American sailors in difficult straits in British prisons. Abducting Lord Selkirk would have been a way to reach that objective. Notwithstanding the failure to capture Selkirk, however, Jones had returned to Brest with two hundred British prisoners, mostly men from *Drake*'s crew. The problem was that there was no place for them to be held, and Jones had neither the inclination nor the means to return them to America.

Admiral Comte d'Orvilliers came to Jones's assistance again, and despite the fact that France and Britain were technically not at war, he agreed to hold Jones's captives in a French prison ship in Brest. Eventually in 1779 the prisoners Jones had taken became part of an exchange for 228 American sailors. Jones's capture of a significant number of British sailors helped precipitate a change in 1780 in British policy concerning Continental Navy prisoners. In that year Parliament legislated that all Continental Navy prisoners would be treated as prisoners of war. Contributing to that alteration in British policy was another of the under-recognized achievements of John Paul Jones.

A by-product of the change in Britain's policy toward its Continental Navy prisoners was that Britain recognized preliminarily the reality of American nationhood. The prisoner-of-war status no doubt changed—and at times saved—the lives of hundreds of those who had the misfortune to be captured while fighting in the Continental Navy. Jones's perseverance in securing the freedom of American sailors was also evidence that he was driven by much more than a need for personal recognition. Jones's fight for the release of imprisoned sailors and advocacy for the payment of his crew's wages and prize money helped to establish the U.S. Navy tradition of taking care of its own.

The problem of getting a ship no doubt preoccupied Jones while in France in 1778 and early 1789 as much as did the Simpson issue, financial needs, and the disposition of his prisoners. Jones had been disappointed in March 1777, when the Congressional order for him to command one of the three new frigates to be built in Boston evaporated. Then hopes for command of a new ship were renewed. As plans were being formed before Jones's eventual assignment to *Ranger*, Robert Morris, the head of the Marine Committee in Congress, wrote to the American commissioners in Paris in May 1777 about getting a ship for Jones. "Our design of sending him is (with the approbation of Congress), that you may purchase one of those fine frigates that Mr. Deane writes us you can get, and invest him with the command thereof as soon as possible. We hope you may not delay this business one moment, but purchase, in such port or place in Europe as it can be done with most convenience and dispatch, a fine, fast sailing frigate or larger ship."[7]

In his letter, Morris even ordered that the commissioners find "some good house or agents to supply him with everything necessary to get the ship speedily and well equipped and manned . . . and never quit until it is accomplished."

That sense of urgency on the part of the Marine Committee had encouraged Jones at the time. The forty-gun *L'Indien,* being built in a private Dutch shipyard, was this ship the committee intended Jones to command.

After Jones had arrived in France in early 1778, however, two forces combined to frustrate yet again the exciting prospect of a frigate. First, there was the ever-present problem of money. Congress was never able to provide the funds for the ship to the commissioners in Paris. As a result, the commissioners sold the brand new ship to France and then worked to have France turn the ship back over to the commissioners for Jones's use. But international politics intervened, and that was the final impediment to Jones getting *L'Indien.*

France was still technically neutral, and Britain applied heavy pressure on both the Dutch and the French to prevent *L'Indien* from finding her way into the Continental Navy. No doubt at this point the British Admiralty was beginning to see the Continental Navy as a significant military factor. All special efforts by the commission—even a direct appeal from Jones to the French minister of marine after Jones's return to Brest—failed to save his prospective ship. *L'Indien* eventually found her way into the South Carolina navy, where she did little to advance the American cause.

During the failing efforts to secure *L'Indien,* Jones had been offered the command of a sixteen-gun corvette by the French; it was an offer he could and did refuse. A sixteen-gun ship met neither the operational requirements for a significant offensive naval action nor his growing sense of self-esteem. He did continue, however, to advance plans for aggressive naval action against the British—those efforts were his best lobbying arguments for a good ship. The various plans ranged from an attack against Glasgow (which in all probability would have been suicidal), attacks against Baltic convoys, a raid on the west coast of Africa, and a raid against the Newfoundland fisheries.

By September of 1778, Jones was becoming more desperate. He knew that he needed something more than the reliable and now departed *Ranger* or the sixteen-gun corvette offered by the French to meet his operational needs and advance his career. He had to be wondering if he would ever get a ship worthy of his ambitions. On the thirteenth of the month, he wrote a long and complaining letter to French Minister of Marine Antoine de Sartine. The minister was a former police officer who had garnered the attention of King Louis XVI with his administrative abilities. His orientation was bureaucratic and political, rather than naval and strategic, and he became an ongoing factor in Jones's quest for a good ship. Toward the end of the letter, Jones put it on the line with Sartine: "I do not wish to interfere with the harmony of the French marine; but if I am still thought worthy of your attention, I shall hope for a separate command, with liberal orders:—if, on the contrary, you have no farther occasion for my services, I have only to ask for the Alert, and a few seamen, with permission to return in that small vessel to America before winter."[8]

Then on 21 September he wrote to the Duke de Chartres, and after six paragraphs that began with "I," he made his point: "In my present mysterious situation here, I am considered an officer in disgrace."[9] He began on that same point in a letter to Franklin on 19 October: "I have been, and am in the eyes of Brest and the French marine, considered as having incurred your displeasure and being consequently in disgrace. . . . The Commissioners' refusal of my bill, my journey to Paris without any visible reason, the cabals and misrepresentations of Lieutenant Simpson, and my present inactivity, are held to be so many circumstantial proofs; and my dishonor is now so firmly believed everywhere that it is in vain for me to assert the contrary."[10]

On the same day, he even wrote a long letter to the King of France, chronicling his effort to secure a ship and ending, "As your majesty, by espousing the cause of America, has become the 'protector of the rights of human nature,' I am persuaded that you will not disregard my situation, nor suffer me to remain any longer in this insupportable disgrace."[11]

Increasingly Jones was pursuing a scattergun approach to getting a ship. The individual American commissioners in Paris were each targets; the king and the minister of marine were targets; individual French officials were targets. And although it was unusual for a naval captain to pursue such an objective directly with foreign nations, the American commissioners did not seem to mind. They had plenty to deal with in their pursuit of broad support and money for their new nation. The times were unusual, and Jones was never reluctant to push his own cause up to and even beyond customary political limits.

On the face of it, the commissioners' failure to make stronger efforts to get Jones back to sea in a decent ship was a mistake, particularly since the Continental Army and Navy had been suffering defeat after defeat. Jones overcame the continuous disappointments and embarrassments during this period, however, maintaining an unbreakable belief in his navy and his nation. Convincing evidence of this was contained in a letter of 15 November to his friend, Thomas Bell, captain of a privateer temporarily in Lorient. Bell's negative description to Jones of matters in Philadelphia and the sorry state of the

Continental Navy could well have pushed Jones over the edge of frustration, perhaps even out of the navy. Yet Jones's letter of response was optimistic. It also contained an uncanny prediction that demonstrated a grasp of broad national strategy. Despite the unhappy state of the American Revolution at that time, and particularly Jones's difficulties in France, he drew an encouraging conclusion about Philadelphia and—for his time and circumstances—an absolutely astonishing prediction about the American navy:

> Your account of the Situation of Philadelphia and our Poor Marine distresses much—but let us not altogether despond. Tho' I am no prophet, the one will yet become the *first* City, and the other the *first* Navy within a much shorter space of time than is generally imagined. When the Enemies land force is once conquered and expelled the Continent, our Marine will rise as if by Enchantment, and become within the memory of Persons now living, the wonder and Envy of the World.[12]

Finally toward the latter months of 1778 matters took a turn for the better, and Jones surely was sensing this when writing to Robert Morris of the Marine Committee about the efforts of Sartine, the French minister of marine. Jones reported that Sartine had authorized Jacques Donatien Le Ray de Chaumont to purchase a ship that would be to his liking, and that the prospects for his getting to sea before the spring were good. The key in the situation would turn out to be Chaumont, the confidant to the French king, shipbuilder, fleet owner, speculator—and the husband of the woman purported to be Jones's initial lover in France in late 1777.

Chaumont had been in the hunt for a ship for Jones and had come up with several possibilities. Among them was a former French East Indiaman, *Le Duc de Duras.* The merchant ship appealed to the French because she could be purchased on credit. That made it Chaumont's kind of deal, but Jones wanted to continue to shop. At one point, he wrote to Chaumont, "I wish to have no Connection with any ship that does not sail *fast,* for I intend to go in harm's way."[13] That phrase neatly reflected Jones's essentially aggressive combat doctrine, and it still lives in U.S. Navy tradition today.

Finally, by the end of 1778, Jones made up his mind that *Le Duc de Duras* would have to do, and in February of 1779, Sartine confirmed that the king was willing to turn over *Le Duc de Duras* to Jones. At last, Jones would finally command a frigate, one that would outgun, if not outsail, most of the other ships of her class that she might meet in combat. There was undeniably an ego-enhancing aspect too; he had joined a special group of fighting captains from the age of sail, those who commanded frigates.

Frigates were the smallest of the main classes of naval combatants of the age of sail. They generally mounted between twenty-eight and forty-four guns, and were very frequently commanded by aggressive captains who relished independent operations and were definitely not risk-averse. In the British Navy's warship classifications of the time, they were listed as fifth- and sixth-rate ships, the two smallest ships among the British Navy's rated warships. In comparison, fourth-rate ships generally carried fifty to sixty guns and were considered to be the smallest of the ships of the line, third-rate ships mounted sixty-four to eighty guns, second-rate ships carried ninety to ninety-eight guns, and first-rate ships carried one hundred guns or more.[14]

The unusual utility of the frigate in the age of sail was noted by no less successful a naval leader of the time than Vice Admiral Lord Horatio Nelson. Nelson wrote about his lack of these multipurpose vessels with emotion while commander in chief of the British Mediterranean fleet in 1798: "Was I to die at this moment, 'Want of Frigates' would be found stamped on my heart."[15]
In honor of his friend and patron, Jones chose the French translation of Franklin's nom de plume, "Poor Richard," for the name of the frigate he would command. The rough French translation of that nom de plume "Bonhomme Richard" is "kindly and wise old uncle Richard." It was an odd name for a ship of war commanded by an aggressive and hard-edged naval officer. Jones had been particularly struck, however, by one bit of advice from Franklin's collection of maxims written under that assumed name. It was Franklin's advice in *Poor Richard's Almanac* to a man who "wishes to have any business faithfully and expeditiously performed, to go on it himself" that struck a responsive chord in Jones.

In selecting the name *Bonhomme Richard,* Jones also helped to establish what would become the U.S. Navy tradition of naming certain of its ships in honor of particularly supportive politicians. Following her brief and violent Continental Navy career, and after finding her final resting place in the North Sea, the unlikely name *Bonhomme Richard* would echo and re-echo in U.S. naval history, once as an aircraft carrier that served in three different wars before being decommissioned in March 1992, and currently as an amphibious command ship.

Le Duc de Duras had been launched in Lorient for the French East India Company in 1765. She was one of a number of French ships that were designed to serve in the French merchant marine in peacetime and in the navy during wars. And while she had been worked hard, she still had some service life left. Her length overall was 145 feet, her beam was almost 37 feet, and she had a high, slanted poop deck, distinguishing her somewhat from most of her British Navy counterparts. From a distance, her overall design seemed to emphasize curves, rather than angles. As a result, she had a look of harmony with the sea rather than a look of aggressiveness. But her looks belied her potential to deal destruction.

Le Duc de Duras had made two trips in the China trade and one as a troop transport. After her refitting for the Continental Navy, her main battery—located on her upper deck—consisted of twenty-eight 12-pound guns. There also were six old 18-pound guns on the lower deck, and at the time of her coming battle off Flamborough Head, she had six 8-pound guns on her quarterdeck. Notwithstanding Jones's indication that he would have preferred an armament of thirty guns, all 18-pounders, *Bonhomme Richard* wound up after refitting as one of the more heavily gunned frigates in naval service. And in that respect, she was a vague forerunner of the extremely successful purpose-built U.S. Navy heavy frigates of the War of 1812.

Like any warship, *Bonhomme Richard* was a product of a series of design compromises, and this was particularly true for her, since she was not a purpose-built warship. For example, what she packed in firepower was compromised by her lack of speed and nimbleness. And her bottom was not coppered, denying her the advantage of a relatively new technological advance pioneered by the British Navy. As a result, her speed and maneuverability, already limited by her design, would have been further compromised by the accumulation of marine growth on the hull below the waterline.

Jones would complain about that lack of speed soon after her initial deployment, and it would be a factor in her famous single-ship action to come. As a final part of her refitting, *Bonhomme Richard*'s hull was painted solid black. That hull color would be another visual feature setting her apart from most British warships of frigate size and larger, whose black hulls were distinguished with wide horizontal ochre stripes marking the gun decks.

What really distinguished *Bonhomme Richard,* however, was her internationally unfamiliar flag of thirteen red, white, and blue horizontal stripes and thirteen white stars on a rectangular blue field in the upper left corner. It was a flag that would soon fly over the ubiquitous British Navy "white ensign" as a result of *Bonhomme Richard*'s approaching victory off Flamborough Head, along the northeastern coast of England.

Whatever the pros and cons of *Bonhomme Richard*'s design and performance features, she was a much more formidable fighting machine than anything Jones had previously commanded. With a crew of approximately 380 men, he had crossed over the line to command of a major fighting ship, and it would be up to him to maximize her positive qualities and minimize her negatives in combat. It clearly was uncharted career territory for Jones, and his immediate challenge was fitting out his new command. The process was facilitated by the fortuitous fact that, despite her Continental Navy captain and American national colors, the French underwrote the cost of *Bonhomme Richard*'s preparations for combat.

Among Jones's major orders of business was his armament, beginning with his ship's cannons. During the age of sail, those weapons were far from standardized in design or manufacture. As a result, one of the more troublesome realities was that there were too-frequent design and manufacturing flaws. Those flaws and sometimes just plain age caused naval cannons to burst at times in the process of firing, with devastating effect on their gun crews and anyone in the general vicinity of the explosion. Records indicate that several of *Bonhomme Richard*'s 18-pound guns did burst at the beginning of her battle off Flamborough Head.

The ship's log shows that *Bonhomme Richard*'s 18-pounders were brought aboard on 18 May. They apparently came from local French East India Company armament stores and, unfortunately, were old model weapons. Most of the 12-pounders, a mix of both older and newer weapons, were also loaded aboard on 18 May. By June, the 8-pounders, apparently all new models, and a certain amount of shot also were aboard. The loading of these cannons and their proper mounting and positioning was no minor evolution, since the weight of each cannon ranged from somewhat more than two thousand pounds to four thousand-plus pounds. Finally, a huge amount of personal weapons were loaded, including a variety of muskets, pistols, pikes, cutlasses, swords, hand grenades, and even tomahawks. As it turned out, a single hand grenade among the tons of munitions loaded would play a surprisingly important role in the outcome of Jones's most important battle.

The recruiting of *Bonhomme Richard*'s crew was another of Jones's basic challenges. The officers and men of *Ranger* were gone, and Jones's new command was probably the better for that. Yet recruiting a motivated group of officers and men in France for a ship commanded by an American and sailing under American colors was a special challenge. Among other expediencies, Jones resorted to signing on men who lived on the streets and frequented the taverns of Nantes. He also recruited British prisoners held by the French Navy, some of whom probably were Americans, serving either voluntarily or involuntarily in the British Navy.

As nondescript as the crew was, it was not an unusual group for its time. In the age of sail, when seamen frequently signed on whatever ship would take them, internationally homogenized crews were commonplace. As it turned out, *Bonhomme Richard* wound up with more than ten nationalities represented among her men. Beyond that variety of ethnic and national backgrounds, was a big problem: they all were new to their ship. And it took time and training for a crew, no matter its complexion, to work together efficiently. In hindsight that is based on *Bonhomme Richard*'s performance, it is reasonable to assume that Jones's leadership more than met that very substantial challenge. If his experience as captain of *Ranger* revealed weaknesses in Jones's leadership, the performance of *Bonhomme Richard*'s men under heavy fire reflects exceptional leadership qualities in Jones's recruitment and training of his crew.

One of *Bonhomme Richard*'s strongest combat assets was her contingent of marines. While most frigates of the time probably would have 70 or so marines on board, Jones wound up with 140. They were drawn from one of the Irish regiments serving the French king, men who would be particularly pleased with an opportunity to beard the British lion in its home waters. *Bonhomme Richard*'s marines had three important roles. First, they were critical in commando-type raids ashore. Second, they were effective as marksmen in sweeping the enemy's open decks during close-in fighting at sea. Third, they were essential in the hand-to-hand combat that resulted when ships were grappled together in combat.

Last among the preparations Jones was making were modifications to adapt the ship for serious coastal raiding. Amphibious strikes were always on Jones's mind, and he had proved their value in *Ranger*'s raids against the coasts of the British Isles. The special alterations for *Bonhomme Richard*'s fitting out included preparing quarters for the additional troops she would have embarked and the addition of a main deck structure for use by a combined services planning staff.

While Jones was shaping *Bonhomme Richard* into a versatile fighting machine, he also had to clarify his next mission. During the months he had lobbied for a ship, he continued to put forward various plans. Now that he had command of *Bonhomme Richard,* however, the time for speculative plans was over; the time for action was at hand. The letter of 4 February from the French minister of marine, telling Jones the happy news about *Le Duc de Duras,* also contained his orders from King Louis, and the orders could not have been more sweeping. Jones was authorized "to hoist the flag of the United States," and "As soon as you are prepared for sea, you will set sail without waiting for any ulterior orders."

Sartine's letter relaying the king's orders went on to require Jones to provide a report of his actions and to treat prisoners humanely. And that was it; a naval officer could not ask for more latitude. Jones's orders were the antithesis of political micromanagement of the military and had to please him. The matching orders from Franklin were equally permissive, and Jones referred to them as "liberal and noble minded instructions." So, at this point, Jones finally had secured command of a frigate, and the French were underwriting the cost of fitting it out. In addition, he had extremely permissive orders. It must have seemed to Jones that the anguish of the past months was worth it after all.

As the refitting advanced and discussions of his mission continued, it appeared at one point that there would be a major navy-army amphibious assault, an operation proposed by the precociously brilliant young French Major General, the Marquis de Lafayette. The young French general had a good grasp of naval matters, and Jones and Lafayette, who was also a major general in the Continental Army, pursued the planning together. The first choice for a target was Liverpool on the Irish Sea.

The correspondence between them indicated mutual enthusiasm for the mission and the prospect of working as a team. There appeared to be complete subordination of egos, a genuine mutual respect, and a high degree of anticipation of an important military achievement. Jones wrote to Lafayette, "I shall expect you to point out my errors when we are together alone with perfect freedom." That uncharacteristically humble statement and Jones's behavior during his brief involvement with Lafayette were clear evidence that his ego, substantial as it was, was not all-consuming. It could be put aside for the sake of an important mission.

As events turned out, however, the Liverpool mission never got beyond the planning stages. France and Great Britain were again officially at war, and Lafayette was reassigned to be part of the French invasion of Britain that was being mounted for the summer of 1779. Subsequently Lafayette went on to play a major role with General Washington, and he was one of Washington's generals involved in the final stages of the land war during the American Revolution. Jones and Lafayette would never have another opportunity to work together in a combined operation, but they did manage to maintain their correspondence.

Even after it was canceled, the Jones-Lafayette project had a significant strategic benefit, however, as word of the plan was revealed to the British, probably by Franklin's secretary, Bancroft. The anxiety along Britain's coasts was compounded, and Parliament allocated funds and military assets to meet the threat.

Although Jones had not yet sailed in *Bonhomme Richard,* he was once again inside the enemy's decision cycle.

As spring turned into summer, a squadron was formed around *Bonhomme Richard.* First was the new American-built, thirty-six-gun frigate, *Alliance,* which the Continental Congress had placed under the command of Pierre Landais, a former French naval captain of limited ability and questionable sanity. John Adams had described Landais as a man with an "embarrassed mind," and in combat, the former French officer turned out to be more of a threat to Jones than to the British Navy.

Samuel Adams had arranged for Landais to be made an honorary citizen of Massachusetts, and Congress, pushed by Commissioner Arthur Lee's brother, Richard Henry Lee, had maneuvered his appointment as a captain in the Continental Navy. Some said that the whole idea for the elaborate construct to establish the former French naval officer in the Continental Navy was to counter Jones's growing reputation. In the long run, Landais's behavior would lend considerable support to that theory. If Jones had had serious problems with Simpson as his first lieutenant, he was about to find out just how much worse the leadership problems could be as a commodore with Captain Landais in his squadron.

In contrast to *Alliance* and Landais was the former privateer, the small twenty-six-gun frigate *Pallas,* commanded by French officer Denis Cottineau de Kerloguen, who would turn out to be a true asset to Jones when the combat started. Next in size was the lightly armed twelve-gun brig *Vengeance,* also commanded by a French officer, Philippe Ricot. Finally there was the twelve-gun cutter, *Le Cerf,* commanded by a third and junior French officer, Joseph Varage. Thanks to commissions handily provided by Franklin, all three of the French officers were also officers in the Continental Navy, at least technically. The terms of those dual commissions would, however, quickly become an issue for Jones. The mixed makeup of the squadron's captains was a recipe for a force commander's nightmare.

But on the positive side, Jones finally had command of a frigate, and his squadron had some naval muscle. And it was *his.* He was a commodore with the ability to take the fight to the enemy.

Future U.S. president and member of the American Commission in Paris, John Adams, spent considerable time with Jones during Jones's preparation of *Bonhomme Richard.* Adams provided an interesting observation of Jones at this critical juncture in the commodore's career. Although the two men dined together frequently, Adams was wary of the aggressive young naval officer. At the time, Adams suspected that Franklin was scheming against him, and Jones, seemingly a close associate of Franklin, would not be someone to trust completely. Adams also perceived Jones as eccentric, aggressive, and personally ambitious. But his assessment went deeper: "His eye has keenness and Wildness and softness in it."[16] It was not the softness, but the keenness and wildness that would come into play dramatically in the coming months.

5
A Hard Beginning

"Better is the end of a thing, than the beginning thereof."
Ecclesiastes 7:8

New orders from the French minister of marine arrived for Jones in June 1779. The scale of the new mission did not rise to the level of the combined army-navy assault on Liverpool that had been planned with the Marquis de Lafayette. But the strategic objectives remained the same: attack Britain's maritime lifelines and keep the British population and leaders off balance with raids against their homeland.

The Americans hoped that this new mission would tie down troops and naval units in the area of the British Isles and help reduce the pressure on General Washington's beleaguered army. It was also hoped that this strategy would help dampen popular and political commitment at the Admiralty and Whitehall in London for the war with the American colonies. And despite the early preponderance of military setbacks in the war, particular political and military events sustained the colonies' expectation that separation from Great Britain was achievable, but just barely.

The most important of the political events was the American Declaration of Independence itself, which made it clear on 4 July 1776 that the political tipping point had been reached in the disputes between Britain and her American colonies. In simple terms, that document established that the American colonists were no longer subjects of the king of England, they were citizens of a new nation. There was no longer any likelihood of negotiating an end to the periodic armed conflicts that had been developing over time; the issues would have to be decided in all-out combat. Once the Declaration of Independence was published, the American colonies could not turn back in their fight for liberty.

Undoubtedly, the British military recognized how profoundly the Declaration of Independence had changed things. In September 1776, only months after Congress enacted the Declaration, Admiral Lord Howe arranged a meeting on Staten Island with a Congressional committee consisting of Benjamin Franklin, John Adams, and Edward Rutledge, in an effort to open a door to negotiation by finding a way to negate the Declaration. Howe, in addition to his duties as senior British naval officer in America, had been appointed a commissioner by King George III to, in Howe's own words, "restore the public tranquility and to render his American subjects happy in a permanent union with Great Britain." In his account of the meeting, the admiral illuminated just how critical the Declaration of Independence was from the British point of view: "We could not . . . proceed in any conference of negotiation upon the inadmissible ground of independency."[1] The Staten Island meeting failed.

Arguably the most significant military event that sustained the colonies' hope for freedom from British rule was the victory of the Continental Army at the battle of Saratoga on 7 October 1777. The results of that battle had great psychological impact, shaking the belief that Britain's highly professional military would make short work of the colonials' minimally equipped military forces. The Continental victory at Saratoga cast serious doubt on the presumption in London that Britain could win a protracted war, and Jones's forthcoming deployment in *Bonhomme Richard* was intended to increase that doubt.

Accompanying the growing questions about operational military factors, there was considerable concern at Whitehall and in Parliament about the steadily increasing cost of British military operations in America. From a pragmatic political point of view, Britain had more important problems within its growing empire to deal with elsewhere in the world. Above all else was the ever-present threat from France, a specter that overshadowed all of Britain's other global challenges. The war in America threatened loss of a major piece of the empire; the struggle with France threatened Britain's national existence.

Against that geopolitical background, the French perceived Jones's mission in *Bonhomme Richard* as a means of drawing British troops and naval units away from theaters of primary concern to them. In the summer of 1779, the English Channel was at the top of France's list of military theaters. The idea of invading England was an ever-present vision, an overriding objective that remained a constant for France during the eighteenth and early nineteenth centuries. That vision was a near-reality for France and Louis XVI in the summer of 1779. An important enabling factor for France's invasion plan was the signing of a political-military alliance with Spain. One of the principal objectives of the alliance—perhaps the most important to the French—was to create a combined French-Spanish fleet that could seize control of the English Channel and maintain that control long enough to make an invasion of the British Isles possible.

In the early stages of the invasion plan, the combined fleet actually grew to sixty-four ships of the line, an impressive naval force for its time. Admiral

Comte d'Orvilliers was placed in overall command of this formidable fleet. Britain, on the other hand, with her warships spread out to cover major commitments in the Atlantic, Baltic, Caribbean, Indian Ocean, Mediterranean, and Pacific, was able to gather only thirty-eight ships of the line in the theater. This numerically overmatched force was placed under the command of Admiral Sir Charles Hardy.

From outward appearances, it looked like France would finally be able to mount a successful invasion of Britain, and on 16 August 1779—only days after Jones departed on his deployment against the British Isles in *Bonhomme Richard*—the combined fleet actually anchored off Plymouth. As events turned out, however, the French-Spanish combined fleet was never able to bring Hardy and the British fleet to actual combat, and eventually disease ravaged the French and Spanish crews. The combined fleet disbanded, and the French dream of a cross-Channel invasion of Britain had to be postponed once again.

D'Orvilliers returned to Brest with a disease-riddled-and dispirited fleet in September, arriving only days before Jones would fight his way to lasting fame off Flamborough Head. Jones's coming victory received so much attention in America, Britain, France, and other countries on the Continent in part due to the contrast it made to the failure of the French invasion plan.

In June, French Minister of Marine Antoine de Sartine ordered Jones and *Bonhomme Richard* to escort duty, protecting French merchantmen in the Bay of Biscay. Defending French merchant ships from British commerce raiders and privateers was not Jones's idea of a worthy mission for his proven abilities as an aggressive naval commander—it was entirely too defensive. But the French had provided his ship and were paying his bills. So for the present they gave the orders, and Jones executed them.

Jones and his squadron departed on 19 June, and things did not get off to a good start. It had quickly become apparent to Jones, for example, that *Bonhomme Richard* was slow. For a commander committed to offensive tactics, that was not a happy circumstance. And although shifting ballast and tweaking the rigging while at sea might add a half knot to her speed, it was clear that he would have to compensate for the shortcoming in other ways. Equally troubling was the realization that Captain Pierre Landais was going to be a serious problem.

At the very beginning of the June deployment, Landais had precipitated a collision between *Bonhomme Richard* and *Alliance.* And beyond the damage to the two ships—*Bonhomme Richard* lost her jib and spritsail boom and *Alliance* lost her mizzenmast—Jones had to have realized that Landais was a potentially fatal weakness in his squadron. In other circumstances, he could have had him relieved, but given the politics involved, that was out of the question. Landais remained in the squadron, and he would become a near-fatal problem at a crucial point in a coming deployment for Commodore Jones.

On 1 July, Jones was back in Lorient, writing a report of his operations to Franklin. In the report, he described the success of his escort duties and then focused on a telling encounter with two British convoy escorts. His report cited both a weakness of his ship and a strength that would eventually prove to be an overriding and counterbalancing factor. "They appeared at first earnest to engage, but their courage failed, and they fled with precipitation, and to *my mortification outsailed the Bon homme Richard, and got clear.* I had, however, a flattering proof of the martial spirit of my crew, and I am confident that, had I been able to get between the two, which was my intention, we should have beaten them both together."[2]

It is interesting to note that, despite the motley makeup of his crew and his past difficulties with the *Ranger*'s crew, Jones was developing a respect for the combat potential of the *Bonhomme Richard*'s men. It is also interesting that Jones felt that he could have defeated the two escorts by getting between them, presumably to fight them simultaneously. In the age of sail, engaging an enemy on both sides—being "doubled"—was considered to be an extremely disadvantaged situation. Seeking that position would have been considered reckless in the extreme by naval traditionalists. Jones's concept of converting this tactical disadvantage into an advantage was a stunning example of his emphasis on establishing the initiative in naval combat.

In any event, he closed the report to Franklin on a note that suggests that he also was maturing in his dealings with his civilian leadership in Paris: "I am ready to enter with cheerfulness on any plan or service that is consonant with the common interest, and meets with your approbation; and if I fail, it shall not be for want of attempting to succeed where an opportunity appears."[3]

That upbeat tone would be tested as Jones continued to prepare for his next assignment. He began the repairs required for his squadron's ships. A new bowsprit was required for *Bonhomme Richard,* and *Alliance* needed a new mizzenmast to replace the one lost in her collision with *Bonhomme Richard.* Those were the most obvious repair items but only a fraction of the general repairs and replacements required for Jones's next mission. And although Jones was satisfied with his crew's fighting potential, he had ongoing discipline problems. In addition to routine difficulties, such as petty theft among the men and minor disobedience to orders, there were more serious incidents. Animosity between the French and Americans resulted in fights between the two groups, and the former British Navy sailors that had been added to *Bonhomme Richard*'s crew actually hatched a plan for mutiny. The intent of the mutineers was to take both Jones and his ship to England. For its audacity, it was a plan worthy of the man they hoped to overthrow. The plan was discovered, however, and ended with the leader receiving 250 lashes, a punishment that he somehow survived, only to be imprisoned at the end of his flogging.

During this period in Lorient Jones was sick. Few details are known about his illness, but it is likely that the accumulated frustrations and pressures of his deployments in *Ranger,* the securing and fitting out of *Bonhomme Richard,* the convoy duty in the Bay of Biscay, and the difficulties of refitting and recruiting after his return to Lorient were all contributing factors in the breakdown of his previously strong health.

In August, the French minister of marine sent Jacques Donatien Le Ray de Chaumont to Lorient to hasten Jones's next deployment, and when he arrived, Chaumont immediately began dealing directly with each captain in the American squadron. Jones had to have sensed that he was going to have this kind of problem with Chaumont when he received a letter from him in June on the subject of command of the squadron. It was a letter reflecting both a landsman's and a bureaucrat's frame of reference. The letter may even have been the product of a husband seeking subtle retaliation against his wife's lover:

> The situation of the officers who have accepted commissions from Congress to join the armament of the ship *Bon homme Richard* . . . may be in contradiction with the interests of their own ships; this induces me to request you to enter into an engagement with me, that you shall not require from the said vessels any services but such as will be comfortable with the orders which these officers shall have, and in no case you shall require any changes to be made in the formation of their crews, which, as well the vessels themselves as their armaments, shall be entirely at the disposition of the commandants of said vessels who shall be answerable to those who have armed them. I also beg you to agree, that all the prizes which shall be made, be addressed to such consignees as I shall point out, for the preservation of the interests of all the concerned.[4]

The major problem with the agreement Chaumont was requiring was that it was a license for Jones's captains, who were by no means a "Band of Brothers," to ignore any order that they might not like. It is true that particular agreements within a naval squadron were common in the age of sail, when a squadron might not only be multinational but also might include several variations of privateers. Yet what Chaumont imposed was an intolerable hindrance for a commodore in command of a squadron. It was foolish on the face of it, and it would have been particularly objectionable for a commodore as aggressive as Jones. It took an immense amount of self-confidence, an overriding drive for honor, and a deep commitment to a cause for a captain with Jones's record of operational success to accept Chaumont's requirements. And when Chaumont also stated in the letter that he would control the sale of any prizes that Jones and his squadron captured, he added insult to injury.

Chaumont's letter, perhaps more than any other single piece of evidence, demonstrates the difficulties under which Jones was pursuing his duty in 1778 and 1779. He had been placed in command of a converted merchant ship, manned by a crew that had not been trained to fight together, and he was to operate with captains following their own agendas. In addition, he was required to sign an agreement that no competent squadron commander, by any stretch of the imagination, should have been asked to sign. But Jones did sign; he knew it was his only chance to get back to sea and into action. It was a potentially disastrous compromise brought on by the unique circumstances in the nascent Continental Navy, a service starved for funding, marginally equipped, and minimally trained.

Closely linked to the inherent problems of money, equipment, and people within a new navy was the parallel problem with a civilian leadership that was undergoing on-the-job training in the particular skills required for the effective utilization of a military service. Although deeply—and wisely—committed to the concept of civilian control of the military, the civilian leaders had no experience in how to effectively exercise that control and thus no solid basis for establishing basic guidelines for such leadership. Neither the Naval Committee of Congress nor the American commissioners in Paris could rely on an established culture or past tradition in regard to exercising civilian control of the Continental military services. The problem was an outgrowth of the broad challenge for establishing the general governance of the new nation by Congress.

The situation was redeemed considerably, however, by the Continental leaders, among them George Washington, Benjamin Franklin, Robert Morris, and John Adams, whose instincts, political perceptiveness, and basic intelligence kept them fixed on a naval strategy that was asymmetrical and realistic in its use of such tactics as commerce raiding and commando-like raids against the British Isles.

Franklin's written orders of 30 June reflected a continuation of that strategy and assigned a huge, inverted U-shaped operating area to Jones and his small squadron. The area stretched from the west coast of Ireland, around the top of Scotland, down the eastern coasts of Scotland and England, and into the North Sea opposite Denmark. Franklin ordered Jones, "You are to make the best of your way with the vessels under your command to the west of Ireland, and establish your cruise on the Orcades, the Cape of Derneus, and the Dogger Bank, in order to take the enemy's property in those seas. . . . About the 15th of August, when you have sufficiently cruised in these seas, you are to make route for Texel, where you will meet my further orders."[5]

Cruise of Bonhomme Richard. This chart shows John Paul Jones's successful deployments in the Continental ship *Bonhomme Richard.*
From the author's collection, with special permission of Raisz Landform Maps

The operating area described by Franklin had two particularly relevant features. First, it included the approach and departure routes for merchant ships transiting between the British Isles and the West Indies and the American colonies. Second, significant Continental Navy activity in the area would draw British Navy units into defensive rather than offensive assignments. It was a strategically sound use of limited naval strength, albeit exceedingly optimistic given the size and makeup of Jones's squadron and the tenuous command authority under which he was operating.

Given all the circumstances, Jones probably had no more than a fifty-fifty chance of achieving some meaningful success on his deployment. What could not be anticipated was the pivotal psychological by-product that would result from one relatively brief ship-to-ship action during that deployment. Jones's approaching, unlikely single-ship combat victory off Flamborough Head would be the intensely violent conjunction of a wide array of circumstances and military-political forces that elevated the importance of the event.

Jones expressed misgivings about his orders, particularly about being ordered to return to the Dutch island of Texel and not having a major British port designated for a raid. In a follow-up letter on 8 July, Franklin addressed Jones's questioning in only slightly restrained diplomatic language. He cited the beggars-can't-be-choosers reality of the American situation in Paris at the time: "I have no other orders to give, for, as the Court is at the chief expense, I think they have the best right to direct."[6] What he did not go into was that there was a sound reason for Jones to wind up at Texel—from there, he could escort a convoy that had been bottled up at the island back to France. The convoy was laden with strategic naval matériel, and France was in desperate need of the masts, yardarms, booms, tar, and hemp that the convoy was carrying from the Baltic region.

Undeterred, Jones persisted, taking a different tack. He wrote about the slowness of his ship and asked yet again that he be assigned to a better and faster ship. He also wondered if the plans for an operation with Lafayette might be resurrected. Franklin, a master at the art of political manipulation, countered with a letter to Jones citing a disturbing report he had received from the minister of marine of "the mutinous disposition" of the *Bonhomme Richard*'s crew. Jones then followed with a defensive letter to the minister of marine, placing the blame for the mutinous elements in his crew on Chaumont and claiming that is was Chaumont who "thought it expedient" to add a large number of captured British Navy sailors to *Bonhomme Richard*'s crew. Toward the end of the same letter, Jones assured Sartine that he would get under way within forty-eight hours. Franklin had pulled the strings so that Jones got the message without a direct confrontation.

Jones fired a parting shot, however, in an attempt to wind up on the political offensive, at least with Sartine. He expressed his great surprise to the French minister that unnamed individuals in Lorient had letters describing the areas included in Jones's coming deployment. Jones was, of course, no match in political maneuvering against the likes of Franklin and Sartine, but characteristically, he never surrendered in those political contests that invariably were settled by oblique maneuvers and influence. What he lacked in political sophistication, he compensated for with dogged determination. Jones was practicing "asymmetrical warfare" in a political context.

Finally on 9 August, Jones was under way from Lorient to an outer anchorage of the harbor, with *Pallas, Vengeance,* and *Cerf* in company. *Alliance* and two French privateers, *Monsieur* and *Granville,* joined the squadron there. All seven ships then waited at anchor for the Continental privateer *General Mifflin,* whose captain decided, upon arrival, that he had changed his mind and was not joining Jones's squadron.

While at anchor, Chaumont moved from ship to ship, directing matters on his own, instead of working through Jones as the squadron's commodore. As he waited at the anchorage, Jones surely wondered what he had gotten himself into. He had argued aggressively for a ship and had gotten one; he had argued aggressively for an important assignment and had gotten one. Now he had to produce for his country, his country's ally, and for himself. Given the quality of his ships and men and the constant meddling from Chaumont, it was an immensely daunting prospect.

But just as surely, Jones would have believed that, once under way and separated from the politics and other distractions ashore, he could work his squadron into shape. That was and is "the navy way." One of the reasons for his optimism in that regard would have been—for a change—his senior officers, beginning with Richard Dale, his first lieutenant. Dale had served with distinction in the Continental Navy, had been captured by the British, escaped, captured again, and escaped again. After his second escape, he had wound up in Lorient in 1779, where he volunteered to serve in *Bonhomme Richard.* During the forthcoming battle he would be seriously wounded, but he would survive and go on to become one of the initial captains of the United States Navy when it was established in 1794 and a highly successful commodore before his retirement in 1801.

In addition to Dale's credentials as a combat-experienced officer, there was the important matter of the personal chemistry between the two naval officers.

Dale was calm and even-tempered, in contrast to Jones's short-fused personality. Their contrasting personal qualities would have added an additional, positive dimension to *Bonhomme Richard*'s most senior leadership. After all of Jones's troubles with his officers, Dale would turn out to be arguably his best. And he would be fighting alongside Jones when effective leadership was most critical.

Bonhomme Richard's second lieutenant was Henry Lunt, who had served in *Alfred* and *Providence* with Jones. Lunt was captured by the British, imprisoned for two years, and then freed in Nantes in March 1779 along with other prisoners. Having a reliable friend as his second lieutenant turned out to be a personal pleasure and a bonus derived from Jones's efforts to secure exchanges for Continental Navy prisoners held by the British. In addition, there were ten midshipmen on board *Bonhomme Richard,* all but two of whom were regarded by Jones as effective members of his crew. Including the men of the lower decks, Jones finally had a group that showed potential as a fighting crew, despite their initial lack of homogeneity. Jones's crew in *Bonhomme Richard* was evidence that the Continental Navy was surviving its difficult birth and beginning to emerge as a fighting force that could hold its own in an increasing variety of missions, even against the best opposition.

Before leaving Lorient's outer anchorage, Jones wrote several letters, and two provide important insight into his persona. One was to General Lafayette, dated 13 August, and it illuminates the special bond that often exists between strongly motivated military professionals, even those of different services, different nations, and with powerful egos. At one point, Jones refers to possible future joint army-navy operation with Lafayette: "I am highly honored by your expressing hopes that such an expedition between us will yet take place in the course of this war. I ardently join you in that wish, and assure you that few prospects could afford me equal pleasure, or more entirely gratify my ambition. . . . I expect to sail this evening, and you will perhaps hear of me soon."[7]

The second letter of particular interest, also dated 13 August, was to Franklin. Initially the letter deals with personnel and prize money. And it then turns to the issue of command of the squadron. Although only a brief reference to recruiting for *Bonhomme Richard,* it is an important example of a senior officer in the infant Continental Navy working to establish proper areas of responsibility within the concept of civilian control of the military. Although polite, it was clear: "M. de Chaumont has made an useless journey here, as I had taken all the necessary measures to engage the men that were wanting before his appearance, even at Nantes."[8]

On 14 August, Jones and his squadron sailed from Lorient's outer anchorage. His moment in history was only weeks away, but true to form, new problems began within days, when the French privateer *Monsieur* left his command. Since he had no direct military authority over the captain, there was nothing Jones could do to keep him involved in his mission. During the early stages of the deployment, Jones took several merchant ships. During this open ocean transit of more than three hundred nautical miles, Jones no doubt spent a lot of time drilling the crew in everything from mustering boarding parties to serving the guns.

By 23 August *Bonhomme Richard* had made landfall off the Irish coast at Dingle Bay, in the southwest corner of Ireland. The series of events that followed did not portend the momentously positive deployment to come. The first event was one of a squadron commander's worst nightmares during the age of sail: a complete lack of wind. In this instance, such a calm was double jeopardy for Jones. He had to try to keep his squadron together, and he had to keep its ships off the threatening rocks of the Skelligs, outside Dingle Bay. As the current and swells were setting him closer and closer to the rocks, his barge was lowered to tow *Bonhomme Richard* clear of danger. The coxswain and crew of the barge were Irish, and they took advantage of the situation to abandon the becalmed *Bonhomme Richard* and head for shore and home. The ship's sailing master pursued the deserters in another of the ship's boats and only succeeded in getting lost in a fog. The deployment was just beginning, and Jones had two boats and a significant number of men missing, including his second lieutenant.

The following day, Captain Landais made his first contribution to the mounting mix of problems confronting Jones. He came on board *Bonhomme Richard* and publicly berated his commodore for ordering him to not pursue a potential prize inshore the previous day. He also announced that in the future he would make up his own mind about which potential prizes to pursue and when he would pursue them. Publicly criticizing your commodore would have earned a court-martial in any long-standing navy of the time. But on 24 August 1779 off Dingle Bay, Chaumont's undercutting of Jones's authority over his captains and the often-nebulous lines of authority in Continental Navy ships were at work. Jones tried to make the best of the situation and move on. He was showing an ability to subordinate what had to be his basic reaction as a naval commander to the situation for the sake of the mission.

Next, Jones sent *Cerf* to search for the two missing boats and his second lieutenant, all of which were important parts of *Bonhomme Richard*'s operating capability, and the situation continued to deteriorate rapidly. While awaiting *Cerf*'s return, the weather turned nasty and Jones shortened sail, worked offshore, and rode the storm out. On 27 August, after the storm had moved through, Jones was finally able to assess matters.

Landais in *Alliance* had, as threatened, taken off on his own. *Cerf* had failed in her mission to find Lunt, and her captain, Joseph Varage, had decided on his own to return to Lorient. Varage later claimed that his cutter had suffered too much storm damage, but his departure without any apparent effort to communicate with his commodore clearly was a result of the agreement required by Chaumont that had so seriously undercut Jones's authority as squadron commander. As it turned out, Lunt and his boat crew had been captured while looking for food ashore. He was imprisoned for his second time and died while incarcerated.

The French privateer *Granville* had taken a prize and left the squadron. Like Varage, *Granville*'s captain simply departed on his own. *Pallas* had a broken tiller that would require some time for repair. At that point the squadron had been reduced to *Bonhomme Richard,* the lightly armed French brig *Vengeance,* and the damaged *Pallas.* To cap Jones's problems, the British Navy knew that he was at sea in the area of Ireland and had dispatched two frigates to hunt him down. Just about the only good news was that the two British frigates were searching along the southeast coast of Ireland, rather than along the northwest coast, where Jones was operating.

In unvarnished terms, Jones's mission was a shambles. Any officer who would have decided to abort the mission and return to France under the circumstances Jones was facing could not have been faulted. Jones, however, determined to press on. In his report to Franklin from the Texel after the deployment, he said simply that despite having only *Pallas* and *Vengeance* with him, he was determined to continue the mission. His decision was a reflection of a personal doctrine that had emerged by this point in his career: *Never give up.* It was a doctrine he followed when lobbying for a decent ship and one that would tip the balance for him in his forthcoming battle. It also was a doctrine that would become embedded with good effect in future U.S. Navy tradition.

Taking advantage of fair winds, Jones worked his way past Ireland, reaching the Flannan Islands at the northwest end of Scotland on 30 August. Early the following morning, three sails were sighted, and after a considerable chase to the northeast, Jones, with *Vengeance* in company, captured *Union,* a British merchantman. The *Union* was a letter of marque ship—a privateer with a government license to attack the ships of Britain's enemies—carrying a cargo of uniforms to the British Army in Canada. The capture was made off Cape Wrath, coincidentally one of the rendezvous points Jones had established for the squadron.

Landais in *Alliance* showed up at Cape Wrath at about the same time as the taking of *Union* by Jones. He too had a prize—*Betsy,* a British merchant ship. In a conciliatory effort, Jones assigned the manning of *Union* to Landais. Landais responded by continuing his very visible defiance of Jones's orders, and he sent *Union* and his own prize *Betsy* into Bergen, Norway, one of the ports for prizes designated by the French but not the port Jones had designated for those two particular prizes. On 2 September, *Pallas* (which had left the squadron to make repairs) also rejoined *Bonhomme Richard,* not far from Cape Wrath. On 3 September, Jones started south to take the squadron to the east of the Orkney Islands and down the northeast coast of Scotland. Once again, Landais departed on his own after ignoring an order for a conference on board *Bonhomme Richard.*

At this point, rough weather and the sub-par performance by several of his captains had been ongoing challenges for Jones. But if he was distracted, he was not deflected. Jones pressed on with his mission, and although he might have had difficulty appreciating it at the time, he was achieving some strategic impact. His squadron had taken a number of merchantmen as prizes, and his activities had alerted nearby communities along the way to the possibility of attacks by his squadron. The *London Evening Post* of 20 September reflected the general state of alarm he was creating. "A letter from Cork, Sept. 11, says, 'Not a day passed but we are receiving accounts of the depredations committed by Paul Jones and his squadron on our coast. A report is current this day that he is with his whole fleet at anchor in Bantry Bay, and had with him five prizes.'"[9]

By 11 September, Jones was nowhere in the vicinity of Bantry Bay at the southwestern tip of Ireland; he was off the northeast coast of Scotland. But such was the state of concern and confusion he was creating. A few weeks later, London's *Morning Post and Daily Advertiser* was more dramatic, comparing Jones to a popular stage character: "Paul Jones resembles a Jack O'Lantern, to mislead our mariners and terrify our coasts. He is no sooner seen than lost; Hey! Presto!—like Mungo in the Farce—'Mungo here, Mungo there, and Mungo everywhere!'"[10]

By the middle of September, Jones was off Leith with *Pallas* and *Vengeance* in company, predictably causing panic in the nearby communities ashore. The plan he outlined to Captains Denis Cottineau and Philippe Ricot was bold indeed. He intended to land at Leith, the seaport that serves Edinburgh, and present an ultimatum. The demand would be for the payment of a heavy ransom as an alternative to burning the town. According to Jones, such an attack against the British homeland would be retaliation for British attacks against American civilians, such as the burning of the town of Esopus in the upper Hudson valley of New York on 16 October 1777 and the burning and sacking of numerous towns along the Connecticut coast in July 1779. He also saw such raids as a way to gain added leverage for securing freedom for American sailors held in British prisons. Initially the plan was received with little enthusiasm by the two captains, but with increased stress on the potential ransom, set at 200,000 pounds by Jones, according to his after-action report to Franklin, Cottineau and Ricot finally developed some interest in the attack on Leith.

With the support of his two captains secured, Jones organized a landing force and an ultimatum was prepared. Jones actually beat his way into the Firth of Forth and toward Leith on 16 September, as the local residents frantically prepared to defend their homes against the fearsome American naval raider. Fortunately for the local citizenry, which was virtually defenseless against an attack from the sea, the wind turned dead on the nose for the American squadron. As a result, Jones and his crew were forced to give up the incursion and run before the wind and out of the Firth. The following day, Jones was threatening nearby Kirkcaldy, when nature again intervened with a gale that sprang up as he was about to send a landing party ashore. It could well have seemed that God was on the side of the Kirkcaldy and Leith residents at this point, and Jones abandoned the raid.

Once again, however, one of the main objectives of the mission—raising tension in the British countryside—was advanced. On 21 September, the *London Evening Post* confirmed the concern and confusion Jones was creating. Based on the paper's account, Jones was still perceived as being "here, there, and everywhere."

> Three ships had appeared off Leymouth and Dunbar. Which seemed to be enemies, and had taken two or three vessels, in the mouth of the Firth; the largest was frigate built, and was supposed to carry 40 or 50 guns. . . . It was reported that the above was Paul Jones squadron, but letters received on Friday at Edinburgh from the West Country say, that Paul Jones was on the West coast upon the 13th instant.[11]

Jones was still in an offensive mood as he turned southeast and headed toward Newcastle at the mouth of the Tyne River, his next objective. An effective raid on that harbor would have the added benefit of disrupting the British coal supply for the approaching winter. As he approached Newcastle, some of the circumstances were familiar, but some were different. Once again, he was having difficulty convincing his captains of the efficacy of an attack. Cottineau, in particular, was opposed to Jones's plans to attack Newcastle, and he threatened that both he and Ricot would abandon the squadron if Jones persisted in his plan.

In contrast, however, the officers and crew of *Bonhomme Richard* not only were enthusiastic about raiding Newcastle, they were willing to go it alone if Captains Cottineau and Ricot balked. That was very different from the contrary crew Jones had in *Ranger* and the collection of disparate groups with which he had departed from Lorient a month before. Jones's personal leadership accomplished little with his captains; that relationship was unalterably corrupted by the agreement he had made at Chaumont's insistence in Lorient. On the other hand, his personal leadership clearly had molded a fighting crew in *Bonhomme Richard.* The real proof, at this point, was just over the horizon and only a little more than a week away.

Meanwhile the British Navy was steadily deploying units to seek out and destroy the elusive Jones and his small squadron. The heavy frigate HMS *Ulysses* and the frigate HMS *Boston* had been sent into the Irish Sea in search of him, the ship of the line HMS *Romney* was in the general area, and the heavy frigate HMS *Emerald,* with two smaller ships in company, had left the Nore anchorage in search of Jones. And of greatest significance, the frigate HMS *Serapis* was already athwart his course toward the Texel. The British Navy was slowly closing a noose around Jones and his squadron.

Perhaps it was a belief that a lone attack by *Bonhomme Richard* really was too risky, or perhaps it was his instincts telling him that the British Navy was closing in that caused Jones to bypass Newcastle. In his final report of the mission to Franklin on 3 October he rationalized his uncharacteristic decision: "I am persuaded even now, that I would have succeeded, and to the honor of my young officers, I found them as ardently disposed to the business as I could desire; nothing prevented me from pursuing my design but the reproach that would have been cast upon my character, as a man of prudence, had the enterprise miscarried."[12]

Whatever the reason—or combination of reasons—Jones resumed his southeasterly track, moving along the Northumberland coast. As he proceeded, his presence continued to roil the countryside, and he continued to attack British merchantmen. The *London Evening Post* of 21 September was one of the many newspapers that were following his activities:

> The celebrated American corsair, Paul Jones, had entered the River Humber on Thursday last, and chased a vessel within a mile of the Pier,

> where he sunk, burnt, and destroyed sixteen sail of valuable vessels, which threw the whole town and neighborhood into the utmost consternation; as a very few men in armed boats, might have laid the town in ashes. He had taken nine or ten colliers and other vessels a day or two before he appeared at Hull.[13]

The newspaper report went on to describe Jones's squadron as consisting of a Boston-built forty-gun frigate, a former French East Indiaman of forty-four guns, two new thirty-two-gun American frigates, a new twenty-two-gun American frigate, two eighteen-gun brigantines, and two small tenders! That might have been the squadron of Jones's dreams, but the reality of September 1779 was that the squadron described by the *London Evening Post* was mostly a British nightmare, no less of an effective threat, however, because of the wild exaggeration of the squadron's size. As Jones moved along the coast, the women and children were hastily evacuated from the areas and the militia was mustered to repel the "corsair."

As Commodore John Paul Jones of the Continental Navy once again set his course toward the southeast, he was less than 150 miles from Flamborough Head. A better end than the beginning of his deployment was at hand. The sometimes brilliantly successful and sometimes trouble-filled prologue to his major moment in history was coming to a close. Jones's antagonist for that coming moment of history was not far over the horizon to the southeast, embarked in a British frigate that was named for a god rooted in the misty history of ancient Egypt.

6
A Pivot Point of History

"In Sea affairs, nothing is impossible, and nothing improbable."
Admiral Lord Nelson

One of the most violent events in the American struggle for liberty was the combat between the men of the Continental ship *Bonhomme Richard* and the men of HMS *Serapis*.[1] The battle took place on 23 September 1779, off Flamborough Head, a windswept promontory poking into the North Sea along England's Yorkshire coast. On the face of it, the battle off Flamborough Head could have been no more than a footnote in the history of the American Revolution. It was an isolated struggle, albeit a particularly bloody one, between two ships that weren't even large enough to be classified as capital ships in the age of sail. Within the context of the ongoing world war that surrounded it, how important could that single naval action have been?

In fact, many histories, including those by U.S. authors, simply make no mention of the battle at all. A recent history about "The Struggle to Create the American Republic," for example, does not even list John Paul Jones in its index, nor does it list the battle off Flamborough Head.[2] But a penetrating analysis of the event challenges the land-oriented and dismissive view and reveals the transcending strategic importance of this historically pivotal confrontation between the men of *Bonhomme Richard* and *Serapis*.

In truth, the victory of *Bonhomme Richard* over *Serapis* was to the naval component of the American Revolution what the battle of Saratoga was to the land campaign—it changed everything. The battle's unlikely outcome broadcast to the world that the American Continental Navy not only could fight, it could fight and *win*. In a broader context, *Bonhomme Richard*'s victory eventually became a metaphor for the entire war. Jones's victory showed that a force that is militarily inferior to its opponent on paper can overcome its disadvantages when driven by powerful motivation.

The run-up to the battle began with Jones sighting the topsails of a large convoy of ships to the south of the town of Scarborough—roughly twenty miles to the northwest of Flamborough Head—on 22 September. The convoy, consisting of more than forty ships with extremely valuable cargoes, was a target of opportunity that matched Jones's mission perfectly. As *Bonhomme Richard* chased the convoy to the south, she was rejoined by *Alliance* and *Pallas* on 23 September. With those two ships and the cutter *Vengeance,* Jones had something of a squadron under his command again.

They took several small prizes as they sailed south, and, as an important by-product, once more created turmoil ashore. Scarborough, Hull, and the surrounding Yorkshire countryside were hastily mobilized, and local authorities dispatched frantic messages requesting help from the British Navy. The *London Daily Press* of 21 September gave Jones's actions an economic twist and focused on their psychological impact in Britain: "In consequence of the capture of so many colliers, and the interception of the trade, the price of coals will be enormous. . . . Instead of having the domain of the sea, it is now evident that we are not able to defend our own coast from depredations."[3]

By the afternoon Jones had learned from local pilots that he was in sight of a Baltic convoy. It also became clear that two frigates were escorting the merchant ships. One was the small twenty-gun merchant ship taken up into naval service, HMS *Countess of Scarborough,* with a British Navy captain and probably a civilian crew. The other was the forty-four-gun frigate HMS *Serapis.*

Serapis, destined to become part of the legend that would grow around Jones's actions, was new, and one of her most important features was that her bottom was coppered. That recent technological advance in naval ship design prevented marine growth on a ship's bottom. This in turn meant that a ship with a coppered bottom was significantly faster and more responsive than vessels without this construction feature, such as the *Bonhomme Richard.* And despite that fact that she was rated at forty-four guns, *Serapis,* like many ships of the age of sail, actually carried a number of cannons somewhat different than the number called for in her original design. In fact, at the time of her confrontation with Jones, it is believed that *Serapis* actually mounted between forty-six and fifty cannons. With that many guns, and her two gun decks rather than the single gun deck of most frigates, *Serapis* was right at the borderline between a large frigate and a small ship of the line. During the age of sail, it was not unusual for a fifty-gun ship to fight in the line of battle along with the much more heavily armed ships that carried one hundred guns or more.

In terms of armament, speed, and maneuverability, Jones, in his fourteen-year-old converted merchantman, appeared to be overmatched in single-ship combat with the new, more heavily armed, more nimble, and purpose-built *Serapis.* Counterbalancing the factors in *Serapis*'s favor, Jones's four-ship squadron of the moment was superior to the combination of *Serapis* and *Countess of Scarborough*. *Bonhomme Richard* also had a larger crew complement than *Serapis*. In an additional comparison, Captain Richard Pearson of *Serapis* was a thirty-year veteran in the Royal Navy and had been a captain for six of those years. He also had considerable combat experience. All told, he was a much more experienced naval officer than Jones was, and it is reasonable to assume that his crew was considerably better drilled in gunnery.

As Pearson and the convoy moved slowly south, he saw a large red flag flying above Scarborough Castle, a warning that an enemy was offshore. Pearson put into Scarborough harbor to get additional information, which was quick to arrive with a messenger boat: the threat being broadcast was from Jones and his Continental Navy squadron. That was serious news indeed for a captain responsible for a convoy carrying much-needed naval stores for the British Navy. Pearson immediately returned to sea and placed himself between his convoy and the potential enemy. And given his mission, that was exactly what he should have done.

As the situation became clear, Pearson signaled for the convoy to reverse course to the northwest and move into Scarborough Bay, where the guns of Scarborough Castle would protect them. And with that order, he again successfully responded to his primary mission—protect the convoy—since the maneuver facilitated the two British Navy escorts placing themselves between the convoy and Jones's squadron.

Amid confusion, for which merchant convoys of the age of sail were notorious, the convoy managed to start its retreat toward Scarborough, and by 5:30 in the afternoon of the 23rd, *Countess of Scarborough* had joined *Serapis* between the convoy and Jones. There was nothing special in Pearson's maneuvers; they were basically sound tactics driven by clear circumstances and his primary mission. In his after-action report to the Admiralty, dated 6 October, Pearson reported his initial actions in a sailor's plain language: "I made all the sail I could to windward, to get between the enemy's ships and the convoy, which I soon effected."[4]

As the combatants approached each other, Jones prepared his ship to fight in three basic ways. *Bonhomme Richard*'s six 18-pound guns would fire round shot at the hulls of the British ships, and the 12- and 8-pound guns would fire double-headed shot at the spars and rigging.[5] He had seamen and French Marines (including a lieutenant colonel de Chamillard) positioned on the three small platforms of *Bonhomme Richard*'s fore-, main-, and mizzenmast tops. These men had muskets and small swivel cannons loaded with grapeshot; their job was to first clear the tops of the British ships of their marksmen and then fire down on the British personnel on their exposed decks.

The antipersonnel firepower Jones placed in *Bonhomme Richard*'s tops became a critical factor in the battle. Jones also positioned a number of the French Marines on the relatively high poop deck of his ship. The Marines would provide additional fire down on personnel on the exposed decks of his approaching enemy. Same as Pearson, Jones was preparing nothing radical in the way of tactics; he was reacting to the situation and his capabilities.

As the ships continued to maneuver in the light wind, they slowly drew closer. Jones had ordered his squadron to form a line of battle. As usual, Captain Landais in *Alliance* ignored his commodore's signal. Pearson turned toward the shore and onto a port tack to take advantage of the current. Jones also turned to port to continue closing with *Serapis.* Finally, just about the time the evening moon was rising, they were within hailing distance. Captain Pearson identified himself and asked, "What ship is that?" Jones, who was flying British colors—showing false colors was a common tactic to cause an enemy to hesitate—answered, "Princess Royal," the name of a British East Indiaman. Pearson was viewing the American ships bow-on, a difficult angle for determining the nationality of a ship. He hailed again, "Where from?" Jones tried to stall and, according to *Serapis*'s log, Pearson then threatened, "Tell me instantly from whence you came and who you be, or I'll fire a broadside into you."

In the meantime, Jones's turn to port apparently confused Landais in *Alliance* and Captain Cottineau in *Pallas.* Landais hove to, and Cottineau continued on a course taking him farther out to sea and away from Jones. The confusion demonstrated that Landais and Cottineau were not mentally in tune with their commodore. Captain Ricot in *Vengeance* continued to simply stand off, which was about all he could do with his small ship. That confusion in the ships accompanying Jones simplified the tactical situation immensely for Pearson, because he was able to focus on *Bonhomme Richard.* And as a corollary, there was no way Jones could get at the vulnerable merchant ships—doubtless his primary intent—without dealing with *Serapis.* The two ships slowly moved closer, with *Bonhomme Richard*'s starboard side eventually facing the British ship's port side.

A single shot from a musket in one of the American ship's tops flashed, then cracked and echoed off the one-hundred-foot-plus cliffs of Flamborough Head. As if responding to a starter's gun, *Bonhomme Richard* ran up her American colors, and she and *Serapis* fired virtually simultaneous broadsides into one another. It was an even start to the deadly struggle.

As the cannon flames ripped the dusk, both ships erupted in activity. Gun crews that had poised quietly next to their weapons began the desperate firing, sponging, reloading, ramming, priming, running out, aiming, and firing cycle.

The manufacturing of dead and wounded had begun. In such contests, speed of cannon fire usually correlated with victory. Aboard *Serapis,* Pearson had personally nailed his ensign to its staff; it was now a battle to the death between the men of *Bonhomme Richard* and the men of *Serapis.*

It was not a good sign for the Americans when *Serapis* was clearly first to get a second broadside off. In addition, several of Jones's old 18-pounders immediately blew up, killing or wounding those in the vicinity of the faulty guns. Each captain maneuvered to try to rake his opponent by positioning himself across the bow or stern of his enemy and firing a broadside that would penetrate along the length of the opposing ship. In these maneuvers, Pearson, with the faster and more nimble ship, had the clear advantage, particularly in light wind. Pearson capitalized on his advantage and succeeded in gaining a superior position across *Bonhomme Richard*'s stern several times and then raked her with devastating broadsides. Knowing that he could not survive a standoff battle, Jones then succeeded in laying his ship across *Serapis*'s quarter, and he attempted to board her. Because the American sailors had only a narrow point on *Serapis* to board, however, they were repulsed and Jones bore away.

Next, Pearson attempted to cross *Bonhomme Richard*'s bow in order to rake her again. He turned too soon, however, and *Bonhomme Richard*'s bowsprit became entangled in *Serapis*'s starboard quarter. Having clearly had the better of things based on his speed and maneuverability, Pearson hailed Jones and shouted, "Has your ship struck?" It was not an unexpected question from a captain who believed that his victory was at hand. And it was not an unreasonable question from a captain whose ship was demonstrating its sailing superiority and faster rate of fire.

No captain in Jones's situation could have been seriously faulted for concluding that he was in a losing fight—*Bonhomme Richard* had taken devastating blows—and striking his colors to avoid additional bloodshed. Such an action would have been well within the unwritten code of honor of the age of sail. Jones's response, however, sprang not from logic or even a code of honor, but from his inherent determination and commitment to a cause. He shouted the plain truth: "I have not yet begun to fight."

Some biographers claim that Jones's immortal words were spoken much later in the battle, and some claim that he never used those exact words. But the preponderance of evidence indicates that it was at this juncture in the battle that Jones shouted his now-famous refusal to surrender. The firsthand account of the battle, provided years after the event by *Bonhomme Richard*'s first lieutenant Richard Dale, supports the contention that those were Jones's words. Dale's account also establishes that the exchange occurred when the ships first came together during the battle. He wrote, "*Bon homme Richard,* having headway, ran her bows into the stern of the *Serapis.* We had remained in this situation but a few minutes when we were again hailed by the *Serapis,* 'Has your ship struck?' To which Captain Jones answered, 'I have not yet begun to fight.'"[6]

In any event, no one claims that Jones did not express the basic idea summed up in the words contained in Dale's account. And when all is said and done, it was the idea, not the exact words, that has inspired generations of U.S. Navy sailors.

Jones extricated himself by backing his topsails, and as the ships tore themselves apart, Pearson came about by wearing ship. The two ships were again in parallel positions, with *Serapis*'s port side facing *Bonhomme Richard*'s starboard side. Now it was Pearson's turn to back his topsails, presumably to fall behind *Bonhomme Richard,* cross her stern, and again rake her from that position. Jones countered by turning to starboard and the ships came together for a third time, this time with *Serapis*'s bowsprit entangled in *Bonhomme Richard*'s starboard quarter. Jones realized that he was in a position to negate Pearson's advantages of speed and agility by converting the battle into an eyeball-to-eyeball struggle. And he was among the first to take a hand in the securing of the two ships. Taking a forestay from *Serapis* that had parted and fallen on board *Bonhomme Richard,* he secured it around his ship's mizzenmast.

Slowly the American ship pivoted and her starboard side eventually lay alongside *Serapis*'s starboard side, with the ships lying bow to stern. Jones ordered that grappling irons be thrown over to secure the two ships. More than fifty were quickly in place, indicating that his crew was performing smartly under fire. Pearson did his best to break the embrace but the sharpshooters and seamen in *Bonhomme Richard*'s tops swept *Serapis*'s exposed decks with deadly musket fire and grapeshot. Pearson, in the meantime, anchored his ship, possibly to try to cause the two ships to separate or possibly simply because he was confident that he could win the fight in hand-to-hand combat with Jones's crew. This would not have been a surprising attitude for a British Navy captain, because a common element of the service's combat doctrine was to lay one's ship alongside the enemy and fight the battle at close quarters.[7] For Pearson on this day, however, it was a fatal mistake.

It was a little past 8 PM at this point, and the battle had been raging for slightly less than an hour. The two ships had been drifting with the current toward the northwest, with *Bonhomme Richard* being steadily blasted to pieces by her enemy's more rapid cannon fire and *Serapis*'s crew taking heavy casualties from the deadly accurate musket fire and grapeshot from her enemy's tops, as well as grapeshot from her relatively high poop deck. Both ships were on fire, but the American ship was burning, not just on and above the main deck, but between the main and lower decks as well. In all probability, the fire deep within *Bonhomme Richard* was started when several of her 18-pound guns exploded at the beginning of the battle.

In the confusion, *Bonhomme Richard*'s senior warrant officer, thinking that his captain and first lieutenant were dead, attempted to surrender his ship. Jones, hearing the man shouting, "Quarters, quarters," intervened and knocked him unconscious with an unloaded pistol. Captain Pearson, also hearing the man shouting for quarters, yelled across, "Have you struck? Do you call for quarters?" Jones reply was a slightly longer version than his previous reply to the same question: "No; I'll sink, but I'll be damned if I'll strike!"

Pearson attempted to take *Bonhomme Richard* with a boarding party at this stage, but the Americans' superior numbers came into play. The British boarding party was driven back after the bloody hand-to-hand fighting reached Jones's quarterdeck. The Continental Navy ship was a battered hulk at this point, with many of the British cannonballs passing completely through her hull. In grotesque asymmetry, *Serapis* was almost completely destroyed from the main deck up, and *Bonhomme Richard*'s hull no longer existed as such. The battle had raged for three hours.

As the water rose in *Bonhomme Richard,* her master-at-arms released the British prisoners captured in previous actions. The British sailors were put to work, manning the pumps of the sinking American ship. Although they could have bolted and tipped the balance of the battle against the Americans, the released prisoners surprisingly did no such thing. Perhaps it was a matter of saving themselves from imminent drowning, perhaps it was fear of being shot on the spot, but in any event, the released prisoners were forced to become a positive factor for the Americans.

Then the tide of battle suddenly turned. A seaman from *Bonhomme Richard* who had been dropping grenades onto the main deck of *Serapis* from one of *Bonhomme Richard*'s yardarms, succeeded in dropping one through a main-deck hatch and onto the gun deck below. When the grenade exploded, it ignited large amounts of gunpowder that had been brought up from the magazine to supply the ship's main batteries and accumulated in several areas around the gun deck. The explosions neutralized *Serapis*'s gun deck, silencing her main armament. Suddenly, it was Pearson's turn to confront surrender. His assessment was that with almost all of his guns silenced, rigging wrecked, and main deck swept by enemy fire, the superior numbers of the American ship could not be overcome. In addition, he had successfully carried out his main mission—the British convoy, with its highly valuable cargoes, was safe in Scarborough harbor under the protection of the castle's guns.

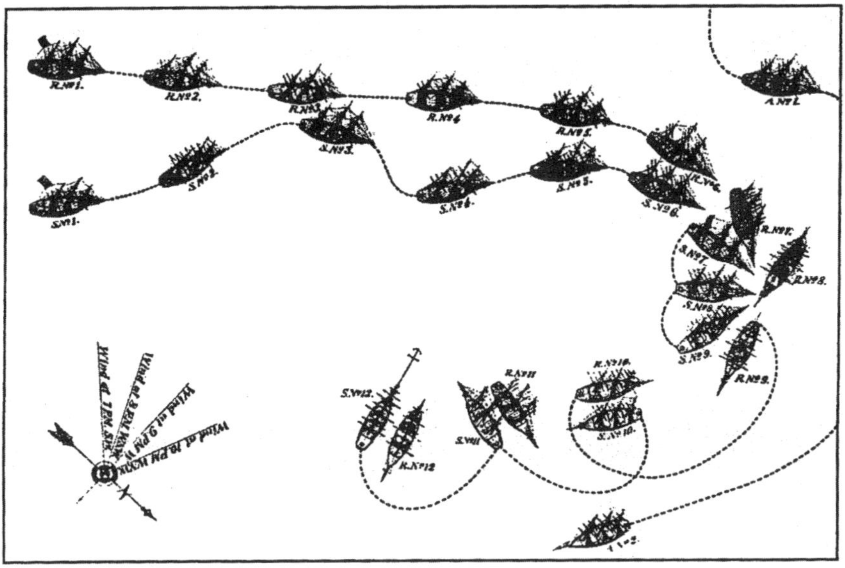

This redraft of an original sketch by John Paul Jones shows the plan of the battle off Flamborough Head in September 1779 between the Continental ship *Bonhomme Richard* and HMS *Serapis.*
From the author's collection

At about 11:15 PM, Pearson made the decision to stop the carnage, and as the fighting ended, it was First Lieutenant Dale who seized a remnant of *Serapis*'s rigging, swung aboard the subdued British frigate, and confirmed the surrender. Captain Pearson was then escorted aboard *Bonhomme Richard,* where he presented his sword to Jones. Acknowledging the bravery of his adversary, Jones returned Pearson's sword to him.

The two officers then adjourned to what had been Jones's cabin and shared a glass of wine. The casualties from the battle were appalling: more than 150 from the American crew of 322 were dead or wounded, and more than 130 from the British crew of 284 were dead or wounded. Jones recorded his reaction in an after-action report to Benjamin Franklin: "Humanity cannot but recoil from the prospect of such finished horror, and lament that war should produce such fatal consequences."[8] There would have been no cause for celebration in those statistics. The men in both ships had done their duty, many at the ultimate cost, and that was that.

Quickly the focus shifted to extinguishing the fires that raged on both ships and attending to the wounded. The latter was a gruesome process, usually conducted in the ship's cockpit with crude instruments and no anesthetics. The surgeon was also responsible for burying the dead.

In fighting the fires, the first priority was to move *Bonhomme Richard*'s powder away from the flames below deck. If her magazine were to explode, it would be the end of both ships and most of the men who had survived the combat. The effort was urgent enough for even the British officers to participate. As a prize crew went about taking control of *Serapis,* a group of French Marines secured the British prisoners in the hold of what was formerly their ship. After the surrender of *Serapis,* the ships were separated, and as they parted, *Serapis*'s mainmast came crashing down, taking most of the ship's spars and rigging with it. Only the foremast, foretopmast, and mizzenmast remained.

Lieutenant Dale was in *Serapis* leading the clearing of wreckage and firefighting, despite a painful leg wound. He finally gained an upper hand in both efforts and ordered the wheel put over in order to move farther away from *Bonhomme Richard.* When the ship failed to respond, Dale quickly dispatched a seaman to see if the rudder had been shot away. The seaman returned to say that both rudder and steering tackle were intact. At about that point in time, *Serapis*'s sailing master approached Dale and asked evenly, "Excuse me, sir, but are you aware that the ship is at anchor?" Most probably, Dale responded with some choice expletives—and perhaps even a grim laugh. Some might conclude that that moment was the beginning of the special relationship that eventually developed over the coming centuries between the U.S. Navy and the British Navy.

Throughout the night the exhausted crew of *Bonhomme Richard* fought to save the two crippled ships. Fortunately, the men of *Alliance, Pallas,* and *Vengeance* were able to assist in the struggle. By dawn of the 24th, the fates of the two wounded ships were still in doubt, but at least the situation had stabilized somewhat. The wounded were being attended to, most of the fires—except for those between decks in *Bonhomme Richard*—were out or under control, and the prisoners had been moved off *Bonhomme Richard* and secured.

In examining the battle off Flamborough Head it is important to also assess the actions of *Alliance, Pallas,* and *Vengeance.* At about 9:20 PM on the night of the battle, Landais in *Alliance* had entered the combat. His first action was to approach the combatants slowly from the southeast. At this time the two ships were grappled together bow to stern. As Landais approached, he turned to cross the stern of *Bonhomme Richard* and the bow of *Serapis.* In that position he fired a full broadside, ostensibly at the bow of the British ship. Unfortunately, he was also firing into the stern of *Bonhomme Richard.* Since the latter ship had already suffered a great deal of damage to its stern and presented a larger target, Landais actually did more damage to *Bonhomme Richard* than to *Serapis.*

Despite frantic yelling from Jones's crew, Landais circled the two ships and fired another deadly broadside, this time into the bow of *Bonhomme Richard* and the stern of *Serapis.* Again he inflicted casualties and damage to both ships. This time, however, he probably did more damage to *Serapis.*

Landais then moved off and remained at a safe distance from the combat until the battle was over. During the entire episode off Flamborough Head, Landais's ship suffered no damage and his crew suffered no casualties. In fact the evidence that emerged after the battle indicated that it was Landais's intention to actually assist in the sinking of *Bonhomme Richard* and then capture the exhausted and damaged *Serapis* himself. In his after-action report to Franklin, Jones was still enraged at Landais: "His conduct has been base and unpardonable."[9]

Captain Cottineau in *Pallas* played a more positive role in the action on 23 September. Early in the evening he engaged *Countess of Scarborough.* It was a decidedly uneven contest. Cottineau's ship was manned by 250 men and mounted twenty-six 8-pound guns and six 4-pounders. His opponent's ship was manned by 125 men and her armament consisted of twenty 6-pound guns. The British ship put up a tough fight, but after being badly cut up by *Pallas*'s superior firepower, she was forced to surrender.

Ricot and *Vengeance* never really entered into the combat, nor would she have been expected to do so. As a lightly armed brig, she was no match even for *Countess of Scarborough.* In all probability, she would have been more of a hindrance than help in the single-ship actions between *Bonhomme Richard* and *Serapis* and *Pallas* and *Countess of Scarborough.*

By the evening of the 24th, despite all efforts, it was clear that *Bonhomme Richard* could not be saved. The winds were freshening and the pumps could not gain on the flooding in her hold. It was only a matter of time. The remaining prisoners and wounded were transferred to other ships, and by the following morning, the last crew members were ordered off. *Bonhomme Richard* was left for the sea to claim. The wind continued to freshen and a driving rain provided an appropriately somber background for the scene. At 10:30 AM *Bonhomme Richard* slipped beneath the surface, with her bow slightly down, still pointing the way for her last transit. She died quietly and came to rest two hundred feet below the surface of the North Sea. As she departed, the wind in *Serapis*'s shattered rigging and the drumming of the rain on the survivor's deck played *Bonhomme Richard*'s dirge.

In the final assessment, the victory of the crew of *Bonhomme Richard* over the men of *Serapis* was not a victory of brilliant tactics or advanced technology. The tactics on both sides appeared to have been straightforward, and in the early stages at least, things probably came down to a matter of how well the maneuvers were executed. Once the ships were locked together, sheer crew numbers and mental toughness were paramount; any advantages in basic ship design became irrelevant.

In the early part of the encounter, Pearson was clearly in the process of pounding his enemy into submission. The tide of battle shifted, however, when Pearson—attempting to fall back and presumably turn to starboard in order to cross under Jones's stern and rake *Bonhomme Richard* with another broadside—ran his bowsprit on to Jones's starboard quarter instead.

Pearson's backing of his sails to fall back and his failed attempt to cross under *Bonhomme Richard*'s stern created one of the more intriguing "what if" moments of naval history. What if Pearson had not backed his sails and had continued on course until he was well clear of *Bonhomme Richard*? Would he have been able to then simply continue outmaneuvering her and pound her to pieces? Was it a basic miscalculation of time, relative speed, and distance by Pearson that caused him to run onto *Bonhomme Richard*? Was there an unanticipated puff of wind that caused *Serapis* to surge ahead and into her opponent? Was Pearson's attempt to cross under *Bonhomme Richard*'s stern checked by Jones's decision to turn to starboard, presumably to cross *Serapis*'s bow as she fell back? If the latter is true, then the issue of gaining the upper hand in the crucial moment of the battle had come down to Jones's quick thinking and his crew's quick reactions.

Pearson's after-action report of 6 October 1779 to the Admiralty did little to throw light on the precise decisions and orders on which the battle turned. He wrote, "I backed our topsails, in order to get square with him again, which, as soon as he observed, he then filled, put his helm a-weather (turned to starboard), and laid us athwart hause; his mizzen shrouds took our jib boom, which hung him for some time until at last it gave way, and we dropped alongside of each other, head and stern, when the fluke of our spare anchor hooking his quarter, we became so close fore and aft that the muzzles of our guns touched each other's sides."[10]

As soon as the two ships were entangled, Jones realized that he had been presented with an opportunity. He seized his chance and made the ships fast. Up to that point, Pearson was winning the battle; from that point on, Pearson probably had considerably less than a fifty-fifty chance of victory. His advantages of speed, maneuverability, and superior gunnery were neutralized. Jones's advantages of superior crew numbers and concentration of fire on the exposed deck, spars, and rigging of his enemy came into play. And eventually, Jones had the quickness of mind and the iron determination to convert those strengths into a hard-fought and deserved victory. The hand grenade through *Serapis*'s main hatch was the final pivot point on which victory turned.

Jones's after-action report to Franklin of 3 October also throws little additional light on the most crucial decisions at the most critical point in the battle. In the portion of his report that dealt with the moments before the two ships came together for the third and final time, he wrote only of general intentions and events.

> I must confess that the enemy's ship being much more manageable than *Bon homme Richard,* gained thereby, several times an advantageous situation, in spite of my best endeavors to prevent it. . . . It was my intention to lay the *Bon homme Richard* athwart the enemy's bow, but as that operation required great dexterity in the management of both sails and helm, and some of our braces being shot away, it did not exactly succeed to my wishes; the enemy's bowsprit, however, came over the *Bon homme Richard*'s poop by the mizzen mast, and I made both ships fast together in that situation, which by the action of the wind on the enemy's sails, forced her stern close to the *Bon homme Richard*'s bow, so that the ships lay square alongside of each other, the yards being all entangled, and the cannon of each ship touching the opponent's side.[11]

As it turned out, Jones's victory consisted mostly of a series of decisions driven by doctrine, that overarching idea that transcends tactics. And like most good combat doctrines, it was one that could later be identified in a single phrase, in this case, "I have not yet begun to fight." It also can be argued that something beyond doctrine supported Jones through the situations when most captains would have capitulated: He was fighting for the cause of liberty, a force that outweighed his need for personal glory and even his fear of death. Jones's victory at the battle off Flamborough Head fit the concept written more than twenty years later by Napoléon Bonaparte: "It is moral force more than numbers that wins victory."[12]

In the aftermath of the battle, Pearson was stigmatized by some, despite the fact that he achieved his main mission: The convoy was saved without a single British merchant ship being captured or sunk. A court-martial acquitted him of wrongdoing and found that he and the captain of *Countess of Scarborough,* Thomas Piercy, had "done credit to themselves . . . against a superior force." In fact, Pearson was eventually rewarded with a knighthood. Despite official exoneration and honors, however, the ignominy of being captured by John Paul Jones, who was universally despised by the British, could not be expunged.

Jones, on the other hand, failed to achieve one of the primary missions of his deployment: to take or sink the merchant ships of the Baltic convoy. Yet because of his raw courage and the timing of his victory, he eventually became a U.S. hero and one of its most noteworthy naval leaders.

The battle between *Bonhomme Richard* and *Serapis* had an audience. More than a thousand people from the countryside had gathered on the cliffs of Flamborough Head to witness the fight. During the night it would have been difficult to determine the actual course of the battle or who was winning. By midmorning of the 24th, with the combatants hove to about six miles off the coast, spectators would have begun to realize that the two British ships had been captured by John Paul Jones. As the news spread, residents in the local area again were concerned about Jones coming ashore with a raiding party. In London and the rest of Great Britain, there was mounting shock and anger at the unlikely outcome of the action between *Bonhomme Richard* and *Serapis.*

London's *Morning Post and Daily Advertiser* of 27 September reported, "The *Serapis* and the *Countess of Scarborough* were obliged to strike." Besides understating the victory, the newspaper grasped at straws concerning the elusive American raider: "There is the greatest reason however, to expect his squadron and prizes will yet fall into our hands as the *Winchelsea,* and three frigates of force are cruising off Yarmouth for that purpose." The squadron described in the *Morning Post and Daily Advertiser,* patrolling nearly 150 miles to the southeast of Flamborough Head, would have a long wait. Jones was already heading almost directly east toward the Netherlands.

Worth noting, not all of the British newspaper coverage portrayed Jones as a cutthroat pirate. On 28 September, the *London Evening Post* gave evidence of a free press in Britain: "It appears that Jones's orders were not to burn any houses or towns. What an example of honour and greatness does America thus show to us! While our troops are running about from town to town on their coast, and burning everything, with a wonton, wicked, and deliberate barbarity, Dr. Franklin gives no orders to retaliate. . . . Paul Jones could have burned Leith the other day, with the greatest ease, and another little town near it; but his orders were peremptory, not to burn any towns."[13]

When news of the battle reached the Admiralty, a powerful squadron made up of the sixty-four-gun ship of the line HMS *Prudent;* the twenty-eight-gun frigates HMS *Amphitrite,* HMS *Medea,* and HMS *Pegasus;* and the twenty-four-gun frigate HMS *Champion* was dispatched on 28 September from Spithead in southern England to find Jones and eliminate him. But it was too late. Despite the crippled state of *Serapis,* which had become Jones's flagship during the journey to the Netherlands, Jones was able to work his way slowly to the east, with *Alliance, Pallas, Vengeance,* and the additional prize, *Countess of Scarborough,* in company.

Along the way, the problem of command of the squadron resurfaced. Jones wanted to go to the French port of Dunkerque, so the prisoners he had collected during his deployment could be brought directly to France, avoiding the political complications of dealing with the disposition of prisoners in neutral Holland. His captains amazingly overruled him, however, on the basis of the squadron's original orders from the French minister of marine, and there was simply no way Jones could get the jury-rigged *Serapis* into Dunkerque alone. The squadron put into the Texel on 3 October. The British, who had been unable to intercept Jones because of poor intelligence, eventually set up a blockade of the Texel with the fifty-gun HMS *Jupiter* and three frigates. Jones was back on the European continent safely, but the Royal Navy had him in a corner.

With the British patrolling off the Texel, the French marine minister Antoine de Sartine's plan for Jones to escort a trapped French Baltic convoy from that port back to France was blocked. In addition, the neutral Dutch were unhappy that Jones was in one of their harbors with two British prizes and hundreds of prisoners, including a senior British Navy captain. Coming events proved Jones's judgment to have been correct—it would have been better all around for him to put in to Dunkerque. The situation was an example of the negative results of political leaders' overzealous efforts to micromanage deployed naval forces. The error was compounded by the failure to establish the commodore's clear authority over a squadron that was bound to confront unforeseen events.

Because of the drama associated with the victory off Flamborough Head, it is easy to lose sight of the full achievements of Jones's deployment around the British Isles in *Bonhomme Richard.* Although he was not the first Continental Navy officer to take the American Revolution to the British Isles, Jones was the first to mount sustained raids on those coasts. (The first American officer to raid Britain was Captain Lambert Wicks in the eighteen-gun Continental Navy brig *Reprisal.* Wicks, traveling with a small squadron, had taken a significant number of prizes in 1777 in the English Channel.) In slightly less than two months, Jones circumnavigated the British Isles and captured and sank a substantial amount of enemy merchant shipping along his way. He then ended his deployment with a decisive combat victory against a powerful frigate of the British Navy. Adding to the drama of his accomplishments, he did it all with a fourteen-year-old converted merchant ship and a squadron made up of captains over whom he had been given tenuous authority.

Jones had done much more than win an unlikely single-ship victory. More important, he had carried out an extended difficult mission that had far-reaching strategic implications. The military accomplishments of *Bonhomme Richard*'s deployment came at a time when the defeat of one of the Continental Navy's few remaining operational units could have been the final bad war news that shattered the American will to fight on against Great Britain.

Jones's victory contrasted with three naval reversals the Americans suffered in late summer and fall of that year: (1) the collapse of the French plans for the invasion of Britain (2) the disastrous American amphibious operation against the British at Penobscot, Maine (at a cost to the meager navy of a frigate, brig, and a sloop of war), and (3) the failure of a combined American-French force to retake Savannah, Georgia. Because of the confluence of all of those negative circumstances, the news of Jones's victory at the battle off Flamborough Head reverberated thunderously, not only in the cities of America and Great Britain, but also in Paris and other European capitals.

Jones's achievements in *Bonhomme Richard* had a positive and sustaining psychological impact in America and a corresponding negative psychological impact on British public opinion and on the British political and military leaders in London. In historical perspective, the battle off Flamborough Head was an example of an apparently minor military victory that had a disproportionate effect on history. It was the kind of phenomenon that matched an idea expressed by Admiral Lord Nelson, writing from HMS *Victory* in 1804, "In Sea affairs, nothing is impossible, and nothing improbable."[14]

7
Victory's Aftermath

"The problems of victory are more agreeable than those of defeat, but are no less pressing."

Winston Churchill

Jones arrived at the deep-water anchorage for Amsterdam, the island of Texel, on 3 October 1779. He was seventy-five miles from the city, by way of a shallow, shifting, and tortuous channel through the Waddenzee and Isselmeer. The long and challenging route from Jones's isolated anchorage at the Texel to Amsterdam, where he would finally experience the first wave of public acclaim for his victory off Flamborough Head, was symbolic.

Jones had returned with his two British Navy prizes and more than five hundred prisoners, but as was the case when he returned from his successful deployment in the Irish Sea in *Ranger,* there were no congratulatory messages from either his American civilian leadership in Paris or his French sponsors. Instead of a triumphant welcome, there was only a renewal of the subtle political maneuverings that he had dealt with between his successes in *Ranger* and his deployment in *Bonhomme Richard.* He was back from his true element, the sea, and was quickly on the more indirect and frustrating ground of diplomacy.

One of the first things Jones did at the Texel was to write a lengthy report of his deployment for Benjamin Franklin. He didn't want to make the same mistake he had made when he returned to Brest in *Ranger* in May 1778, when he provided an opportunity for Arthur Lee to take him to task for not providing a detailed report of his mission in the Irish Sea.

In addition to providing a chronology of events in his report, Jones made a point of describing just how difficult his command and control situation was during the mission. He stated unequivocally that he would never again agree to take a squadron to sea without absolute command authority over his subordinate captains. He pursued the issue further with an angry indictment of Captain Landais, who had not only attacked Jones during the battle with *Serapis,* he had failed to attack the British convoy after Jones had captured *Serapis* and Captain Cottineau had captured *Countess of Scarborough. Alliance* had suffered no casualties and could have wrecked havoc among the unprotected merchant ships. His failure to do so was an inexcusable military mistake of inestimable magnitude.

Once the report was sent on its way, Jones turned his attention to his diplomatic problems. From the moment his victorious squadron anchored, the Dutch government was unhappy with Jones's presence. That presence not only generated very public stress in the Netherlands' shifting relations with the British, it brought no compensating commercial, political, or military benefits. From the Dutch government's point of view, it appeared increasingly likely that the British would prevail militarily in America, particularly in light of the series of reverses suffered by the Continental Navy during 1779.

Despite an emotional attachment to the American cause of liberty, the practical and trade-oriented Dutch did not want to be on a losing side, particularly if it meant opposing the world's most powerful navy. As a result, they were particularly sensitive to British diplomatic demands triggered by Jones's arrival at the Texel. It simply was not a good time for an American commodore to show up with two captured British ships and hundreds of British prisoners.

The French also were unhappy, because the Dutch—a major carrier of French trade that could not be carried safely in France's own ships—were unhappy. When the Dutch government decided that Jones must leave the Texel, the French ambassador ordered the French ships that had been deployed with Jones—and fought off Flamborough Head under the American flag—to return to their French colors. In addition he convinced Jones to fly the French colors over his two prizes, *Serapis* and *Countess of Scarborough.*

But when the French ambassador tried to get Jones to claim that he had fought under a French letter of marque, Jones blew up. Enough was enough. Not only would the French letter of marque reduce Jones to the status of a privateer, it could be interpreted as a de facto admission of the non-status of America as a nation. The French proposal was counter to Jones's deepest motivation. He described it as an unworthy proposition on "a dirty piece of parchment" and rejected it out of hand.

Even Franklin was unhappy with the situation, since it was creating a whole set of unwelcome diplomatic problems for him. The French were critically important to America as an active ally, and the Dutch had significant potential as a future ally, particularly as a source of financial assistance to America. Franklin could not, as a diplomat, ignore those realities, notwithstanding the magnitude of Jones's accomplishments in *Bonhomme Richard.*

The British appeared to be the only ones who were drawing political benefit from where the American squadron wound up after its deployment. With Jones at the Texel, the British could not only continue to block the trapped Baltic convoy that the French needed badly, they also had the infamous John Paul Jones almost within the grasp of their squadron patrolling off the harbor. And capturing or killing Jones would wipe out his embarrassing combat win over *Serapis.*

The British took full advantage of the situation and argued aggressively that Jones did not represent any recognized nation, and therefore he should not be provided sanctuary from his pursuers. The British continued to claim that he was no more than a pirate and demanded that *Serapis* and *Countess of Scarborough* be returned to them. Fortunately for Jones, the Dutch diplomatic discomfort was counterbalanced by two factors beyond the actual diplomatic negotiations. The first was that the government of the Netherlands, centered in the slow-moving States General, was not designed for fast decisions. Thus it was not likely to take quick action in Jones's controversial circumstances. The second factor working for Jones was the immense and very visible public popularity he had achieved in the Netherlands, a phenomenon that became apparent soon after his arrival. Public opinion was arguably the key factor working for Jones.

When Jones appeared on the streets of Amsterdam, cheering crowds followed him, and he was accorded an enthusiastic ovation when he appeared at the theater. Songs were written in his honor, some of which have survived to this day as Dutch folk music. And those public expressions of popular opinion gave Jones much-needed leverage in the situation. In net, it was a case of the deep inertia of the Dutch government and strong favorable public opinion in support of Jones combining to stalemate the intense British diplomatic pressure.

The British, badly stung by the defeat and capture of *Serapis* and *Countess of Scarborough,* were predictably incensed at the public acclaim for Jones in Amsterdam and the lack of immediate action by the government of the Netherlands. British national pride and honor were at stake. But of even greater importance to the British was how their country's relations with present and potential allies would be affected by the British Navy being bested by an upstart Continental Navy officer in a converted French merchantman. At a time when alliances were a crucial element in Britain's struggle with France, that concern made John Paul Jones a particularly important diplomatic challenge for the British.

The British tried to have Jones arrested by Amsterdam officials as a common thief, but the local authorities—no doubt mindful of Jones's exceptional public popularity—would have none of it. In the meantime, the French ambassador counseled Jones to maintain a low profile while the diplomatic negotiations continued. He also instructed him not to move without word from the French minister of marine.

Several issues required Jones's immediate attention, however, and first among them was Captain Landais. Not only was there the problem of his continued disobedience to Jones's orders during the recent deployment, Landais was in physical danger from the surviving crew members of *Bonhomme Richard,* men who had been the recipients of several of his broadsides off Flamborough Head. Jones took action and summarily relieved him of command of *Alliance,* replacing him with the ship's first lieutenant. Landais reacted characteristically and defied Jones's order. Jones then sent Captain Cottineau to transmit his order to leave the ship within twenty-four hours. Landais continued in character and challenged Cottineau to a duel for offending him by delivering the message. The duel with rapiers resulted in a serious wound for Cottineau.

Landais then went to Amsterdam where he began ordering supplies for the refitting of *Alliance.* When his credit was refused he began writing a series of abusive letters to Jones and challenged him to a duel. Jones accepted, and as the challenged party, he exercised his prerogative and selected pistols as the weapons. Since Landais lacked skill with handguns, he chose instead to leave Amsterdam and go to Paris, where he continued to bedevil Jones and cause embarrassment for Franklin. Fortunately for Jones, Franklin gave Landais extremely short shrift. Franklin's letter of 12 March 1780 to the former captain of *Alliance* left no doubt about his opinion of Landais; it was uncharacteristically undiplomatic:

> I think you then so imprudent, so litigious, and quarrelsome a man, even with your best friends, that peace and good order, and consequently the quiet and regular subordination so necessary to success, are, where you preside, impossible. . . . If, therefore I had twenty ships of war in my disposition, I should not give one of them to Captain Landais. The same temper which *excluded* him from the French marine would weigh equally with me; of course I shall not replace him in the *Alliance.*[1]

Another issue requiring Jones's immediate action was the disposition of the prisoners held by the American squadron. Jones had wanted to get into Dunkerque from the Texel quickly in order to arrange an exchange for American naval prisoners held by the British. Once he realized that he was not going to get out of the Texel quickly, his efforts shifted to getting the prisoners ashore locally for humane and practical reasons.

At the same time, however, the British ambassador was trying to prevent the transfer ashore of the five hundred British prisoners on pretexts that argued against common sense—that is, if one was truly interested in the welfare of the prisoners. The British ambassador provided a transparent summation of these pretexts: "The Weather, the fears of the infection on the shore, the difficulties of knowing how to treat with these Piratical people without committing His Majesty's Dignity, all have conspired to puzzle the Business."[2] It was clear, notwithstanding that bit of diplomatic flummery, that the British saw the prisoners less as a humanitarian issue and more as a means of making life difficult for the Continental Navy commodore they had cornered in Holland.

The larger issue of the prisoners was reflected in the specific problem of Captain Richard Pearson, who was becoming increasingly surly in captivity. On 15 October, Pearson wrote haughtily to Jones demanding to know what was being done in the way of a prisoner exchange for himself and his men. The tone of Pearson's demand made it clear that he was not addressing his captor as a fellow naval officer, but as the brigand the British government claimed Jones to be.

Jones had treated the prisoners, and particularly the British Navy officers, as well as possible under the circumstances. Pearson, for example, had been paroled and had found quarters ashore after the squadron anchored at the Texel. But when Jones delivered Pearson's furniture and tableware from *Serapis* to him at his quarters, Pearson returned them with a rude note saying that he could not accept the items from a "rebel." Pearson later accepted the items when sent in the name of Captain Cottineau, who was still a French naval officer, despite having received a commission in the Continental Navy as well.

Although Pearson's behavior could be passed off as that of an officer deeply distressed at the loss of his ship to a significantly less experienced officer in an inferior ship, he introduced an additional dimension to the situation. He was attempting to make the case, as publicly as possible, that his defeat had come at the hands of an *unworthy* opponent, rather than a commissioned naval officer.

Jones continued to treat Pearson with consideration, however, and even eight years after the action off Flamborough Head, Jones referred to Pearson as "an officer of the first grade in personal courage and professional skill, and a gentleman without reproach." In doing so, Jones demonstrated that not only was he the better fighter, he also appeared to be the better man. For Jones, who was born with no social status, who was a naval officer whose primary training was in the merchant service, and who had been publicly slighted by his own civilian leaders, Pearson's behavior was more painful than a saber slash. It undoubtedly reinforced Jones's fixation on achieving official public recognition of his status as a senior officer in the Continental Navy and official public recognition of America as a nation.

The situation with Pearson in the Texel showed how tightly Jones's status as a senior American naval officer and recognition of America as a nation were linked. And the attitude of Captain Pearson was a nasty and very personal reminder for Jones that his professional recognition and recognition of America as a nation were tenuous. Doubtless, Pearson's behavior also multiplied Jones's motivation to prove himself against the British Navy. In still another—and broader—sense, the situation between Jones and Pearson was a microcosm of the British attitude that fueled the run-up to the revolt of its American colonies.

The extent of those problems of national and personal recognition was vibrantly underscored in portions of an official letter from British Ambassador to The Hague, Sir Joseph Yorke. The letter not only demanded that the Dutch government transfer Jones's two prizes to the British, it went on to also described Jones as something other than a dedicated and skilled naval officer in the service of a legitimate nation. Yorke wrote, "The undersigned, ambassador extraordinary and plenipotentiary of the King of Great Britain, has the honor to communicate to your High Mightinesses, that two of his Majesty's ships, the *Serapis* and the *Countess of Scarborough,* arrived some days ago in the Texel, having been attacked and taken by force by a certain Paul Jones, a subject of the king, who, according to treaties and the laws of war, can only be considered as a rebel and a pirate."[3]

For one who believed he was fighting in the cause of liberty and for a nation whose situation was "new in the annals of mankind," Yorke's scornful characterization of Jones as "a rebel and a pirate" would have deepened his motivation far beyond even what Captain Pearson had accomplished by his haughty behavior. And although Jones commented on the British ambassador's civility during a chance meeting, Yorke's further reference to Jones as a subject of King George III would have, in all probability, been the most motivating characterization of all for Jones.

Despite the British legal arguments and their insults, Jones was able to achieve a partial success in the prisoner issue. In October he was permitted by the Dutch to transfer the prisoners from his ships to a fort at the Texel where they were in the custody of French Marines. Jones had succeeded in providing humanitarian treatment for the British prisoners. He did not, however, succeed in exchanging his prisoners for a like number of Continental Navy sailors held by the British. That was a failure Jones would have felt deeply in light of his ongoing personal mission on behalf of American sailors being held under harsh conditions as "traitors" by the British. In a mean twist of fate, the prisoners taken by Jones were eventually used by the French to secure the freedom of Frenchmen held by the British.

In a more positive vein, Jones eventually had the satisfaction of seeing Pearson used individually in successful American efforts to gain the liberty of Gustavus Conyngham, the courageous captain of the fourteen-gun privateer *Revenge,* initially out of Dunkerque and then out of Philadelphia. Conyngham was commissioned in the Continental Navy and, like other Continental Navy captains for whom there were no available commissioned ships, he operated as a privateer under a letter of marque from the Continental Congress. In his initial deployment, he sailed from Dunkerque along the English and Scottish coasts, returning along the Irish coast to Spain. He also was successful in privateering operations against Britain in the Caribbean.

Conyngham had achieved great success against British commerce, taking sixty merchantmen before being captured by the British Navy and confined to the infamous Mill Prison in England in early 1779. In November of that year, Conyngham escaped with thirty fellow American prisoners by tunneling under the prison walls and then managing to reach the Netherlands. At the Texel, he met Jones. Ambassador Franklin had been working hard to prevent Conyngham's return to the British by the Dutch, and with Pearson as part of prisoner negotiations, Franklin finally had the additional leverage he needed to ensure Conyngham's freedom. Jones eventually had the satisfaction of greeting his fellow officer personally on board *Alliance,* after his exchange.

During the political maneuverings while he was at the Texel, Jones also faced the ongoing challenge of refitting his squadron and its prizes. Influential civilian support was needed and a significant person involved in that effort was Charles Guillaume Frederic Dumas, a Swiss writer and sometime commercial agent for America in the Netherlands. In addition to his involvement in refitting Jones's squadron, Dumas was marginally helpful as a source of information about the Dutch government's machinations with its various subplots in regard to Jones's presence in Holland.

Dumas was also the father of a thirteen-year-old daughter, Anna Jacoba, who caught Jones's eye. When she met Jones, Anna Jacoba was at an age at which discussion of marriage was often considered appropriate, but by all appearances, she was no more than an amusing flirtation for Jones. He wrote about her in October 1779 in a letter to Edward Bancroft in which he described both of Dumas's daughters. The older of the two, about whom little is known, he referred to as "a fine lady." But apparently Jones found Anna Jacoba to be more attractive "because one might prevent some little Errors from taking root in her mind which the other seems to have contracted." That evaluation is subject to numerous interpretations, few of which flatter Jones. In the end, the flirtation seemed to produce little more than some embarrassingly bad poetry by Jones, and arguably the most significant aspect of the relationship was that it gave Jones's biographers yet another "romance" about which to write.

As winter began to set in, matters were not improving at the Texel for Jones. For one thing, he was again having problems with the crews of his ships. The officers and men of *Bonhomme Richard* had lost much of their clothing when their ship was destroyed off Flamborough Head. The crew of *Alliance* was not in much better shape, and no one had been paid, except for a token of one ducat, which did nothing but incense the recipients. In addition, the Dutch were increasing their pressure to force Jones out of the Texel, and, as a result, his squadron was dispersed. *Pallas* and *Vengeance* reverted to their French Navy identification, and *Serapis* and *Countess of Scarborough* were turned over to the French. The latter was eventually sold as a merchantman in Dunkerque, and the former was eventually refitted for the French Navy and deployed to the Indian Ocean. Jones shifted to command of *Alliance,* which was in poor material condition after the eccentric Landais's tour as her captain.

It is not difficult to imagine Jones's state of mind at this stage. He had served in the Continental Navy for four very active years, led a series of successful naval raids against the British Isles, captured and sank many British merchantmen, disrupted British military planning, and defeated a new British frigate in single-ship action of tremendous psychological importance. But in the process, he was increasingly confronted with a hard fact of life: while his senior political leaders often sat at lustrous mahogany conference tables negotiating life and death, he went to sea to personally engage in a life-and-death struggle. He and his crew faced the grapeshot that could tear an arm off, cannonballs that could—and often did—cut one in two, lethal musket balls, and the danger of drowning. Ashore, rather than acknowledging his accomplishments, Jones's civilian leaders frequently treated him as a pawn at best and as a politically embarrassing annoyance at worst. Jones was patronized—until he might be needed again.

By December, Jones clearly had had enough. He was worn out from his very active deployments in *Ranger* and *Bonhomme Richard,* the battle with *Serapis,* and politics. On 5 December he wrote to Robert Morris, a member of the Marine Committee in Congress, indicating that he anticipated being ordered back to America in *Alliance.* It is not difficult to perceive his deep disappointment between the lines; his letter was just short of a clear-cut demand that he be ordered back to America and the direct control of Congress:

> By the within dispatches for Congress, I am persuaded you will observe with pleasure that my connexion with a Court (of France) is at an end, and that my prospect of returning to America approaches. The great seem to wish only to be concerned with tools who dare not speak or write truth. I am not sorry that my connexion with them is at an end . . . all the honors or profit that France could bestow should not tempt me again to undertake the same service with an armament equally ill composed and with powers equally limited. . . . I shall hope hereafter to be usefully employed under the immediate direction of the Congress.[4]

As December advanced, the Dutch pressure on Jones to leave the Texel mounted. The French ambassador had ordered Jones not to move from the Texel, but the Dutch had dispatched Vice Admiral Pieter Hendrick Reynst with a squadron that included several ships of the line to graphically emphasize their desire that he leave forthwith. The Dutch admiral took an overbearing tone with Jones that skirted the edge of insult. On 17 December, he wrote to Jones, bristling at Jones's ignoring of his summons to appear before him on board his flagship.

Later in his letter, Reynst demanded to know what flag *Alliance* was under, and when Jones would be leaving the Texel. His letter then went on to assume that *Alliance* was under the French flag, in effect, answering his own first question. He further demanded that Jones present his commission from the French King and render a gun salute to the Dutch admiral.

Jones calmly refused to be intimidated and answered in measured terms, also on 17 December: "I have no orders to hoist the Flag of France on board the *Alliance.* Nor can I take upon me to hoist in this port any other than American colors. . . . In the meantime, it is my wish to find a favorable opportunity to sail from hence. . . . Should I receive new orders I shall not fail to communicate my situation to you."[5]

Jones continued to ignore Reynst's bluster and, at one point, defiantly offered to take on any three of the admiral's ships in combat. In the meantime, he went about the big task of getting *Alliance* ready for sea. Toward the end of the month, *Alliance* was in good enough condition to take to sea, and Jones got the break from the weather that he needed. He did not wait for orders from Franklin or the French Ministry of Marine or for permission from the Dutch government. Nor did he notify the pretentious Admiral Reynst of his intentions. He made a bold decision and bolted from the Texel on 27 December, while the British blockading squadron was temporarily blown off station by heavy easterly winds.

By 11 AM he was free of the anchorage and of the British Navy squadron assigned to contain him and racing to the southwest on a reach, generally the most favorable sailing angle for a square-rigged ship. The wind continued to build during the day, and Jones sped on. He was on the thin edge of safety with the amount of heavily reefed sail he kept aloft, and at one point, he blew out his fore topsail. But he sped on. Then, during the early hours of the 28th the wind moderated. Jones shook out the reefs from the sails *Alliance* was carrying and clapped on more sail. By that evening, *Alliance* passed a British fleet, comfortably anchored at the Downs, to the northeast of Dover. Jones was close enough to see the British ships' anchor lights. There wasn't a captain in that fleet who wouldn't have given several years' pay to get Jones, but for a second time within forty-eight hours, Jones eluded the British Navy.

By noon of the 29th he was free of the English Channel, with the safety of the French coast on his port hand and the ample maneuvering room of the Atlantic to starboard. Seizing the initiative had paid off once again. Jones had taken a risky decision on his own and escaped the grip of the British Navy and the political entanglements in the Netherlands.

Jones and *Alliance* sailed into the Bay of Biscay and as far south and west as Cape Finisterre. No doubt feeling better about things, he was searching for prizes to cap his victory off Flamborough Head, but he had little success. In the meantime, tensions were again building within his crew. One of the principal sources of friction this time was the combination of *Alliance*'s original crew, mostly New Englanders, with former crew members from *Bonhomme Richard,* a mixed group of at least twelve different nationalities, including, American, Bengalese, English, Fayalese, French, Irish, Neopolitan, Norwegian, Portuguese, Scottish, Swedish, and Swiss seamen. The split involved both the wardroom and the lower decks, and it erupted in challenges to duels between officers and less gentlemanly fights among seamen. Finally, in nasty weather on 16 January, Jones put into La Coruña on the Spanish coast, where he set about replenishing his ship and effecting needed repairs and alterations after quelling yet another incipient mutiny.

By the end of January 1780, *Alliance* was ready for sea again, but her crew was not. After leaving La Coruña on 27 January, Jones announced that he was planning another three weeks of commerce raiding in Biscay Bay before returning to Lorient. His officers argued against his plan, however, and convinced him that the time had come to get back to Lorient. The transit across the Bay of Biscay was slow going in heavy weather, and the mentally and physically exhausted officers and crew of *Alliance* finally anchored in the roadstead outside Lorient on 10 February. Jones, almost as if he dreaded his return to land, kept *Alliance* at the outer roadstead for more than a week, finally moving to the inner anchorage on 19 February. By this time he was suffering from problems with both his eyes, and once his ship was settled in the anchorage, he moved ashore to the home of his friend James Moylan.

Now back in France after the battle off Flamborough Head, Jones had a revealing confrontation with his second lieutenant, Henry Lunt. Lunt was a seasoned officer who had served with Jones in *Alfred* and *Providence,* before serving under him in *Bonhomme Richard.* Lunt had risen from seaman to commissioned officer, had accumulated considerable combat experience, been captured by the British, and escaped from Mill Prison, all before signing on *Bonhomme Richard.* But most important of all, he had fought effectively and bravely with Jones off Flamborough Head. That was a unique bond, and it was, therefore, particularly distressing for Jones when Lunt asked to be released from *Alliance.* It was even more distressing when he stated the reason in a note to his captain. Lunt's note might have shown a lack of education, but more important, it reflected honesty, sincerity, and loyalty. Lunt wrote to Jones, "Sir you have treated [me] with disrespect all the Late Cruze. . . . I have often Said it & say it still, I would Sooner Go in a Warlik Ship with Capt. Jones than any Man Ever I saw if I Could be treated with Respect, But I Never Have Been; wich Makes me Very uneasy & Discontent."[6]

Lieutenant Lunt's letter is a reflection of the very important matter of Jones's relationships with his officers and men. Uniformly, it was agreed that Jones could be mercurial and harsh, even prone to physical reinforcement of his orders at times. But Lunt did not seem to be talking of instances of frustration or temper in his commander; he appeared to be saying that Jones had shown a consistent lack of respect for him. That accusation raised a very basic question concerning Jones's leadership.

Jones was being accused of the same fault he attributed to his first commanding officer, Dudley Saltonstall, when Jones was first lieutenant in *Alfred.* On 14 April 1776, he had written on the subject to member of the Continental Congress Joseph Hewes, and although he did not directly connect Saltonstall with his comments in the letter, it was clear that his observations were aimed at his former captain. In the letter to Hewes, Jones had written, "It is certainly in the interest of the service that a cordial interchange of civilities should subsist between superior and inferior officers; and, therefore, it is bad policy in superiors to behave towards their inferiors indiscriminately, as though they were of a lower species . . . for to be well obeyed, it is necessary to be esteemed."[7]

Fortunately, Jones was somehow able to satisfy Lunt on that question and convince him that his bad temper and constant demands for perfection were not evidence of disrespect. Lunt remained with his captain, but the incident was confirming evidence that John Paul Jones, notwithstanding the many positive aspects of his leadership, would not be among the small group of naval heroes in history to be greatly beloved by those who served under them.

On 19 February, the same day Jones moved into the inner harbor of Lorient, Franklin wrote from Paris telling him that Congress had ordered his return to America in *Alliance.* He was to carry an important military cargo of arms and cloth for army uniforms, plus three passengers: Samuel Wharton, an American merchant; Ralph Izard, an American diplomat; and Arthur Lee, who had been no friend while Jones was operating from French ports. It was a mundane and potentially irritating mission, particularly since Jones would be forced to put up with the devious Lee during the weeks of transit. Difficulties with Lee began immediately when he demanded that Jones carry an inordinate amount of his personal baggage in *Alliance.* Jones quickly rejected the request because of the space limitations in his ship, and no doubt he did so with some relish. The one positive aspect of his new orders was that Jones would presumably be returning to the direct control of Congress. The prospect of escaping the diplomatic morass in France to the less "sophisticated" politics of Congress would have been good news indeed for Jones.

As winter moved toward spring, work on *Alliance* progressed. Many basic alterations had to be accomplished, some due to Landais's incompetence, some due to normal wear and tear at sea, and some due to initial design and construction flaws. Notably, there was no battle damage to repair from the ship's involvement in the battle off Flamborough Head. Problems with the ballasting, size of the spars, and positioning of the masts were among the major refitting projects accomplished by *Alliance*'s crew. And, as usual, funding was a serious problem. Franklin wrote emphatically to Jones, who had suggested that the French underwrite the cost of refitting his ship, about how limited the Commission's funds were and how he was bearing the entire cost of refitting *Alliance.*

Jones was authorized by Franklin to proceed with the work, provided he was extremely attentive to controlling costs: "For God's sake, be sparing! unless you mean to make me bankrupt, or have your drafts disregarded for want of money in my hands to pay them."[8] Ultimately, Franklin paid for all of the work on *Alliance.* But he balked at the coppering of the ship's bottom, which had been among the major refitting items desired by Jones.

Jones was also dealing with a problem that was, by now, all too familiar: *Alliance*'s crew had received neither its pay nor its prize money. Franklin advanced a small amount to Jones, and a month's salary—out of twelve months due—was distributed to the officers and crew. The French commercial agent Jacques Donatien Le Ray de Chaumont also promised to make a much larger amount available from the French government. Chaumont reneged on that promise, however, apparently because he had diverted the funds to cover his own speculations.

Getting the prize money for *Serapis* and *Countess of Scarborough* also proved to be difficult. Jones wanted Congress to buy the ships, refit *Serapis,* and turn her over to him; that was not to be. The French offered to buy the ships, which would have generated prize money relatively fast. But *Alliance*'s crew argued against that offer, believing that they would do much better if the ships were sold at a commercial auction. Waiting for the ships to sell at an auction stretched out the process considerably, with a commensurate delay in any proceeds for the crew. As it turned out, the crew would have done better if the ships had been sold to the French. As the negotiations over the prize money for the crew were taking place, the men could see both ships being dismantled before their eyes in the harbor.

Jones wanted the pay and prize money issues settled: "Though my crews were almost naked, and I had no money to administer to their wants, yet my constant applications to court for two months produced no relief, no payment whatever, either in salary or prize money."[9]

The problems over the crew's pay and prize money dragged on, however, while the political pressure mounted for Jones to be ready for departure to America. At this point, the pressure came mostly from Franklin's secretary, Edward Bancroft. But Jones wanted to resolve the pay and prize money problems before leaving. He determined to travel to Paris for that purpose and probably also to determine—and influence—the reaction of the French court to his victory off Flamborough Head. His decision to go to Paris would precipitate important changes in the course of Jones's life, particularly for the short term. He departed from Lorient for Paris on 15 April. The coming experience would be very different from that of previous visits.

8
Paris and Celebrity's Cost

> "It is no doubt a good thing to conquer on the field of battle, but it needs greater wisdom and greater skill to make use of victory."
>
> Polybius

Jones arrived in Paris on 17 April 1780, and was welcomed by American commissioner Benjamin Franklin. Their first call in Paris was on French Minister of Marine Antoine de Sartine. Sartine had been involved—not always positively—in securing a ship for Jones. He also was involved in virtually all of the decisions concerning Jones's missions following his arrival in France in *Ranger.* Under the circumstances, Jones might have anticipated an enthusiastic welcome from his ally. On the contrary, Jones received a surprisingly cool reception from Sartine and the French naval officers at the Ministry.

Jones wrote about the meeting and how Sartine "gave us a reception cold as ice, did not say to me a civil word, nor even ask me if my health had not suffered from my wounds, and the uncommon fatigue I had undergone." The minister's lack of enthusiasm for Jones's successes was probably due to Sartine's connection with a political faction in France that opposed alliance with America. Whatever the reasons, it was another in the string of underwhelming receptions for Jones upon returning from significantly successful missions. Despite the unenthusiastic welcome at the Ministry, however, the problems over the prize money for *Serapis* and *Countess of Scarborough* appeared to be nearing resolution. The French minister at least made promises to help get the matter settled.

By 20 April, only three days after his arrival, Jones was ready to return to Lorient and *Alliance.* The ship had been refitted and loaded, and he prepared a final letter to Franklin, asking for official recognition of his accomplishments in *Ranger* and *Bonhomme Richard.* It appears that up to that point, Franklin's only communications with Congress on the subject were in broader reports and in the contexts of a number of difficult issues, such as prisoner exchanges. In a letter of 4 March from Franklin to the president of Congress, Samuel Huntington, for example, there were two mentions of Jones. The first appeared in the opening sentence and referred to "our little squadron under Commodore Jones."

The second appeared at the end of a discussion of Jones's anticipated return to America in *Alliance* and noted, "He has gained immense reputation all over Europe for his bravery."

In Franklin's first mention of Jones, his emphasis was on the squadron, not its commodore. Franklin's second mention, pointing out that the commodore was gaining fame in Europe, could conceivably have had a negative effect on Jones's standing with Congress, where public—particularly foreign—acclaim for a military officer would generally make members uncomfortable. Both of those references failed to provide any specific recognition of Jones's accomplishments, or, for that matter, any acknowledgment of the obstacles that he overcame leading up to his deployments from France.

Jones deserved something more from Franklin, and apparently Franklin eventually did begin to go a bit further on Jones's behalf with Congress. On 1 June, he wrote, referring to how Jones "by his bravery and conduct has done great honor to the American flag." That would have had considerably more impact on Congress than a mention of "our little squadron." Franklin also went on to say that he was "recommending him to the notice of Congress and to your Excellency's protection."[1] Those two references of 1 June, although brief, went beyond a general report of events. They were official specific endorsements of Jones from the senior American representative in Paris, and they would have given Jones's career a deserved boost.

Sartine, who had appeared cool to Jones in April, also redeemed himself somewhat with a long and very positive letter to Congress on behalf of King Louis XVI on 30 May. The letter was devoted entirely to the subject of Jones's exceptional performance of duty and the key lines would have been career enhancing for the victor at the battle off Flamborough Head. Sartine wrote, "The reputation he has so justly acquired will precede him, and that the recital of his actions alone will suffice to prove to his fellow citizens that his abilities are equal to his courage. But the King has thought proper to add his suffrage and attention to the public opinion. He has expressly charged me to inform you how perfectly he is satisfied with the services of the Commodore, persuaded that Congress will render him the same justice."[2]

Jones was moving toward a departure from France on a relatively high note, but a powerful force was gathering, something that would sweep away the plans for his immediate return to America like spindrift in a gale. It also would influence how Jones's career would be perceived over the years, undercutting to some degree his victory over Captain Pearson and *Serapis.*

The force that swept Jones up was celebrity. His capture of *Serapis* and *Countess of Scarborough,* his disruption of British maritime activity, and the turmoil he created along the shores of the British Isles were successes that contrasted sharply with the run of American and French naval failures leading up to the action off Flamborough Head. Jones had filled a desperate need—not just in America, but also in France—for a noteworthy military success against Britain and particularly against the British Navy. As a result, Jones became an instant celebrity of the first magnitude in Paris.

It is clear, however, that Jones did not understand the full implications of his popularity. And as it turned out, there would be an unanticipated personal cost for his newfound celebrity, a price that would draw down the career equity he had built with his achievements in *Providence, Alfred, Ranger,* and *Bonhomme Richard.* Jones was about to learn that celebrity came with a significant price tag.

For six weeks, Jones was embraced by a city where there was no more important measure of personal value than celebrity. Outward appearances, social manners, and self-indulgence were major preoccupations in Paris. Parisian attitudes contrasted sharply with what Jones experienced as a youth and young adult—Scottish emphasis on hard work and public morality and comparable colonial American attitudes. Jones had few if any defenses, particularly in light of the suddenness of his celebrity. And his susceptibility to the rush of adulation in Paris would have been increased by the contrasting lack of significant official recognition when he returned to the Texel from his victory off Flamborough Head.

Among the first events triggered by the waves of sudden public popularity was his induction into a second Masonic group, the Lodge of the Nine Sisters in Paris. Many considered it to be the most prestigious Masonic group in France. Jones was praised extravagantly at his induction ceremony. A French observer of the welcoming oration during Jones's acceptance into the group described how those remarks had placed Jones "on an equity with his rival Pearson." Given Captain Pearson's behavior at the Texel, one wonders whether Jones smiled or winced at that observation. Perhaps there was a bit of both in his reaction. In any event, induction would have an important, ongoing benefit: the influence of the Lodge's members. Voltaire, Franklin, and many of the intellectual leaders of French society were now Jones's brothers in the Lodge of the Nine Sisters, and these were men of profound influence in France.

In the long term, however, perhaps the most significant action of the Lodge of the Nine Sisters was its commission of a bust of Jones by Jean-Antoine Houdon, one of the greatest portrait sculptors of the time. This work, created while Jones was still alive, has been reproduced and copied in numerous media. George Washington, Franklin, and Thomas Jefferson all owned personal copies. Today, copies of the work produced by the Houdon gallery are considered major works of art and are offered at auction in prestigious galleries. A white marble version, made originally for the Lodge of the Nine Sisters and believed to be the only one done in marble, is among the U.S. Naval Academy Museum collections in Annapolis. According to contemporaries, including James Madison, the Houdon bust was an extremely close likeness of Jones, capturing much of his character at the time of his greatest victory. With their commission and his creation, the Lodge of the Nine Sisters and Houdon not only honored Jones while he was in Paris in April and May 1780, they helped to fix his heroic image and perpetuate it in American naval lore.

As Jones's fame spiraled upward, he began receiving formal invitations to such social events as dinners, receptions, the opera, and even a reunion of those who fought off Flamborough Head. He was applauded when he appeared at the theater. Special arrangements were made to recognize his victory over *Serapis.* Franklin introduced him at court, where he was presented to Louis XVI. Queen Marie Antoinette invited him to visit her at her box at the opera. And he barely had time to sit for the artists and sculptors who wanted to immortalize his image. Jones was the center of attraction wherever he went. His extreme popularity was noted in a social column from Paris for the *General Advertiser and Morning Intelligencer* in London on 10 May: "The famous captain Paul Jones actually lodges in this city with Mr. Adams, at the Hotel Valois, Rue Richelieu. Last Tuesday he went to the opera, where he received the applause of the audience who testified their joy to see that intrepid mariner."[3]

His celebrity also drew many informal invitations from women who were attracted by his fame, good looks, and the combination of his chivalrous manner with a reputation as a fearsome naval raider. The scented notes came from a wide cross section of women, some professing hesitancy in writing directly to him and others who were direct in their intentions. One of the more fascinating notes that survived, one that reflected something different from the flattery being heaped on Jones, was from Madame de Saint Julien, a companion of the then-aged Voltaire. Her note scolded Jones sharply, "It is a great pity, my dear captain, that you have less reliability than courage, and that you are not as good at keeping your promises as you are in conquering your foes." Clearly Madame was not impressed with Jones's social manners.

More in keeping with Jones's celebrity status, a Paris society columnist for a London newspaper gossiped in print about "Lady——who possesses all his heart . . . is of high rank and virtue, very sensible, good natured and affable . . . possessed of youth, beauty and wit, and every other female accomplishment." The columnist then summed up the view of what apparently was a significant portion of Parisian women: "He is the most agreeable sea-wolf one could wish to meet with."[4]

Among the better-known relationships with women during Jones's weeks in Paris was that with Madame la Comtesse de Lowendahl. She was the daughter of a Bourbon prince and was married to a count who was an army general. Talented, young, and attractive, Madame de Lowendahl was among the brightest stars in the social firmament of Paris at the time. She also was the "Lady——" described for London gossip column readers. It appears that Jones met the countess at the home of François Genet, who was prominent in Paris society and politically influential. It also appears that Jones and the countess were often simultaneous dinner guests at the Genet home. The resulting correspondence between the two appears to have begun with a flirtatious note from the countess.

When Jones responded with the clear intention to establish a romantic relationship, the countess protested that her note was written as harmless banter. As the correspondence continued, it also began to appear that perhaps her primary objective was to enlist Jones's help in securing an assignment for her husband with General Washington's army. Jones was not deterred, however, and he continued with protestations of his admiration, including a code the couple could use for secret correspondence. Viewed with the objectivity of time, it would be excessive to classify the situation as a meaningful relationship. The countess was trying to manipulate Jones in order to advance her husband's military career, as wives among her social contemporaries were wont to do. Jones, on the other hand, was pursuing a familiar ritual in which both the process and the desired result were recreational. Both the countess and Jones appeared to fail in their ultimate objectives, and that seems fair enough.

A relationship of a different quality, however, developed while Jones was in Paris during the spring and summer of 1780. The identity of the woman involved, known initially only as "Delia," the romantic nickname Jones used for her, was a mystery for many years. It is now known that she was a Scottish woman whose maiden name was Nicolson. She was married to a Scottish expatriate in the Netherlands, Count William Murray. The count used the name Murray-Nicolson after their marriage. No doubt, Jones had picked the nickname for his lover on the basis of a popular song of the day. "Delia" was the subject of that romantic song, which began on a lyrical note: "Return enraptured hours/When Delia's heart was mine," and ended darkly with, "The lovely

Delia flies/While racked with jealous pains/Her wretched lover dies."[5] The beginning and end of the song proved to parallel to a significant degree the relationship between Jones and his Delia.

The affair appears to have begun in May with an invitation for Jones to spend a day and night with the count and countess at their chateau outside Paris. It was one of the many social invitations Jones received, and we have no evidence of why he accepted this particular one. It is believed that the affair began with the first encounter and continued after Jones returned to Lorient from Paris in June.

The letters from Countess Nicolson had a different quality than those received by Jones from other women, and they are the only love letters he is known to have saved. The letters are a clear sharing of genuine emotions, rather than the ritual protestations of affection more typical of the exchanges in Jones's previous relationships. And what the correspondence lacked in sophistication was more than balanced with honest passion. The countess's letters were especially poignant, particularly after a six-day assignation with Jones outside of Lorient in late June or early July. In her first letter after that tryst she reflected the combination of joy and torment of unconditional passion: "It was only the belief in your love that gave me the courage to leave you. At the moment when you disappeared from my sight I thought I should die of despair. . . . What would I not give if you were free to remain in France! . . . I am dying to rejoin you, never again to separate from you."[6]

Over time, the Countess Nicolson's letters continued to focus on her unhappiness at being separated from Jones. His correspondence, in contrast, begins to lack the intensity of hers, and with their separation, they drifted apart. There is a copy of a letter Jones wrote from Portsmouth, New Hampshire, in December 1781 to "his most lovely Delia," telling her of previous letters he has written to her and reporting his activities. He also notes that he has received only one letter from her since his departure from Lorient.

When Jones was back in Paris in 1783, the countess, by then a widow, wrote to him. Initially, she referred to him as "a being who has constituted the misery of my life for four years." And then she implored: "O, most amiable and most ungrateful of men, come to your best friend, who burns with a desire of seeing you. . . . Come, in the name of heaven." They met, but the separation—and probably, Jones's realization that marriage was now an issue—was fatal to the affair. The countess went on with her life, and official records indicate that she left France during the French Revolution, barely escaping the guillotine. Jones went on with his career, driven by his cause and his ambition.

In the final analysis, one occurrence during Jones's stay in Paris in 1780 transcended the romance and the applause: The French king bestowed a title on him. The Order of Military Merit, conferred on Jones by Louis XVI, had three degrees of honor, and Jones received the lowest, with the title of Chevalier.

Jones's award of the Order of Military Merit could be compared to being made a Knight of the Bath in Britain, which carries the title of Sir. Jones frequently used his French title of Chevalier during the rest of his life. Jones's modest origins, the merchant marine path to his navy commission, British references to him as a pirate and cutthroat, and the imperious treatment he received frequently from naval officers of other nations all would have led him to use the new social label he had received from the king.

With his new title, Jones also received an elaborately decorated sword with a gold hilt from King Louis. As a symbol of his new title, one would think that Jones would have been extremely reluctant to part with the sword, but in fact, he offered to give it to Countess Lowendahl for her keeping. Fortunately she declined, knowing what Jones expected in exchange for the weapon. Based on her refusal, the sword remained with Jones, and after his death, it passed through a series of owners, eventually finding its way back to Jones at his final resting place in the United States.

Despite the distractions of his celebrity in Paris, Jones did continue to push Franklin and the French for a new and larger mission against the British Isles. On 1 June, however, he received a note from Franklin, ordering him to get under way in *Alliance* with his passengers and his important military cargo for General Washington. When he returned to Lorient, the circumstances with *Alliance*'s crew had deteriorated. His men were aware that Jones had been living high in Paris, while they sat in Lorient with no money.

When he came aboard *Alliance,* he mustered the crew and told them that there was no specific timetable for the payment of their prize money and no funds to cover their past-due pay. One can imagine the comments among the crew when they were out of earshot of their captain. After their deployment in *Bonhomme Richard* and return to Lorient, their captain had chosen to live ashore, where he was spending considerable time romancing Countess Nicolson. They, on the other hand, were living and working in *Alliance.* That contrasting circumstance no doubt contributed to the crew's belief that Jones was not trying very hard to secure their prize money and back pay.

Jones had allowed simmering problems to come to a boil on board his ship, and a final unfortunate set of circumstances caused them to spill over.

Captain Landais had been ordered by Franklin to return to America to face a court-martial concerning his behavior while he was commanding officer of *Alliance.* The order for the court-martial was based on Jones's charges, supported by telling written testimony from his officers. Landais was in Lorient, waiting to take passage in a privateer.

The final element in the disaster for Jones was Arthur Lee, who also was in Lorient awaiting his departure for America in *Alliance.* Lee concocted a clever plan and set it in motion by convincing Landais that he was still legally the captain of *Alliance.* If he could physically take command of *Alliance,* Lee argued, he could sail her to America. Once there, Landais would be in a position to make his case with the support of the officers and crew of the ship, who presumably would be so happy to be home that they would overlook Landais's behavior during their deployment with *Bonhomme Richard.* With a document prepared by Lee, the two conspirators convinced *Alliance*'s increasingly receptive officers and crew that Landais was still their captain and that they would fare much better under him than under Jones. Landais and Lee also reinforced the idea that it was Jones who was delaying the payment of their money. Even officers who had previously provided written testimony against Landais were swept up in Lee's machinations.

Lee, as part of the political faction in America that opposed Franklin and anyone associated with him, was motivated by his deep hatred for the senior American representative in Paris, and he was happy to seize an opportunity to embarrass him with Congress. And Jones was, in his view, a tool of Franklin. Lee summed up his attitude in a letter to a political ally in New England: "It is perpetually Dr. Franklin's practice to employ his wicked tools . . . to accuse others of the crimes of which he was guilty."[7] It was an interesting example of the politics of personal destruction, practiced even in America's early history.

Landais, clearly mentally unhinged, saw an opportunity to return to America to face his court-martial with some semblance of his standing, and he was malleable in the hands of the politically skilled Lee. *Alliance*'s crew, most of whom were from the Merrimack River valley of Massachusetts and New Hampshire, simply wanted their money and to go home. Jones was faced with a situation much like the one he faced with the crew of *Ranger* in the spring and summer of 1778.

When Landais's mental instability and the near-mutinous state of *Alliance*'s crew were joined to Lee's purpose, Jones was the loser, and his own lack of a keen sense of duty to his ship and his crew was the enabler. While he was lauded for six weeks in Paris, his lack of judgment precipitated something Captain

Pearson, with the powerfully armed and efficiently manned *Serapis,* was not able to accomplish: Jones lost his ship to an enemy.

Lee did the groundwork, and in early June Landais simply went on board and declared himself in command of *Alliance.* One of the worst aspects of Landais's takeover was that he immediately imprisoned the former members of *Bonhomme Richard*'s crew, correctly assuming that they were loyal to Jones. Those innocent victims of the Lee-Landais plot, men who had fought valiantly off Flamborough Head, were transported to America as prisoners.

Even after Landais had taken over *Alliance,* Jones still had a chance to set things straight. But instead of confronting Landais on board the ship and reestablishing his own firm control, he left for Paris to seek new authorization to take command of what was, in fact, his own ship. It was an uncharacteristic move by the man who, as a merchant marine captain, had quickly settled a dispute with a mutinous crew member with the thrust of a sword. Three factors possibly contributed to Jones's behavior. First, some evidence suggests that he saw the situation as an opportunity to get a better ship than *Alliance;* perhaps a refurbished *Serapis* could be reclaimed from the French. Second, it is possible that Jones thought he could avoid a political problem that would undercut his achievements during his deployments in *Ranger* and *Bonhomme Richard.* As it turned out, he was not able to get a better ship—he wound up in a ship smaller than *Alliance.* Nor was he able to avoid career damage from the situation with Lee and Landais. Finally, the third factor is that Jones was seriously distracted by all the praise showered upon him during his six weeks in Paris. It was not the only time in history that a brilliantly successful military leader's judgment was clouded by public adulation.

As events turned out, once Landais took command of *Alliance,* the situation deteriorated quickly. Jones tried desperately to put his own actions in a favorable light. For example, he wrote an ill-advised letter to Edward Bancroft criticizing both Bancroft and Franklin. He also wrote to Robert Morris in Congress, this time praising Franklin, blaming Lee, and claiming that it was a desire to avoid "Bloodshed between Allied Subjects of France and America" that had caused him to yield his command of *Alliance* to Landais. When he referred to a desire to avoid bloodshed, Jones was perhaps referring to the option of having the French sink *Alliance* to prevent her departure from Lorient. But the real problem was the series of missteps on Jones's part that had brought matters to that point. On 21 June 1780, Jones wrote to Franklin with the same claim he made to Morris: "He [the commander of the port] had even sent his Orders in the evening before I was aware to fire on the *Alliance* and Sink her to the Bottom if they attempted to approach and pass the Barrier that had been made across the entrance of the Port . . . Your Humanity will I know Justify the part I acted in Preventing a Scene that would have rendered me miserable for the rest of my Life."[8]

Franklin, who had been active in trying to sort out the tangled political mess over command of *Alliance* in Jones's favor, did not give him the benefit of the doubt. He wrote a sharp rebuke and short leadership lecture to Jones on 5 July:

> If you had stayed on board where your duty lay, instead of coming to Paris, you would not have lost your ship. Now you blame them [Jones's friends] as having deserted you in recovering her. Though relinquishing to prevent mischief was a voluntary act of your own, for which you have credit hereafter, if you should observe an occasion, to give your officers and friends a little more praise than is their due, and confess more fault than you can justly be charged with, you will only become the sooner for it, a great captain. Criticizing and censuring almost everyone you have to do with, will diminish friends, increase enemies, and thereby hurt your affairs.[9]

Franklin, although a civilian and not without his own personal shortcomings, had administered the kind of strong counsel that most young naval officers receive from their seniors at early stages in their careers. In understanding Jones, it is important to note that his career had no such junior officer stage. He had been commissioned in the Continental Navy as a lieutenant and advanced almost immediately to captain.

One final chapter of the sorry events involving Landais's takeover of *Alliance* was written when the crew was finally paid. Before Landais's departure for America, Lee had convinced the American commercial agent in Lorient to advance the pay for the ship's crew. The agent, J. D. Schweighauser, an ally of Lee's, advanced more than $6,000 for distribution to *Alliance*'s crew. Franklin refused to honor the payment, and Schweighauser was never able to recover his advance.

Finally, on 8 July, *Alliance* moved out of the outer anchorage of Lorient, and Landais was on his way to a court-martial that would end in his dismissal from the Continental Navy. Jones was left to fight the blame game, lobby for a new mission, and prepare for his departure for America in another ship.

The French had captured the twenty-gun sloop of war *Ariel* from the British in 1777. In the summer of 1780, she was turned over to Franklin to transport the military supplies destined for the Continental Army that had been left behind at Lorient by Landais. Franklin appointed Jones as commanding officer and urged him to load *Ariel* and depart for America as quickly as possible. Being appointed to the sloop of war was a significant comedown from the frigates *Bonhomme Richard* and *Alliance.*

Notwithstanding pressure from Franklin to depart for America, Jones did what he generally did with a new command—he set about improving the ship's rig, ballast, and armament. By the middle of July, Jones was beginning to reload the ship, and two merchant marine brigs, *Luke* and *Duke of Leinster,* were chartered by Franklin to accompany Jones with the military cargo that could not be accommodated in *Ariel.* In the meantime, Jones continued to lobby to lead a major raid against the British Isles at some future time after his return to America.

During August, the winds were unfavorable and apparently the delay provided Jones with an opportunity for a dalliance with the young wife of James Moylan, the friend with whom Jones stayed after his return from the Texel to Lorient in February 1780. There also are accounts of his visits to prostitutes while *Ariel* sat in Lorient. By now, Jones's fleeting relationships and one-night stands with women were a firmly established pattern.

Finally the winds were favorable, and in clear weather with the wind out of the north-northwest on 7 October, *Ariel* departed from Lorient's outer harbor, with the fully laden *Luke* and *Duke of Leinster* in company. But Jones's overdue return to America was to be delayed once more. There was one more payment to be made for his six weeks of celebrity in Paris, and it would be a heavy one. Before he had cleared the coast of France, Jones and the ships with him were slammed by a ferocious gale, a storm that far exceeded the routinely rough weather that was not unusual at that time of year off the coast of Brittany.

At first the wind was out of the west-southwest, then out of the south, and then out of the southwest. Its strength grew to sixty knots, nearly seventy miles per hour, and gusts would have been even more powerful. At that strength, gusts hit with a jarring solid impact. When the storm struck, sails would have been reefed, then double reefed, then sequentially doused, until, according to *Ariel*'s log, the ship was carrying only a double-reefed foresail to provide steerageway to the ship. Under those conditions the slightest mistake by the captain or a weakness in the ship's equipment would likely cascade into destruction and death.

In some ways, *Ariel*'s struggle against the storm was beyond even armed combat between ships; during combat there would be at least an approximate parity between the opponents. In winds of the magnitude Jones was facing, the ship was at the razor edge of being completely at the mercy of the storm. Even the best of seamen in the best of ships could be overcome by such a storm, and as the struggle went on, the deadly danger would make minutes seem like hours and hours seem like eternity. At times, *Ariel* was driven over so far by the ferocious gusts that the tip of one of her yardarms pierced the surface of the sea. As the ship hesitated in that position, heeled over on her beam-ends, *Ariel* and her men teetered on oblivion.

Jones's situation would have been bad enough in the open sea, but on the night of 9 October the wind was driving him inexorably toward the rocks off Penmarch Point. Because the ship was so heavily laden with military equipment and because she was taking on so much water Jones was not able to claw his way off the coast. He had only one chance for survival: anchor. Even at anchor, the ship was driven steadily closer to the rocks. Jones ordered the foremast to be cut away, and then the mainmast was sacrificed, taking the mizzenmast with it as it crashed. At last, *Ariel*'s anchor took hold. For two days and nights, the ship rode out the storm in that precarious position, with her crew manning the pumps furiously around the clock.

When the weather cleared, *Ariel*'s shaken crew rigged a jury mast with a single yard, bent a single sail onto the yard, and cut the anchor cable. *Ariel* crept slowly back toward Lorient. Now the fact that she had been close to Lorient when the storm struck worked in her favor. As the ship approached the outer anchorage the crew would have been unusually subdued; to a man, they understood where they had been.

At mid-morning on 12 October, *Ariel* picked up a pilot in the outer anchorage and slowly eased back into Lorient. The ship was a wreck and her crew was exhausted, but they were fortunate. The coastline and even the harbors along the shores of Brittany were strewn with shattered ships and dead men. Jones had risen to the challenge with incredible skill and courage, and his crew and the battered *Ariel* had also met the challenge.

When Jones wrote to Bancroft on 17 October, he ranked the storm among the many he had seen during his years at sea: "I shall only say, it far exceeded all my former ideas of tempest. We must console ourselves that no lives were lost,—an event remarkably fortunate under such circumstances." *Ariel*'s officers prepared a longer, more descriptive account of the event, including a verbal picture of some of the most terrifying circumstances: "By this time the storm had become so violent that the lee fore yard-arm was frequently under water. The lee gangway was laid entirely under the water, and the lee side of the waist was full. The water in the hold flowed into the cockpit, notwithstanding the utmost efforts of the chain pumps."[10]

It took nearly two months to replace *Ariel*'s masts and rerig the ship. Not surprisingly, Jones used the time to lobby for another ship. He took advantage of the circumstances to argue that another ship would enable him to start back to America sooner. The French frigate *Terpsichore* was his primary target. All of Jones's letter writing was to no avail, however, and when it was suggested that Jones should go to Paris to pursue his efforts to secure a bigger ship, he resisted that temptation. It seems he had learned at least one lesson from the mess with *Alliance*, Lee, and Landais.

On 18 December 1780, with important military cargo and reduced armament to accommodate that cargo, Jones again departed from Lorient for America. It had been three years since he had arrived at Nantes in *Ranger*. During that time, he significantly advanced the American naval strategy against Great Britain and his own career. In addition, the King of France had elevated him to the status of Chevalier. But there is no doubt that any feeling of satisfaction he might have felt was tempered with a sense of greater achievements left to be realized. There was still a war going on, and now he had considerable personal fame to leverage. How he would leverage it remained to be seen, but the word "admiral" surely had emerged at the back of his mind.

In December 1775 *Alfred,* converted from the merchant ship *Black Prince,* became the first ship of the Continental Navy. She mounted twenty-four guns, was rated as a small frigate, and was named for the Saxon king Alfred the Great.
Courtesy of the family of Nowland Van Powell

The twenty-four-gun Continental ship *Columbus* was part of the first squadron of the American navy. She was the former merchant ship *Sally*.
Courtesy of the family of Nowland Van Powell

In May 1776 the ten-gun sloop *Providence* was placed under the command of John Paul Jones.
Courtesy of the family of Nowland Van Powell

The Continental ship *Bonhomme Richard,* a former French East Indiaman, deployed from French ports against the British Isles under the command of John Paul Jones.
Courtesy of the family of Nowland Van Powell

Bonhomme Richard's victory over HMS *Serapis* in September 1779 shocked Europe and America.
Courtesy of the family of Nowland Van Powell

This little-known portrait of John Paul Jones was made from an engraving by Henri Toussaint.
From the author's collection

IN CONGRESS.

The DELEGATES of the UNITED STATES of *New Hampſhire, Maſſachuſetts-Bay, Rhode-Iſland, Connecticut, New-York, New-Jerſey, Pennſylvania, Delaware, Maryland, Virginia, North-Carolina, South-Carolina,* and *Georgia,* TO

John Paul Jones, Esquire,

WE, repoſing eſpecial Truſt and Confidence in your Patriotiſm, Valour, Conduct, and Fidelity, DO, by theſe Preſents, conſtitute and appoint you to be *Captain* ~~of the armed~~ ~~called the~~ in the ~~Service~~ *Navy* of the United States of North-America, fitted out for the Defence of American Liberty, and for repelling every hoſtile Invaſion thereof. You are therefore carefully and diligently to diſcharge the Duty of *Captain* by doing and performing all manner of Things thereunto belonging. And we do ſtrictly charge and require all Officers, Marines and Seamen under your Command, to be obedient to your Orders as *Captain* And you are to obſerve and follow ſuch Orders and Directions from Time to Time as you ſhall receive from this or a future Congreſs of the United States, or Committee of Congreſs for that Purpoſe appointed, or Commander in Chief for the Time being of the Navy of the United States, or any other your ſuperior Officer, according to the Rules and Diſcipline of War, the Uſage of the Sea, and the Inſtructions herewith given you, in Purſuance of the Truſt repoſed in you. This Commiſſion to continue in Force until revoked by this or a future Congreſs.

DATED at *Philadelphia October 10th 1776.*

By Order of the CONGRESS,

John Hancock PRESIDENT.

ATTEST. *Cha Thomson secy*

From the Original in possession of Col. John H. Sherburne, Author of "The Life and Character of John Paul Jones."

In October 1776, John Paul Jones was officially commissioned a captain in "The Navy of the United States of North America." Previously, he had merely been commissioned to specific ships.
From the author's collection

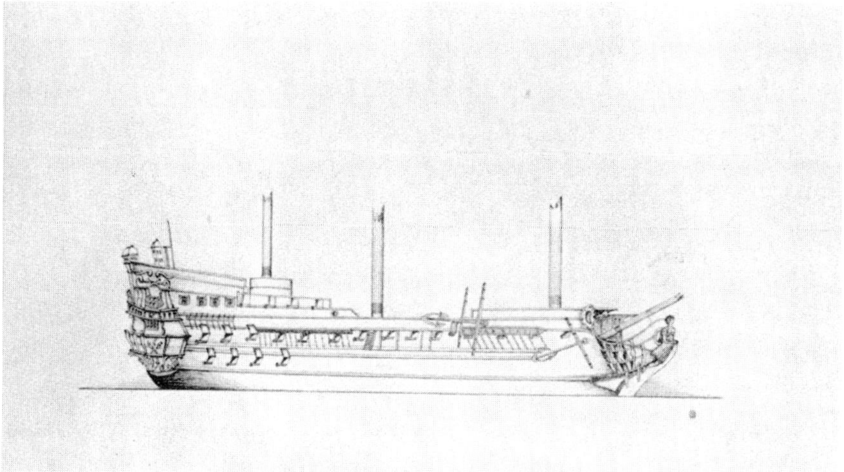

In this rare sketch of *Bonhomme Richard* her high poop deck and starboard armament are clearly visible.
From the author's collection

In April 1778 John Paul Jones—in the Continental ship *Ranger*—triumphed over HMS *Drake,* setting the stage for his later victory off Flamborough Head.
From the author's collection

In the battles of the Liman at the mouth of the Dnieper River in June 1788, Jones led the Russian fleet of the Empress Catherine in a series of victories over a Turkish fleet. These were the sole actions of Jones as a fleet commander.
From the author's collection

9
Homecoming

"Things at home are crossways."
William Carleton

Jones's voyage back to America was counterintuitive for him. Instead of seeking potential confrontations with the British Navy and opportunities for taking merchant ship prizes during the transit, it was important for him to avoid delays and direct contacts with British naval and merchant marine units. His mission was to deliver desperately needed military matériel for Washington's army without delay. Thus he sailed a southerly route across the Atlantic from Lorient to Philadelphia, a track outside the most active shipping lanes for British merchantmen and warships. But during the latter part of his transit, he had a noteworthy encounter with a British man-of-war.

At a point roughly one hundred miles northeast of the West Indies, *Ariel* was spotted and pursued by the twenty-gun British privateer, *Triumph.* Normally, *Ariel* and the British ship would have been a fairly even match. However, *Ariel* was deeply laden with her cargo of military supplies and her armament had been reduced to accommodate that cargo. In that state, Jones was at a distinct combat disadvantage to *Triumph.*

Risking his mission to take on a more heavily-gunned privateer, particularly with the reduced fighting capability of his ship, would not have been good military judgment on his part, and under the cover of darkness, Jones did his best to escape the British ship. By morning, however, the ships were much too close for Jones to escape, and as he had done on other occasions during his career, Jones sought to gain the initiative by deception and bluff. When the ships were within hailing distance, he began by claiming that he was a British Navy captain and demanded that the captain of the British privateer come aboard *Ariel* with his ship's papers. John Pindar, the British captain, was smart enough to refuse that order, but he was clearly in doubt about whether the ship he had overtaken was friend or foe.

Finally, Jones gave him five minutes to comply with his demand, and when Pindar did not meet the deadline, Jones raised his American ensign and quickly crossed *Triumph*'s stern. From that advantageous position, he poured a devastating broadside into the British ship. Jones had negated his opponent's speed advantage by subterfuge, successfully seized the initiative, and delivered a telling first blow—a brilliant piece of tactical work on Jones's part. Pindar struck his colors after only ten minutes of heavy action.

But suddenly, it was "turnabout is fair play." While Jones was having a boat lowered with a prize crew to take possession of *Triumph,* Pindar quickly trimmed up as much sail as possible and sprinted away from his captor. Once out of reach of *Ariel*'s guns, Pindar simply outran his adversary. Jones had started the confrontation with a successful ruse; Pindar ended it the same way but with a significant difference. In the age of sail, it was an accepted practice to conceal your identity to gain an advantage over an opponent, but it was considered dishonorable to flee or renew fighting after a captain had struck his colors. Pindar had violated an important unwritten code of naval warfare.

Jones surely took little comfort in Pindar's violation of the unwritten but very real naval code. He had lost a prize that would have added a dramatic close to his deployments in *Ranger* and *Bonhomme Richard.* Adding insult to injury and more important to Jones, he had been outwitted by his adversary. His disappointment was evident as he later described the event in his journal: "The English captain may properly be called a knave, because, after he had surrendered his ship, begged for and obtained quarter, he basely ran away, contrary to laws of naval war and the practice of civilized nations."[1]

As it turned out, however, the action between *Arial* and *Triumph* was not memorable as an example of either tactical skill or bad form for a naval officer. It was noteworthy because it was the last battle fought by John Paul Jones under the American flag. And during this last battle in an American ship, he had won another single-ship action against the British Navy, but in the end he was outwitted with an extension of the kind of tactics he had routinely used against his enemies. It was typical of Jones's career—for every triumph something happened that undercut the satisfaction Jones would have otherwise enjoyed.

After the action with *Triumph* and in a final incident before reaching Philadelphia, Jones was confronted with another in the series of many mutinies he faced during his career. Reminiscent of the earlier incident in *Bonhomme Richard,* the British sailors in *Ariel*'s crew were the ones who were planning to seize the ship. As before, however, Jones was able to thwart the uprising.

Finally, on 18 February 1781, Jones, *Ariel,* his passengers, and his military cargo—some of which found its way to the battle of Yorktown—were safely anchored at Philadelphia. Jones was back where his Continental Navy career had begun, and at that point he was no longer enmeshed in the complex and frustrating control of the French authorities and American representatives in Paris. He was back under the close control of Congress, and he enjoyed the substantial career leverage of his dramatic successes while operating from French ports. Jones had every reason to believe that bigger and better commands and missions were ahead.

The first business at hand was the unfinished matter of Captain Landais. As could have been predicted, *Alliance*'s transit back to America was chaotic. Landais was in constant conflict with his officers and even with his ally Arthur Lee. He spent days at a time isolated in his cabin, astonishingly providing no on-deck command leadership to his crew for those extended periods. In the absence of coherent underway leadership, the officers and crew of *Alliance* feared for their ship's safety. In addition, Lee continually insisted on special treatment, creating even more strains among the crew. Despite her problems, *Alliance* managed to reach America. But not surprisingly, she wound up in Boston instead of her intended destination, Philadelphia. And she arrived with First Lieutenant Arthur Degge in command, instead of Landais.

A court-martial was quickly convened, and Landais was tried. Because Jones had not yet returned from France and was not available to testify, Landais was tried neither for his behavior during the deployment of *Bonhomme Richard* nor for his takeover of *Alliance* in Lorient. He would, in fact, never be tried on those allegations. The officers and crew who were involved in *Alliance*'s voyage to Boston were available, however, so the court-martial focused on Landais's behavior during that transit to America.

Fortunately the president of the court-martial was John Barry, one of the Continental Navy captains who, like Jones, had a well-earned reputation for superior seamanship and success in combat. Barry was a no-nonsense naval professional who was not susceptible to the political maneuvering of Lee, Samuel Adams, and their friends. And he showed none of the jealousy toward Jones that was harbored by some of his fellow Continental Navy captains. As a result, Landais's actions during his return to America were enough to do him in at the trial. The court's action was unequivocal. Landais was cashiered from the Continental Navy, and the efforts of Lee and Samuel Adams to embarrass Franklin and Jones through the *Alliance* affair were cut off.

When Jones arrived in Philadelphia; Congress supplied him with a list of questions on the matter that he answered without difficulty in writing. As a result, in April 1781, the final report of Congress on Jones's deployment in *Bonhomme Richard* gave Jones the kind of praise he craved and deserved:

> The United States in Congress assembled, having taken into consideration the report of the Board of Admiralty of the 28th of March last, respecting the conduct of John Paul Jones, Esq., captain in the navy, do *Resolve,* That the thanks of the United States in Congress assembled, be given to Captain John Paul Jones, for the zeal, prudence, and intrepidity with which he has supported the honor of the American flag; for his bold and successful enterprises to redeem to captivity the citizens of these States who had fallen under the power of the enemy; and in general for the good conduct and eminent services by which he has added lustre to his character, and to the American arms.[2]

Jones would have been particularly pleased with the reference to his efforts on behalf of Continental Navy sailors held in British prisons. The sailors' plight was a highly emotional issue for him, and he had made efforts to secure their freedom an ongoing part of his activities in Paris, with limited support from his civilian leadership there.

In a letter to Jones in May, General Washington concurred with Congress's approbation, but with a between-the-lines—and no doubt well-founded—recognition of the potential political dangers that could be associated with an aggressive and popular military leader. Washington wrote, "Whether our naval affairs have in general been well or ill conducted, would be presumptuous in me to determine. Instances of bravery and good conduct in several of our officers, have not, however, been wanting; delicacy forbids me to mention that particular one which has attracted the admiration of all the world, and which has influenced the most illustrious monarch to confer a mark of his favor, which can only be obtained by a long and honorable service, or by the performance of some brilliant action."[3]

Eventually, John Adams also added to Jones's accolades. In a letter from The Hague on 12 August 1782, he praised the decision of Congress to place Jones in command of the ship of the line *America,* which was under construction in Portsmouth, New Hampshire. Of particular interest, Adams also emphasized America's need for a strong navy, and he associated Jones expansively with more than his combat capabilities. He linked Jones to his country's future naval power:

> The command of the *America* could not have been more judiciously bestowed, and it is with impatience that I wish to see her at sea, where she will do honor to her name. Nothing gives me so much surprise, or so much regret, as the inattention of my countrymen to their navy: it is a bulwark as essential as it is to Great Britain. It is less costly than armies,

> and more easily removed from one end of the United States to the other. . . . Indeed, if I could see a prospect of half a dozen line-of-battle ships under the American flag, commanded by Commodore Paul Jones, engaged with an equal British force, I apprehend the event would be so glorious for the United States, and lay so sure a foundation for their prosperity, that it would be a rich compensation for a continuance of the war.[4]

In any event, Landais's dismissal from the American navy ended the potential threat to Jones's career represented by the Frenchman's takeover of *Alliance* in Lorient. Landais's court-martial ended one of the more bizarre subplots in Jones's life. The officer surprisingly managed to return to service in the French Navy, despite his mental incapacity. Then after his retirement from the French Navy, he lived out his life in quiet poverty in New York City and apparently died there in 1818, at the age of 87.

If the Landais court-martial and the official praise by Congress and men like Washington and John Adams were good news for Jones and his career, the general state of the Continental Navy at that time was not. Not surprisingly, the British Navy had wiped out the initial Continental Navy of converted merchantmen by the end of 1779. Then a major portion of the remaining fleet, which was tiny by international standards to begin with, had been lost in the British capture of Charleston in May 1780. That disaster was followed by still other important losses. The twenty-eight-gun frigate *Trumbull* had been all but destroyed in battle with a British privateer in June 1780, and in March 1781, the eighteen-gun sloop of war *Saratoga* was lost in a storm with all hands. Even as the American Revolution wound down, the losses continued, and in April 1781, two British frigates captured the thirty-two-gun Continental frigate *Confederacy*.

Underscoring the Continental Navy's steady loss of ships during the Revolution was the pivotal and most conspicuous naval action of the war, the battle of Chesapeake Bay on 5 September 1781. There was not a single Continental Navy ship involved in what was described by one naval historian and author as "one of the greatest naval victories of all time."[5] In that battle, a totally French fleet under the command of Vice Admiral François de Grasse provided the final crucial naval component to Britain's defeat in the American Revolution. De Grasse seized control of the approaches to Chesapeake Bay, establishing decisive naval superiority at a crucial time and place and thereby preventing the relief by sea of General Charles Cornwallis at Yorktown. Thus came into play the third and final element of the American naval strategy during the

American Revolution: seizing local naval control of a strategic area at a crucial time. But not a single American ship took part in the action.

In contrast to the Continental Navy's generally low state of affairs as the revolution was coming to an end were some promising signs for the future U.S. Navy. One was the fact that in the political infighting for commands and other forms of recognition, merit was holding its own against seniority as a major consideration. For example, after the removal of Landais as captain, John Barry was given command of the purpose-built frigate *Alliance,* one of the few remaining operational assets of the Continental Navy at the time. Barry had distinguished himself in combat from the war's outset, in contrast with a number of officers who although senior on the original navy list of captains either lost their ships or were unable to escape British blockades and get into action.

The approximate balancing of merit with seniority by early Congresses helped establish a positive tradition for the appointment to command in the formative stages of the American navy. It was a balance that roughly paralleled practices in the British Navy and contrasted with practices in other navies, in which seniority and political influence (and during the French Revolution, political correctness) played inordinately important roles in the advancement of their naval officers.

Another positive note for the struggling American navy of the time was the emergence of Robert Morris as the civilian head of the service. Congress dissolved its Board of Admiralty in June 1781 and assigned the primary political responsibility for the navy to Morris, who was also finance minister. Then, in September, Congress confirmed his appointment as Agent of the Marine.

As a representative from Philadelphia, Morris had consistently emphasized the importance of a navy from the earliest days of Congress. He was also a brilliant financier and one of the best administrators in that body. And Morris's appointment was particularly important to Jones, since he had been one of Jones's strongest supporters in Congress from the beginning of his naval career. Despite his sad ending in poverty and obscurity when he died in 1805, Morris was one of the most effective Congressional advocates of a Continental Navy during the many difficult days of the American Revolution. His political contributions to the establishment of an American navy place Morris among the small group of individuals, including Washington and John Adams, who are candidates for the title of "father of the American Navy."

Consistent with his past behavior and notwithstanding the low point in America's naval strength in 1781, Jones began lobbying for his next ship as soon as he returned home. He focused on the most prestigious command of all—the Continental Navy ship of the line *America.* The seventy-four-gun *America* was one of three ships of the line authorized by Congress in November 1776, and she was under construction at Portsmouth. Her designer was Joshua Humphreys, the shipbuilder who later designed and built the heavy frigates that were exceptionally successful against the British Navy during the War of 1812. Her builder was Colonel James K. Hackett. *America* had a good pedigree, was an important step up in terms of fighting power, and would have made an impressive flagship for Jones.

As a ship of the line, *America* was considered a capital ship during the age of sail, and she was an important—and, at the time, expensive—advance for American naval prestige and operational potential. She was the only one of the three ships of the line authorized by Congress in 1776 that would be completed. Captain John Barry supervised the initial stages of her construction, but lack of funds caused the building process to lag badly. As a result, when *Alliance* returned from Lorient and Jones left her, Barry was given that command. Then, when Morris took up the assignment as civilian leader of the Continental Navy in June 1781, he was ordered by Congress to get the construction of *America* completed. Within three days of that order, Jones was selected as the ship's commanding officer and the man to get the construction and fitting-out job done.

There is no doubt that it would have been difficult for Jones to contain himself on hearing the news. He was, at that point, just a step away from command of his country's first ship of the line, and his admiral's star was almost within his grasp. Becoming his country's first admiral would have been the ultimate political victory for Jones over his detractors and his enemies within the Continental Navy. It would have been the perfect sequel to his Order of Military Merit and title of Chevalier bestowed on him by the King of France. In his enthusiasm, Jones made plans to use a figure of Liberty, with her right hand pointing to heaven, for *America*'s figurehead. It was an appropriate expression of the commitment to the cause of liberty that was at the center of his career motivation.

If Jones perhaps thought the turn of events were too good to be true, he would have been right. Although his political detractors had failed to turn the *Alliance* affair against him, the energies of other enemies, this time from within the Continental Navy, were now directed against Jones's promotion to flag rank. His antagonists were two fellow Continental Navy captains with political connections, James Nicholson and Thomas Read.

A committee of Congress had recommended that Jones be advanced to the rank of rear admiral. When Nicholson and Read heard of the recommendation, they began lobbying against the final Congressional confirmation that would have resulted in Jones's advancement. Their motivations were more than suspect. Nicholson had the distinction of losing the new twenty-eight-gun frigate *Virginia* to two British ships in the Chesapeake in 1778 and the new twenty-eight-gun frigate *Trumbull* to two other British ships off the Delaware Capes in August 1781. Read's career was less dramatic, but also unimpressive; he had never even gotten to sea in a Continental Navy combat command.

The arguments of Nicholson and Read to Congress were twofold. First, Jones was junior to a number of officers on the navy's seniority list, including, of course, Nicholson and Read, and second, aspects of Jones's private life made him unworthy of such a distinction. The first part of the argument against Jones was based on fact and raised the issue of seniority versus achievement in determining promotion to admiral.

The second objection to Jones's appointment as a rear admiral was based on innuendo, and it introduced the issue of personal character as a factor in the selection of a Continental Navy flag officer. Jones's reputation with women, whether relevant or not, had caught up with him and was being used to detract from his career achievements. Nicholson further proposed to Morris that command of *America* be offered to each senior officer of the Continental Navy in turn, based on seniority only. Such an approach would have completely negated the role of operational success in the selection process. It was a rigid formula that would have seriously discouraged captains from taking risks.

Fortunately, the latter proposal failed when Congress unanimously confirmed Jones's appointment to command of *America,* but his appointment as the first American admiral was successfully blocked.[6] It would be 1862 before the appointment of the U.S. Navy's first admiral was made, and that long delay paralleled the early period of American history during which some in Congress seriously questioned the value of a significant navy. In fact, some in Congress questioned whether the nation should have a navy at all. Consistently supporting the latter position were Congressmen who claimed that the country could not afford the cost and who further claimed that an American navy would actually precipitate conflicts with other naval powers. Those arguments, under varying circumstances, have continued to surface periodically into the present century.

In addition to lobbying for a new command during the months after his return from France, Jones was also occupied with efforts to obtain the money

Congress owed him. Jones would not receive that money until December 1782, when he received more than $20,000 for back pay and expenses. But with his new command uppermost in his mind, Jones finally left Philadelphia for Portsmouth and *America* on 12 August 1781. For Jones, the important thing was that as captain of *America* and presumably a commodore of a squadron whose flagship would be that new ship of the line, he could take on increasingly important missions. After taking a circuitous route to avoid the British Army, he arrived in Portsmouth on 31 August and turned his attention to completion of the ship's construction. It would be a daunting task with a deeply disappointing outcome for Jones.

Jones took lodging at the Marquis of Rockingham Tavern, and in October he moved to a boardinghouse.[7] With his newfound fame, he fit comfortably into the Portsmouth community, finding many old acquaintances and friends and making many new ones. Among the old acquaintances was Colonel John Langdon, Congress's naval agent in Portsmouth. Langdon had been one of the major obstacles in efforts to complete the construction and fitting out of *Ranger* before her departure for France in 1777, and he was playing a similar role in the construction of *America.*

By the time Jones was named captain of the ship and had arrived in Portsmouth, construction was at a standstill, and Langdon was threatening to discharge the workers. The basic problem was the old one, lack of government funding, compounded by Langdon's unwillingness to risk his own financial interests to press on with *America*'s construction.

At a time when many of those who were committed to the cause of the American Revolution were risking not just their lives but their fortunes as well—Jones had advanced his own funds at times to get to sea—Langdon's approach was strictly business. At one point, when it was apparent that the British were planning a raid to burn *America* in the shipyard, Jones once again used his own money for government purposes, and he hired a security force to protect the ship. He even shared the duty as captain of the guard. Fortunately, Jones's makeshift defense of *America* was visible enough to prevent a British attack.

The hand-to-mouth nature of the ship construction project was typical for the times. In fact, the Continental Congress's financial situation was so bad during the American Revolution that, at one point, Finance Minister Morris actually stopped paying army salaries. He rationalized that it was sufficient return for soldiers to be clothed and housed! The fact that America was able to field any military forces at all underscores how important the cause of liberty was in motivating the officers and men of the nation's first army and navy.

By the summer of 1782, *America* was nearing completion, and Jones's dream of commanding a ship of the line was close at hand. Suddenly, fortune turned against him. The French ship of the line *Magnifique* struck a rock while entering Boston harbor and sank. In a generous act toward an important ally, and coincidentally an act that eliminated what would have been a substantial ongoing military expense, Congress voted on 3 September to replace *Magnifique* with *America*. The French accepted, and with *America* went Jones's last, best opportunity for another major Continental Navy command.

Jones received the official news by letter from his friend Morris, dated 4 September: "The enclosed resolution will show you the destination of the ship *America*. . . . I know you so well as to be convinced that it must give you great pain, and I sincerely sympathize with you." Morris went on in an attempt to focus Jones's attention beyond his order to complete *America* for the French: "When that is done if you will come hither, I will explain to you the reasons which led to this measure and my views for employing you in the service of your country."[8]

It was a heavy blow, and Jones might well have resigned his commission at that point, but he pressed on with the construction and fitting out. Finally, the ship was ready for launching, which was a special challenge in its own right. The shipyard at Castle Rock Island was awkwardly positioned on the Piscataqua River for the launching of a ship the size of *America*. But with considerable skill, Jones managed the launching on 5 November, and the ship was then turned over to the French with appropriate ceremony.

America was broader and shallower than French-designed and constructed ships of the line and was never a favorite of French captains. In 1786 the ship was surveyed and found to be full of dry rot, due presumably to the use of unseasoned wood by Colonel Langdon in construction. She was condemned and broken up, a most inglorious end of a very short career for a ship of the line, many of which in the British Navy lasted through decades of heavy service. For France, *America* was a token of gratitude for French aid in America's struggle for independence. For the new United States, *America* was a prime example of the erratic development of its early naval strength.

Toward the end of 1782, Jones began lobbying for a radical new assignment. *America* was gone, serious negotiations were taking place to end the war with Britain, and no other major Continental Navy commands were in sight. So Jones chose a new approach, and his choice revealed that he was able to grasp naval matters beyond his own quarterdeck, matters that included tactics, command and control, officer training, and even the political realities of naval ship construction. He was also thinking beyond the war against Britain, to the peace that was approaching and what it would take for the American navy to survive its infancy.

Many of those thoughts and specific proposals were contained in a letter to Morris of 22 September. One of his suggestions involved "forming a proper corps of sea officers, by teaching them . . . naval tactics in a fleet of evolution." Jones was willing to economize by utilizing frigates instead of ships of the line for the training squadron he was proposing. In addition to teaching fleet tactics on board ship, he proposed visits by the fleet to dockyards, where there would be an opportunity for prospective officers to learn about ship construction, fitting out, and supply. He appealed to logic: "We cannot, like the ancients, build a fleet in a month." But he also argued with humility: "I however feel myself bound to say again, I have yet much need to be instructed."[9]

As usual, Jones was aiming high, but despite his prestige and the soundness of his arguments, Congress was unwilling to commit to the considerable expense of building and maintaining such a fleet and training program. Instead, they assigned Jones to go to sea with a French fleet to learn as much as possible from that experience. On 4 December they formalized his assignment: "*Resolved,* That the Agent of the Marine be informed that Congress having a high sense of the merit and services of Capt. J.P. Jones, and being disposed to favor the zeal manifested by him to acquire improvement in the line of his profession, do grant the permission which he requests; and that the said agent be instructed to recommend him accordingly to the countenance of His Excellency the Marquis de Vaudreuil."[10]

Jones wasted no time getting to Boston, where de Vaudreuil's fleet was preparing to depart for an amphibious attack on Jamaica. He was well received on board the French flagship, *Le Triomphant,* and on Christmas Eve of 1782, de Vaudreuil's fleet with Jones embarked left Boston. Jones was among a group of experienced and congenial French naval officers, plus a considerable number of French Army officers, some of whom had fought at Yorktown. It was a rich environment for learning.

The first phase of the French plan of attack involved linking up with a second French fleet and also with a Spanish squadron. Like many elaborate and unrealistic French plans for combining fleets for a concerted attack and particularly for the long sought-after invasion of the British Isles, this one never came together.

De Vaudreuil sat and waited for weeks in Porto Cabello, Venezuela. Despite the heat, humidity, and a debilitating fever Jones developed—probably caused by malaria—he continued learning all he could from the French officers. In the early spring of 1783, word reached de Vaudreuil that the basics of a treaty had been worked out, ending the American Revolution and, at least temporarily, the conflict between France and Britain. As a result, he sailed north to Haiti, where Jones began his recovery from malaria and took passage for America in a merchantman.

In May 1783, Jones was back in Philadelphia, and he completed his recovery at a Moravian sanatorium in Bethlehem, Pennsylvania. During his stay with de Vaudreuil's fleet, Jones had gone a long way toward filling gaps in his naval knowledge created by his abrupt transition from a merchant ship captain to a Continental Navy officer.

During 1781 and 1782 and the events of the Landais court-martial, the construction and commissioning of *America,* and the assignment with de Vaudreuil's fleet, a little recognized side of John Paul Jones matured. He emerged as arguably his country's first uniformed apostle of sea power. He had been inclined to lecture his civilian leaders on naval matters from his earliest days as a commissioned officer. Now he had credibility as a proven combat leader and a hero on the European continent, and that credibility bolstered his opinions.

Jones's ongoing concern for the broader aspects of a navy could be seen clearly in the letter he wrote to Morris on 22 September 1782. In that revealing document, he ranges over a wide variety of subjects, indicating that he had a long view of his navy and its role as an element of maritime power. He started his analyses in a historical context that recognized the implausibility of the Continental Navy: "The beginning of our navy, as navies now rank, was so singularly small, that I am of opinion it has no precedent in history. Was it a proof of madness in the first corps of sea officers, at so critical a period, to have launched out on the ocean with only two armed merchant ships, two armed brigantines, and one armed sloop, to make war against such a power as Great Britain?"[11]

Jones did not answer his own question, leaving the reader to call to mind his achievements as a response. The letter to Morris then went on to introduce the subject of the evolution of naval tactics, mistakenly claiming that the British were forced to imitate French tactics. He next discussed the very important subjects of command and control at sea, the ranks that should be established in the navy, a naval "constitution" for seagoing personnel as well as those assigned ashore, the educational value of duty with other navies, and ship construction.

Jones's letter to Morris in 1782 was astonishingly expansive, coming from a captain in a navy that had no capital ships, no flag officers, and that had been all but destroyed by its first opponent. It was a letter from an officer who could look beyond present circumstances and a narrow definition of his professional duty, one who was continuously trying to fill the gaps in his own knowledge. It was the kind of thinking that would evolve slowly in the American navy, and then burst forth at the end of the nineteenth century, with institutions focused on professional study, such as the U.S. Naval War College and the U.S. Naval Institute and with proponents of broad concepts of sea power, such as Rear Admiral A. T. Mahan, author of the globally respected and universally translated "bible" of sea power, *The Influence of Sea Power Upon History.*[12]

At a time when the cumulative number of ships in the navies of individual states exceeded the number in the Continental Navy, Jones nonetheless saw the American navy as much more than an ad hoc naval service assembled to win a war for independence. He instinctively saw it as the beginning of a geopolitical force that would evolve into a powerful instrument of national policy for a future global power. In one of his earlier letters on naval matters, written in October 1776 to Morris, he put his argument for a sound system of payment for American sailors in that kind of a context. Although his problem was the immediate manning of his ship *Providence,* he invoked the broadest—and yet concise—perspective for his reasoning: "And without a respectable navy—alas! America!"[13]

Even while addressing mundane naval issues, Jones saw the importance of the navy to his country's future more clearly than most of his more sophisticated and better-educated political contemporaries, several of whom saw the navy in an inward-looking, regional perspective. Jones also had a broader naval vision than his more politically influential naval contemporaries, who tended to restrict their thinking to immediate matters of seamanship and naval tactics. On 10 October 1783, toward the end of a long, complaining letter about how Congress had mistreated him, his vision burst through his bitterness: "In a time of peace it is necessary to prepare, and be always prepared for war by the sea."[14]

In his plainspoken and often irritating way, Jones was the precursor of thinkers like Mahan, who at the end of the nineteenth century would begin to put naval power into a geopolitical context. Jones set the stage for officers of the U.S. Navy to understand more than the tactics and technology of their profession. But in his own time, his country and its leaders still had many lessons to learn concerning maritime power, just as he freely admitted that he did.

10
Peace and Paris

"Success has always been a great liar."
Nietzsche

By November 1782, Great Britain and America had agreed to a provisional end to the American Revolution, and on 3 September 1783 the war officially ended with the signing of the Treaty of Paris of that year. John Adams, Benjamin Franklin, and John Jay were the American signatories. The first article of the Treaty described the end of the American Revolution in surprisingly plain language: "His Britannic Majesty acknowledges the said United States, viz., New Hampshire, Massachusetts Bay, Rhode Island and Providence Plantations, Connecticut, New York, New Jersey, Pennsylvania, Delaware, Maryland, Virginia, North Carolina, South Carolina, and Georgia, to be free sovereign and independent States, and that he treats them as such, and for himself, his Heirs, and Successors, relinquishes all Claims to the Government, Propriety, and territorial Rights of the same and every Part thereof."[1]

The last article of the Treaty of Paris of 1783 held out a hope that would be realized, not in the short term, but after a century had passed and the interests of the United States and Great Britain became parallel: "There shall be firm and perpetual Peace between his Britannic Majesty and the said States, and between the subjects of the one, and the Citizens of the other."

After seven years of violent struggle, the United States had secured its independence from Great Britain. And Jones had been a significant player in establishing that sovereignty. At the age of thirty-six, he was famous in America and on the European continent for his psychologically crucial victory off Flamborough Head and for his strategically important successes in taking the war to the British homeland. But despite being an international hero, it was not a good time for him. Above all, he no longer had the emotionally charged cause of American liberty—the palpable force characterized as "the enthusiasm of liberty" by Alexander Hamilton—to energize his career. In addition, the American navy was at low ebb, and he had no ship. In fact, the new United States was turning to the question of whether it needed, or could afford, any navy at all.

For the short term, the issue of federal funding of a navy was overriding. The war had been financed by the confederation of thirteen separate American colonies with private funds, paper money, and foreign loans. And in fact, without the ability to levy taxes, debates about the need for a navy were academic. By 1785, *Alliance,* the last ship of the Continental Navy, was sold. It would not be until the U.S. Constitution became legally binding in June 1788 and the United States federal government was given the right to levy taxes that a U.S. Navy was a practical possibility. And it was not until two years after Jones's death, when Congress authorized the building of six new frigates in March 1794, that the U.S. Navy became a reality.[2]

In the meantime, Jones had the financial resources to settle down as a landowner. And for a brief period, on the premise that he would be close to the port of New York, he explored the possibility of buying a farm in New Jersey. But not surprisingly, his planning soon shifted to a return to Paris, where he had become one of that city's leading celebrities during the spring and summer of 1780. The question was how to get there in an official capacity and with the government underwriting the cost. Jones's efforts to get Congress to establish a squadron to train naval personnel and show the flag in Europe were totally unrealistic at the time. Ultimately, the answer turned out to be a diplomatic mission as an agent for securing the prize money still owed in Europe to the crews of *Ranger, Bonhomme Richard,* and *Alliance.*

Although he still held an active captain's commission in the American navy, Jones's new assignment would require skills other than military. Now he would be required to employ written and verbal arguments, rather than cold steel and cannon fire, to secure fair financial settlements for his shipmates and himself. Now the government bureaucrats and politicians of France and elsewhere in Europe were his antagonists, rather than the professionals of the British Navy. It was not a joyful transition, but on the other hand, it was an assignment for which he had accumulated some experience. On 1 November 1783, Congress made his assignment official.

The appointment of Jones as agent included the allowance of an agent's commission on the prize money, in addition to his share as commodore of the squadrons involved. The Congressional action of 1 November ended with a resolution with the key to Jones's return to Paris: "That the agent of marine provide Capt. Jones with a passage to France in the ship *Washington.*" He would also carry dispatches for John Adams, then-ambassador to Great Britain. The thirty-two-gun frigate *General Washington,* with Jones embarked, left Philadelphia for Europe on 10 November 1783.

The fact that Jones was sailing not as a commodore or even as a captain of his own ship was mitigated somewhat by the fact that Captain Joshua Barney was in command of *General Washington.* Barney was an outstanding naval officer who had distinguished himself in more than thirty naval engagements during the American Revolution. In the process he was imprisoned three times and escaped twice. Barney would go on to also earn fame in the War of 1812. The two had met as young Continental Navy officers during the assault on New Providence in 1776, and in addition, they had both begun their careers at sea in the merchant marine. In an interesting parallel with Jones's early experience in the merchant brig *John* in 1768, Barney had actually captained a merchant ship at sixteen years of age, when his captain died suddenly at sea.

During the weeks of *General Washington*'s transit eastward, the two officers devoted considerable time discussing naval matters and reminiscing, much of it during the wintry night watches on *General Washington*'s quarterdeck, the weather side of which was by strict naval tradition Barney's private domain. Within the invisible but impenetrable walls of that small space, only those with official duty there and those invited by the captain dared to tread. The ability of the two members of America's small fraternity of successful naval combat leaders to compare notes on such professional subjects as navigation, combat tactics, and—one can assume—the politics of a naval career would have been a special pleasure for both men.

After the voyage, Barney would observe that his fellow naval officer was generally depressed, something not very surprising in light of Jones's fading career prospects as a seagoing military leader. Jones was still a young man, but with each changing of the watch during *General Washington*'s underway routine and after each conversation with Captain Barney, the realization that his glory days in an American navy were over undoubtedly became more and more oppressive. Jones was suffering from the problem that must inevitably be faced by all successful military leaders—he was losing control of his own destiny because his courage and military brilliance were no longer in demand in America and his performance now had little to do with his future.

During the voyage, Jones also had the company of an army engineer, Major Pierre-Charles L'Enfant. The French-born major had joined the Marquis de Lafayette to serve in General Washington's army during the American Revolution. In addition to a shared acquaintance with Lafayette, L'Enfant had a connection that was of particular interest to Jones at the time; he was a founding member of the Society of the Cincinnati, an organization of American and French military officers who served in America during the American Revolution.

The society, whose name commemorates a fifth century BC Roman "citizen soldier," was established in 1783 and originally consisted of twenty-three of the fifty-four signers of the U.S. Constitution. George Washington was the group's first president. Jones actively sought membership in the society as a way to enhance his status. Being accepted in that group would support his ongoing drive for recognition as a professional naval officer and his related craving for social recognition. In time, he elected to membership, presumably with the help of L'Enfant.

Although *General Washington*'s planned destination was France, Jones convinced Barney to drop him off in England. The reason for Jones's request is not known for sure. One possibility—perhaps probability—was that the dispatches Jones was carrying to John Adams were of sufficient urgency and confidentiality to warrant direct delivery to their destination. Whatever the reasons, they were sufficient to convince Barney, who modified his orders and delivered Jones to the English coast, despite the concern he expressed for Jones's physical safety in England. Jones sloughed off Barney's concern with a bit of bravado flavored with a dash of bitterness: "It will not be the first time if I have to traverse all England with the bloodhounds upon my track."[3]

The landing was in early December, probably at a Channel fishing village near Plymouth. From there, Jones made his way by coach to London, where he delivered the dispatches. On 10 December, London's *Gazeteer and New Daily Advertiser* noted Jones's arrival in England with an intriguing demonstration of domestic intelligence capability but also with considerable confusion about his itinerary: "On Friday evening, about nine o'clock, the celebrated Paul Jones arrived in town from Paris, with dispatches from American Congress . . . after delivering his dispatches on Friday evening, he set out the next morning at three o'clock for Paris, to proceed from thence to America."[4]

Five days after stepping ashore in what had been hostile territory until very recently, Jones was back in Paris. It would be his home, with some significant interruptions, for the next three years.

Jones immediately turned his attention to his prize money mission. He reestablished an effective working relationship with Benjamin Franklin, who was still minister plenipotentiary, but the new relationship lacked some of the warmth of the days during the war with Britain. Most significantly, Franklin and the United States government no longer needed highly visible military accomplishments from Jones. For Jones's part, he was convinced that Franklin could have done more in supporting him in his difficulties with Captain Landais,

Arthur Lee, Sam Adams, and their political allies. Notwithstanding the changed circumstances, however, Franklin buttressed Jones's negotiating leverage with his personal authorization to seek the prize money due the officers and crews of *Ranger, Bonhomme Richard,* and *Alliance.*

Jones began with French Minister of Foreign Affairs Comte de Vergennes and Minister of Marine Maréchal de Castries, and he quickly found that one of the initial obstacles to his mission was Jacques Donatien Le Ray de Chaumont. It was the same Chaumont whose wife was alleged to have had an affair with Jones in late 1777 and who had so muddied the chain of command of Jones's squadron before its spectacular successes in 1779. Jones's romantic affairs had been a factor in his failure to advance to rear admiral. Now there was a chance a past indiscretion could become a barrier to the success of his diplomatic assignment.

Chaumont was the French agent appointed to handle the sale of the prizes Jones's squadron captured in the summer and fall of 1779. Chaumont had long since sold the prizes in question; they had brought approximately $91,400 in prize money. After a considerable deduction by Chaumont for his expenses, approximately $56,700 remained, and not a penny had been distributed to Jones or the men of his squadron. Chaumont claimed that he was holding the money because the French government owed him a larger sum. Chaumont's devious claim did not work in the adjudication Jones precipitated.

The French government even claimed a portion of the money for the expense of holding the prisoners that had been captured by Jones's squadron. Jones overcame that claim by pointing out with considerable emphasis that the British captives he had taken had been exchanged for *French* prisoners, not captive Americans, contrary to his wish and expectation. In his legal dealings Jones demonstrated the same stubborn determination that had been a crucial element of his professional naval accomplishments.

After Jones beat back other questionable arguments, the minister of marine signed an agreement acceptable to Jones regarding the payment due. But further delays and evasions continued to emerge. A specious claim on behalf of the officers and crew of *Alliance* surfaced from an associate of Arthur Lee in Lorient. Predictably, the French government took full advantage of the claim to hold up the money. Jones pursued the matter doggedly, however, and in September 1785 the minister of marine again agreed to pay the money over to Jones.

In July 1786, Jones certified to Thomas Jefferson, who had replaced Franklin as the U.S. plenipotentiary in Paris, that he had received slightly more than $36,200 in gold from the French government. After he had deducted monies that he had advanced to the crew of *Bonhomme Richard,* his expenses in France, and his personal share of the prize money as commodore of the squadron, Jones turned $22,435 over to Jefferson, who certified it as the correct settlement. Jefferson, who had not been paid since his arrival in France, then sent an IOU to Congress for the amount. Eventually Congress and Jefferson agreed that Jefferson would use the funds secured by Jones for Jefferson's own pay and expenses and that Congress would appropriate an equal amount to be paid out to the men of Jones's squadron as prize money.

On 11 October 1787, more that eight years after the military actions involved, Congress confirmed Jones's negotiations and authorized distribution of the prize money among the crews of the three American ships that had sailed under his command in the British Isles theater. The chasm separating the original sale value of the prizes and the final amount that was eventually distributed, combined with the money's tortuous path, was a shabby early chapter in the relationship between America's political leadership and the new nation's military forces. On the other hand, it was not at all unusual for prize money in the age of sail to be delayed for years and eroded by a variety of expenses that were often inflated by agents and other intermediaries.

As an adjunct to his efforts to secure the prize money due in France, Jones tried to get prize money for three ships captured by his squadron that Captain Landais had sent into Bergen, Norway, which was under Danish rule at the time. Jones tried working through Danish representatives in Paris and London, and then, in the spring of 1787, he left for the Danish court in Copenhagen to pursue the issue. His trip was cut short unexpectedly by private business matters, however, and he returned for a brief stay in the United States.

He spent the summer of 1787 in New York City, where he took lodging on the waterfront of the East River, at the foot of what is now Dey Street. The accelerating postwar growth of the early U.S. maritime industry was clearly in evidence in the forest of tall masts in the East River that he could see from his doorstep. It is not clear how much of his time was devoted to his business affairs and how much was devoted to lobbying Congress, which was meeting in New York at the time.

One of his preoccupations was a report by Congress's Treasury Board questioning expense claims related to his mission in France to settle the prize money issue. The board, which was influenced by Jones's nemesis Lee, also seemed intent on rehabilitating Captain Landais. Jones was successful in rebutting the board's report and Congress reaffirmed Jones's accounting of the prize money in question. In addition to defending his performance as the agent in Paris designated to negotiate prize money, Jones made an unsuccessful attempt to resurrect his promotion to rear admiral.

On 16 October, in a more positive vein and shortly before his return to Paris, Congress unanimously voted that he be awarded a special gold medal "in commemoration of the valor and brilliant services . . . in the command of a squadron of American and French ships under the flag and commission of the United States, off the coast of Great Britain, in the late war." The one-of-a-kind medal was designed in Paris and showed a portrait of Jones on the front and a depiction of the battle between *Bonhomme Richard* and *Serapis* on the reverse. The Congressional action also contained a resolution that asked Louis XVI to permit Jones to "acquire greater knowledge in his profession" by embarking with French fleets. With Congressional approval of his efforts in Paris and a significant new honor in hand, Jones was back in Paris by December 1787.

While Jones was in Paris fighting for the prize money due the officers and men of his squadron, he also became active in a series of commercial ventures. Based on his early business successes as a merchant ship captain, it was a logical direction for him to take while he was without a naval assignment. As Jones himself pointed out, however, the sharp business instincts he had demonstrated as a merchant ship captain had atrophied during his naval service. In December 1783, Jones had written to a friend in Virginia, referring to his diminished business instincts and his need to earn some income. Jones also complained of the delay and erosion of his prize money, pointing out how pieces of it disappeared as it passed through the hands of agents who did not fairly serve those who had taken the prizes in combat. He also pointed out how the devaluation of Continental paper money had further reduced the prizes' value.

Among the ill-conceived business projects that Jones embarked upon to solve his financial problems was one that involved shipping goods from France to John Ross, a friend in Philadelphia, for sale in America. The deal ended in acrimony based on what Jones perceived as Ross's nonperformance, and Jones lost the upfront money he invested to secure and ship the goods.

Another more unconventional scheme involved setting up a company to secure sea otter pelts from North America for shipment to China, where the pelts would be traded for Chinese products to be shipped to Europe and sold at a presumably huge profit. That project never got past the preliminary stages, which was probably fortunate for Jones. Jones also invested in the Bank of North America and in land companies, with little apparent return.

One of the ironies of Jones's postwar business failures was that the end of the war opened up a period of accelerating commercial activity for many American merchants. Once the Treaty of Paris was signed in 1783, business activity based on U.S. foreign trade and the domestic economy surged. And as the war had been a period when many American fortunes were depleted, the postwar period became a time for restocking old fortunes and making new ones.

The Industrial Revolution was taking shape, the shift toward consumer-driven economies was gathering momentum, and America's energy was shifting from war fighting to entrepreneurial activities. As a corollary, Americans were beginning to capitalize on burgeoning overseas trade, despite the limiting effects of Britain's Navigation Acts and predatory attacks on American merchant ships by various nations' privateers—including those of former ally France.

In politics, Congress was turning to the need to strengthen the federal government and deal with the national debt with which the new United States began its existence. One historian captured how the accelerating U.S. commercial vitality of the late eighteenth century, particularly as it was expressed in ocean commerce, carried on into the nineteenth century: "Merchants developed new markets overseas, and their ships served them with what Tocqueville was to describe as 'a sort of heroism in their manner of trading,' undercutting British and European competition and outrunning their vessels with 'clipper' ships; the merchant fleet, spreading its sails in every sea, increased at a rate almost matching the growth of population in the new Union."[5]

Another modern historian focused on the significant commercial benefits of not having any major external threats to the new nation after the American Revolution ended: "In the four years of peace that followed, prosperity was widespread and growing, and the United States had faced no immediate foreign threats."[6] Sadly, Jones did not catch the initial stages of the rising tide of commercial opportunity triggered by the emergence of the United States as a nation, notwithstanding the role he played as a catalyst in the process. For Jones, the energizing cause of liberty was not replaced by the challenges and rewards of business success.

While Jones demonstrated that he had lost much of his business acumen, he does not appear to have lost his ongoing romantic inclinations, and it would not be unreasonable to assume that he would reestablish his relationship with Delia. But that was not the direction he took. Despite the initial passion of the relationship, the romance lacked durability as evidenced by a December 1781 letter that Jones wrote to Countess Nicolson from Portsmouth, New Hampshire.

In it, he complained about receiving only one letter from her and he did not include expressions of affection.

When he returned to Paris in late 1783, Jones apparently felt no need to rush to Delia. So Delia wrote to him, "Is it possible that you are then so near to me and that I am deprived of the sight of a mortal who has constituted the misery of my life for four years? . . . come to your best friend, who burns with the desire of seeing you . . . Come, in the name of heaven."[7] Perhaps the greatest inhibition for Jones's renewal of the romance was the fact that Delia was by then widowed and quite possibly contemplating marriage—or at least an exclusive relationship—with him. In any event, it was not Delia to whom Jones turned for female companionship in Paris in 1783.

Next in Jones's serial romances was a relationship with a Frenchwoman who was clouded in considerable mystery. It is difficult to determine, for example, when and where the romance was triggered. It appears that Jones met her socially at some point after his return to Paris in late 1783, and she appears in early literature about Jones only as "Madame T——."Subsequent evidence from correspondence among Jones, Jefferson, and Franklin established that she was the widow of an Englishman named Townsend, and she claimed to be the illegitimate daughter of no less a personage than the late King Louis XV. Her mother abandoned her at an early age and left her—with little more than a questionable claim to royal blood—in the care of the Marquise de Marsan, who raised her.

When the Marquise died, however, Madame Townsend was left without friends and financial resources. Her cloudy lineage, financial plight, and relationship with Jones were revealed in a letter in September 1787 from Jones in New York to Thomas Jefferson in Paris, asking that Jefferson assist Madame Townsend. Jefferson acted quickly on receipt of Jones's letter, and he wrote to Madame Townsend offering his assistance. When she asked Jefferson for a loan, however, he pulled back. When Jones returned from New York to Paris several months later, he was reunited with Madame Townsend and went to considerable length to clear up her debts.

There were two noteworthy differences between Jones's previous romances and his relationship with Madame Townsend, and the first was mutual need. Jones, whose naval career was at an apparent impasse and whose business career was neither psychologically nor financially rewarding, finally needed more than recreational sex. Madame Townsend was financially insecure, and she looked to Jones for financial and psychological support. As a result, this relationship lacked the superficial sophistication of Jones's previous affairs and appears to have been grounded in more significant human feelings.

The second difference in the relationship was the strong chance—perhaps probability—that Madame Townsend bore Jones's child. Although there is no incontrovertible evidence of Jones's fatherhood, the tone of a letter he wrote to her sometime before 1787 suggests that he was writing about his own son. The letter refers to her "sweet godson" and contains Jones's plea that she "cover him all over with kisses for me," with his addition that "they come warm to you both from my heart!"[8]

Sadly, the differences between Jones's love for Madame Townsend and his previous dalliances did not add much longevity to the relationship; there was no marriage to give permanence to the romance. A year after his return to Paris and reunion with his lover, Jones wrote to Jefferson from Russia asking what had happened to her. The story of Madame T——ends abruptly at that point.

By the time Jones returned to Paris from New York in 1787, he had carried out the first half of his mission to pry loose the prize monies owed by France to the officers and men of *Ranger, Bonhomme Richard,* and *Alliance.* But although he had put some efforts toward the task, he had not recovered the prize money from Denmark for three ships Landais had sent into Bergen in 1779. The ships were the two valuable privateers *Betsy* and *Union,* and a somewhat less valuable merchant ship *Charming Polly.* The three prizes, captured by the crews of *Bonhomme Richard* and *Alliance,* had been sent to Bergen based on instructions from Chaumont.

In January 1788, Jefferson wrote to Jones reaffirming his appointment as the U.S. agent to resolve the prize money issue with Denmark, and on 4 March, Jones arrived in Copenhagen. On 11 March he wrote to Jefferson that, despite several days of illness, he was in Copenhagen and had been making the appropriate diplomatic contacts. In addition, he wrote that he was "infinitely indebted to the attentions I received from the minister of France." He also took the opportunity to report on a matter of somewhat lesser importance; he had ordered the smoked beef that Jefferson desired, and his friend could look forward to receiving it through the American agent at Le Havre-de-Grâce.

By the end of March it was clear to Jones that pressure exerted by Britain on the Danish court had had its effect. The Danes claimed that Jones did not have sufficient diplomatic authority to carry out the negotiations, and they shifted the negotiations to Paris and Jefferson. They also maintained that Denmark was obliged by treaty with Britain to return the ships in question to British control.

The prize money issue with Denmark clearly would not be resolved quickly, and Jones wrote to Jefferson, saying bluntly that his business in Copenhagen was at an end. In a blatant effort to placate Jones, King Christian offered him a small annual pension in return for his respect of Danish neutrality during his commerce raiding missions. Jones, to his credit, refused the offer.

During Jones's mission to Copenhagen it was apparent that both the King and Count Bernstorff, the Danish minister of foreign affairs, had their eyes on a future lucrative trade treaty with the United States. In the best diplomatic tradition of verbal obfuscation and with future commercial relations with the United States in mind, Bernstorff tried to convince Jones to not go away angry. On 4 April, Bernstorff wrote to Jones, "If it has not been possible, sir, to discuss definitively with you, neither the principal object nor its accessaries, the idea of eluding the question, or of retarding the decision, had not the least part of it. . . . We desire to form with them [the United States] connexions solid, useful, and essential; we wish to establish them on bases natural and immovable."[9]

Despite the smooth-tongued protestations in Bernstorff's smoke screen, Denmark never did stop "eluding the question," and after decades of wrangling, Congress eventually assumed the obligation for payment of the Danish prize money to Jones's heirs and those of the officers and men of *Bonhomme Richard* and *Alliance.* They also saw fit to pay the disgraced Captain Landais $4,000 for his share of the money, despite his having been discredited and dismissed from the service for cause.

In addition to the fact that his dealings in Copenhagen were dead in the water, Jones had another reason to want to be free of the prize money assignment. In one of his final letters to Bernstorff, Jones alluded to the fact that he could not delay his departure from Copenhagen because of a promise he had made to the Russian Empress Catherine.

Although it was not in the American navy, Jones was about to have an opportunity to achieve two major career goals—advance to rear admiral and command a major fleet. And with some irony, he was following in the footsteps of many British Navy officers who were unable to secure active commands in their own navy at that time.

On the one hand, he must have felt that the situation indicated at least a small area of parity with the officers of his former enemy. And that would have been important in his never-ending drive for professional credibility. On the other hand, the cause of liberty was no longer at the center of his career. There was nothing faintly republican about the country he would be serving, and Catherine was as absolute an autocrat as one could find in history. It surely was a situation of contradicting feelings for a man with Jones's highly emotional personality.

11
In Command of a Fleet

"Admiral: the title and rank of a senior naval officer, often referred to as a flag officer."

Encyclopædia Britannica

The possibility of advancement to rear admiral can be a healthy motivator for an officer, or it can be a fixation that distorts a positive attitude that previously fueled an exceptional career. Although Jones never reached the point of total fixation on reaching flag rank, it clearly was a powerful drive that was close to becoming an end in itself. Following his victory off Flamborough Head and at frequent intervals after that, he lobbied Congress hard for the promotion. But by the time he returned to Paris from New York in 1787, it was apparent that his opportunities for advancement beyond the rank of captain in the U.S. Navy had passed. Although a strong case could be made that he was the leading candidate for flag rank, the required circumstances just never came into confluence.

As that door was closing, however, another was opening. Catherine II, whose Russian rule extended from 1762 to 1796, clearly had expansionist aims, and her aims raised significant maritime challenges for her. One of those challenges, the second Russo-Turkish War, had broken out in 1787, and Her Imperial Highness was strongly interested in having Jones command a Russian fleet against the Turks. Catherine, who was highly intelligent, notorious for her sexual voraciousness, and politically shrewd, knew that senior naval officers who would win in combat were not easy to come by.

In early 1788, the Russian ambassador in Paris, Baron Johan Matias Simolin, broached the subject to Thomas Jefferson, and Jefferson gave Jones a strong endorsement. Jefferson's support also included the admonition that Jones must have sufficient authority to serve effectively in whatever fleet he would command. It also appears that Jones's friend, David Lord Elcho, known in Paris as M. le Comte de Wemyss, proposed him for a commission in the Russian Navy in 1785, but at that time Jones was occupied with securing prize money from France. By early 1788, however, the situation had changed. Jones was available and Russia was at war.

Finally, circumstances were working in Jones's favor for his advancement to flag rank, and on 1 February 1788, Simolin interviewed Jones at a meeting in the Paris home of another Jones supporter, Chevalier Lewis Littlepage, a Virginian who had served under the French in the American Revolution. Jones expressed interest in the possibility of serving in the Russian Navy but stipulated that his service must be as a rear admiral. Even if an assignment in a foreign navy was not his preferred path to that special level of achievement, it was an option that opened up new professional opportunities for the victor at the battle off Flamborough Head. On learning of Jones's willingness to serve in her navy, Catherine was blunt about her motivation: "He will get to Constantinople."[1]

In April of 1788, Jones wrote to Jefferson on the subject, referring to him as "the author of the honorable prospect that is now before me." In the letter, he rationalized his decision to pursue an appointment in a foreign navy: "I have not forsaken a country that has had many . . . proofs of my steady affection; and I can never renounce the glorious title of *a citizen of the United States!*"

In fact, there is little doubt that Jones felt that his country had, in a professional sense, turned away from him. And further on in the letter to Jefferson, Jones specifically pointed out that America "has no public employment for my military talents." Then, he got to the key point: "Instead of receiving lessons from able masters, in the theory of war, I am called to immediate practice; where I must command in chief, conduct the most difficult operations, be my own preceptor, and instruct others." His signing on with Catherine the Great's navy wasn't simply a matter of rank, it was a matter of facing the ultimate challenge of naval leadership: leading a fleet in combat. Jones's professional ambition drove him to seize his opportunity in Catherine's navy.

In 1787, Catherine was facing two specific naval challenges, one in the Baltic Sea and one on the northern littoral of the Black Sea. In the Baltic, Russia's objective was to avoid being crushed between the naval powers of Britain and France, whose ongoing applications of their naval muscle were impinging on the oceangoing trade of other nations. With Catherine's initiative, Russia, Denmark, and Sweden—all of which were nominally neutral in the ongoing struggle between Britain and France—had formed the League of Armed Neutrality during the American Revolution. The league's purpose was to counter British attempts to hinder France's trade with the Baltic countries. Subsequently, the league was expanded to include Prussia and Austria in 1782 and Portugal in 1783.

In an interesting historical side note, Jones had suggested in a letter to Jefferson, and later in a letter to the Marquis de Lafayette, that it would benefit America to join the League of Armed Neutrality. The fact that the United States did not join the alliance was fortuitous; the League of Armed Neutrality was, for all intents and purposes, shattered by two later events. The first was Admiral Horatio Nelson's strategically important victory over Denmark at the battle of Copenhagen in 1801; the second was the assassination of Catherine's son, Czar Paul, the same year.

Russia's naval challenge along the northeast littoral of the Black Sea had little to do with diplomatic maneuvering and much to do with military reality. There, Catherine and her navy were fighting the second Russo-Turkish War, a continuation of Russia's historic territorial expansion southward, with the objective being not just territory but primarily access to warm-water ports. Acquiring Constantinople was the far edge of Catherine's expansionist goal to the south. Her comment that Jones would "get to Constantinople" was evidence of just how important that gateway to the Aegean and the Mediterranean was to her ambitions.

As Catherine pushed Russian influence and annexation through the Ukraine and the Crimean Peninsula, she was confronted with a particularly critical problem at the estuary—known as the Liman—of the Dnieper and Bug rivers. At Ochakov, the point at which the Liman entered the Black Sea, the Porte of Turkey had constructed a powerful fort. In that strategic position, Turkey effectively checked Russian access to the Black Sea from two major southern rivers and eliminated the strategic leverage that access represented. It was a classic case of using the control of a maritime choke point to exert crucial military leverage, and Catherine knew that control of the Liman was essential to Russia's future expansion to the south.

Because of its strategic importance, the taking of Ochakov was attempted early in the second Russo-Turkish War by the commander in chief of Russia's army and navy, a petty Russian noble, Prince Grigory Aleksandrovich Potemkin. The Prince was not only Catherine's trusted political and military adviser, but also her lover for many years, giving him political power that approached that of the empress. Despite having a Russian field army at his disposal, Potemkin failed to dislodge the Turks from Ochakov. In his frustration, he went so far as to suggest to Catherine that she abandon the entire Crimea. She rejected that proposal out of hand.

Notwithstanding his questionable military leadership, Potemkin was no mere lapdog to the empress. He was politically audacious and cunning, and he wielded tremendous power in the governing of Russia; he would play a role second to none in Jones's Russian service.

Potemkin's mediocre military leadership of the Russian Army was matched by the poor state of the Russian Navy at the time. The officer corps of Catherine's naval service was made up of a mixture of Russian nobles and military mercenaries from Britain, France, Spain, and other European nations, and its seamen were poorly trained and lacking in discipline. Catherine knew her navy lacked coherent leadership. In fact she had tried unsuccessfully to persuade a Dutch admiral Jonkheer Jan Hendrik van Kinsbergen to reorganize the leadership of her navy. Catherine turned to Jones for a specific strategic objective: the breaking of the Turk's hold on Ochakov.

The British naval officers in Catherine's service reacted immediately to rumors of her invitation to Jones to serve in her fleet. The British officers united in a letter of protest to Catherine, citing their low opinion of Jones's character and threatening to resign their commissions if Jones became an admiral in their adopted navy. Jones might have had a reputation as an exceptional combat leader, but he was still struggling for acceptance as a member of the global fraternity of professional naval officers. Fortunately for Jones, Sir Samuel Grieg, the senior British admiral in Catherine's naval service, quashed the letter. None of the British officers were involved in the Liman campaign anyway.

Jones's journey to his initial meeting with Catherine in Saint Petersburg was a major challenge that he overcame with typical determination. He started in mid-April 1788 from Copenhagen and proceeded to a small port north of Stockholm. From there he planned to cross the lower Gulf of Bothnia in a packet boat to Finland. Unfortunately that route was blocked by ice. Undaunted, Jones chartered an open 30-foot boat with a local Swedish crew and a smaller tender for an alternative plan. His intention was to sail southward along the coast of Sweden and then around the ice and into the Gulf of Finland. After a day's voyage south, Jones forced the boat's crew at gunpoint to leave the coast and turn east. Finally, after four days and the loss of the tender, the group landed at Revel, now known as Tallinn, on the coast of Estonia. Jones described his unlikely voyage in a letter to his friend the Marquis de Lafayette. In a mildly boastful way, Jones was touting his skills as a seaman: "After about four or five hundred miles of navigation, I landed at Reval, and having paid the [Swedish] peasants to their satisfaction, I gave them a good pilot, with some provision, to reconduct them to their home. My voyage was looked upon as a kind of miracle, being what never had been attempted before, unless in large vessels."[2]

The same letter described how Catherine received him at their first meeting on 6 May with distinction that would not normally be accorded a foreigner at her court. He pointed out that her reception included his appointment as a rear admiral in the Imperial Russian Navy. It had required going almost halfway around the world from America, and his commission as a flag officer was in a foreign navy that was headed by an autocrat, but Jones finally had the title and accompanying status of an admiral.

In return for the empress's warm welcome, Jones presented Catherine with a copy of the U.S. Constitution, which she said, with surprising prescience, would "influence every other government." According to Jones, the British in Saint Petersburg generated the only discordant notes associated with his welcome at the Russian court. He dismissed their reaction to his arrival, however, with the claim that "their vexation, which, I believe, was general, in and about St. Petersburg, gave me no pain." In fact, it's probable that the irritation he was causing the British officers in Saint Petersburg would have given Jones more than a little pleasure.

Less overt, but more dangerous than the animosity of Catherine's British naval officers, was the undercurrent of court intrigue and backbiting that was triggered by Jones's visit and appointment as rear admiral. The Prince de Ligne, a confidant of Potemkin, wrote caustically to Emperor Joseph II of Austria about Jones's new assignment: "The jealousy felt here at seeing a volunteer . . . in charge of all this is extreme, and will increase when it becomes known that Potemkin has persuaded the Empress to take Paul Jones into the service of Russia. . . . He will arrive here next week; an excellent acquisition, so they say. We shall see; but I think him only a corsair."[3]

Within a month of Jones's first meeting with Catherine he was on his way to the Liman of the Dnieper. Catherine left it to Potemkin to determine how Jones would be employed. And Potemkin, who had received Jones with civility, explained to him that initially he had planned to place him in command of the Russian fleet at Sevastopol, but because of a change in circumstances in that theater, he was instead placing him in command of the fleet in the Liman. To smooth Jones's way into his new command, Potemkin appointed one of his own staff officers, a Spaniard named Don José de Ribas, to accompany Jones to the Liman.

Notwithstanding his outward spirit of cooperation, Potemkin placed Jones in another situation with unclear lines of authority. Whether Potemkin did this deliberately or out of incompetence is not known. It is quite possible that Potemkin was jealous of the enthusiasm shown by Catherine for the employment of Jones, particularly for a mission against the Turks in which he had failed. Whatever his motivation, Potemkin's positioning of Jones was reminiscent of Chaumont's handiwork before Jones departed from Lorient in *Bonhomme Richard* in 1779. Only now the stakes were much higher because command of a fleet, not a squadron, was involved.

One of Jones's first command problems was with another Russian rear admiral, the German-French Prince of Nassau-Siegen. Nassau-Siegen was an adventurer who was in command of the oared small craft—referred to as the flotilla—in the Russian naval force at the Liman. He had earned his military reputation as an army officer, and he had no successful experience in naval actions. In fact, when he met Jones every naval operation with which he had been associated had failed. But he was a friend and confidant of Potemkin. And despite Jones being commander in chief of the Russian fleet at the Liman, Nassau-Siegen looked to Potemkin for his orders, rather than to the American Jones. This turned out to be a fatal flaw in command and control, since Jones's fleet and the Russian flotilla were required to operate in close coordination.

After Jones's deployment in *Bonhomme Richard,* he had been emphatic about never accepting command in another situation where his authority was not clear. Yet that is exactly what he was doing at the Liman. Clearly, the lure of admiral's stars and the opportunity to prove himself in command of a fleet were too powerful for him to resist.

Another early problem was with the Russian rear admiral Count Nicholas Mordvinov, the British-trained commander of the naval base at Kherson. Kherson was located on the Dnieper about eighteen miles from the Liman, and it was a major support base for the operations with which Jones would be involved. Mordvinov had fought the Turks in the first battle for Ochakov in 1787, and he was openly contemptuous of his American counterpart when Jones arrived at Kherson. He refused to provide either the situation briefing for Jones ordered by Potemkin or the admiral's flag that would have been flown by the naval commander in the Liman theater.

Finally, when Jones arrived in the Liman in his flagship, the Russian *Vladimir,* he had an emotional confrontation with the ship's captain, Brigadier Panaiotti Alexiano. Alexiano, a Greek serving in the Russian Navy, had anticipated receiving the command that Catherine and Potemkin had assigned to Jones, and he greeted his new commander in chief with a threat to resign because of his perceived ill treatment. And he threatened to take *Vladimir*'s officers with him.

Jones was facing two huge problems relating to the people around him. The first was the questionable professional military abilities of Potemkin,

Nassau-Siegen, and others with whom he would have to work. The second and more serious problem was loyalty. It was clear that those senior or comparable in rank to Jones had no loyalty to him and evident that the loyalty of those he was to command was questionable.

It appeared, however, that Jones was determined to take a positive approach to the circumstances. Perhaps he was paralleling the attitude Vice Admiral Horatio Nelson would sum up concisely in 1805, when he joined the British Navy's Mediterranean fleet: "I am not come forth to find difficulties, but to remove them."[4] In hindsight, Jones's positive approach helped him to get on with the job initially. In the long run, however, it cost him dearly in terms of how his performance in the Russian Navy would be perceived following two separate battles of the Liman.

Just as when he served in *Bonhomme Richard,* Jones was faced with a rare professional opportunity that was compromised by a dangerously unclear command situation. And the risk to Jones in that circumstance was compounded by the fact that he was facing the tough and experienced Turkish Admiral Hassan el Ghazi—often referred to as Captain Pasha—who had led the Turks in the first battle for Ochakov in 1787.

If the circumstances of Jones's command authority were less than ideal, his tactical environment at the Liman was even worse. To begin with, he was operating in a restricted littoral area with which he was totally unfamiliar, and there appeared to be little intelligence to mitigate that circumstance. In addition, because Jones's fleet was to support Potemkin's army as it tried to take the Ochakov Fort, Jones was involved in a major joint army-navy operation. That latter factor complicated his tactical situation exponentially.

The tactical situation that Jones faced would have been daunting even for an experienced admiral. Jones, however, had no prior experience as a fleet commander; all of his knowledge of major fleet operations was theoretical. And because he had entered the Continental Navy as a senior lieutenant, rather than as a young midshipman, he did not even have the firsthand grounding in fleet operations that a young officer would normally absorb in the British, French, Spanish, or other major navies of the time.

Perhaps the most challenging tactical factor for Jones was the Liman itself. The estuary extended on a nearly east-west axis from a fleet anchorage at Shirokaya, where the Dnieper River flowed in at the eastern end, to the opening to the Black Sea, which was thirty miles to the west. At the western end on the north bank, the Turkish fort at Ochakov dominated the short and narrow exit to the sea. On the tip of a peninsula that formed the southern edge of the Liman was a Russian installation, Fort Kinburn. The fort was almost directly opposite and to the south of Ochakov and was the headquarters of General Aleksandr Suvorov. One of the first joint army-navy actions of the campaign was the installation of two Russian gun batteries on a sand spit adjacent to Fort Kinburn, a suggestion made by Jones and agreed to by Suvorov.

At its widest, the Liman was approximately eight miles across, and toward the middle it narrowed to a width of about five miles. Its average depth was eighteen feet, and mud and sand banks rimmed the shores. Potemkin's future army headquarters for surrounding the Turkish fort at Ochakov was located just a short distance to the northeast of the fort, on the north shore. Farther to the east and roughly four miles from Ochakov was the narrow point where Jones would deploy his fleet at anchor in the campaign's opening phase. Just a short distance still farther to the east was the mouth of the Bug River, which Potemkin would have to cross to attack Ochakov.

The shallow and restricted waters of the Liman bore no resemblance to the areas in which Jones had operated in a single ship or as the commodore of a small squadron. The raid on New Providence, his commerce raiding off the northeast coast of the American colonies, the commerce raiding around the British Isles, and the battle off Flamborough Head were all blue-water operations. Even his operations in the Irish Sea, including the single-ship action between *Ranger* and *Drake,* involved considerable maneuvering room. The operational and combat experience that he had in the waters off the Atlantic coast of the American colonies and the waters surrounding the British Isles contrasted profoundly with what he faced in the Liman. Theory and basic combat instincts would have to carry the day for Jones, and he could not expect any helpful input from Nassau-Siegen or Alexiano, both of whom would have been happy to see Jones fail.

The precise order of battle is difficult to sort out from the varying reports. The Russian naval forces and the Turkish naval forces each had two basic elements. One element was the relatively few deep-draft ships that included three-masted ships of the line and frigates, along with some two-masted brigs and other smaller ships. These ships provided the heavy guns of the force. Jones's flagship *Vladimir,* designed to mount sixty-six guns, actually carried only twenty-four, reducing it from a ship of the line in terms of firepower to the equivalent of a small frigate. The second element in the naval forces was comprised of a flotilla of scores of smaller, shallow-draft, and mostly oared boats. The flotilla acted as a mobile naval strike force. The Russian and Turkish forces had a measure of asymmetry in that the Turks had more deep-draft ships, and the Russians had more shallow-draft boats.

Jones uncharacteristically—but wisely—chose to fight his squadron from a defensive position and at anchor, demonstrating an ability to shape his tactics to the situation. His squadron became in effect a line of fixed gun batteries. He anchored his ships across the narrow point of the Liman, just to the west of the mouth of the Bug River. In this restricted area, the superior Russian flotilla could be employed to advantage against the weaker Turkish flotilla. Plus the more numerous Turkish fleet, restricted by the narrow and shallow point Jones picked to defend, would find it difficult to bring its superior numbers to bear against the Russian fleet. In addition, in the position Jones chose, he was able to prevent the Turkish forces from taking control of the lower Bug River. Potemkin's army would have to cross that area to get to Ochakov, and Jones's defensive position would help protect the army's path. Jones was inviting Hassan el Ghazi into a bottleneck where the tactical advantage would reside with the Russians.

Despite the fact that he considered himself under the direct command of Potemkin and not Jones, Nassau-Siegen agreed to Jones's plan, and on 30 May 1788, Jones wrote to Potemkin to establish a beginning point for his actions. In his report, Jones wrote, "I have the honor to send your Highness herewith the report on the present strength of Her Imperial Majesty's Squadron in the Liman of which I have taken Command at Your Orders. I have sent a Copy of this report to the Admiralty at Kherson and to the General and Chevalier de Suvorov. . . . To-day, with the prince of Nassau, I expect to take the strongest position possible, opposite the first Village to the east of the Bug."[5]

As events turned out, Jones finally selected a position just to the west of the mouth of the Bug River, and by 16 June, the Russian forces were in position. Then, several hours after midnight on 17 June, Hassan el Ghazi accepted Jones's invitation to battle by advancing his flotilla past Ochakov and into the Liman. The first battle of the Liman had begun. Nassau-Siegen attempted to get elements of his flotilla behind the Turkish units that had moved into the estuary, but he was driven back to the original Russian defense line.

Hassan el Ghazi then made a major attack on the morning of 18 June with most of his flotilla and some of his fleet against the Russian line, first attacking the right flank of the Russian position. Jones anticipated the sequence of events, and he adjusted his line by being rowed in a cutter through the Russian force during the action. As he moved through the Russian fleet, with cannon fire thundering and flashing and the smoke of battle swirling around him as he shouted his orders, Jones presented an unusual picture of a fleet commander. But it was the only way he could communicate with individual units in a fleet that had no practical system of tactical communication. As it turned out, Jones's one-on-one command and control solution was a crucial factor in the eventual turn of events. And it was the kind of pragmatic adjustment to difficult circumstances that had marked the combat successes of Jones and his fellow Continental Navy captains.

As the battle developed, Jones was able—with help from a fortuitous wind shift—to move units on the left flank of his line forward. With that maneuver, he put the Turkish forces in a withering crossfire. Hassan el Ghazi realized he was in the jaws of a trap, and after losing three boats in the action, he withdrew. Round one went to Jones and the Russians.

Before the action, Jones had extended himself to inform Potemkin of his plans and immediately after the action, he again reported to Potemkin, making a special effort to give credit to Nassau-Siegen and Alexiano. In his report, Jones wrote,

> At eight o'clock, when the Prince of Nassau and I were in a Cutter, looking over our position and reconnoitering a little closer to our enemy, their Flotilla began to fire on us very vigorously. At the same time the first division of their Flotilla advanced along Shore and attacked our reserve, stationed between our ships and the Coast. We took their fire for some time without response, but, seeing the engagement was growing serious, I did my best to help the Prince make the necessary manoeuvres. Then I hurried along the line to bring up all the Batteries and other boats of the Flotilla . . . the Turks, on their part, had brought up the second division of their Flotilla, and I hoped for some time that this would be a decisive battle; but the arrival of our Second division on the Battle-line put the Turks to rout and, with the wind against Us, we pursued them as far as their Squadron. . . . The Prince showed great coolness and intelligence. . . . Mr. Alexiano came in another Cutter and helped us preserve good Order. I saw the Turks lose two Boats (others say three), which blew up. . . . I was greatly pleased by the conduct of the officers; they were brave and orderly; and I do not think the Captain Pasha, who commanded in person, will eat his dinner with pleasure.[6]

Jones's positive approach to the difficult command situation had paid important short-term dividends. The Turks had not been able to establish any control beyond Ochakov, the Russian force had stood up well in combat, and both the Russian squadron and flotilla were still fully effective fighting units.

On 27 June, Hassan el Ghazi mounted another attack, and the second battle of the Liman was on. This time there was nothing cautious about Captain Pasha's tactics. With a favorable southwest wind filling his sails, he blew in from the Black Sea and through the entrance to the Liman with everything he had in his command and with trumpets blaring, cymbals clanging, and shouts for Allah's help echoing through his fleet. Jones and the rest of the Russian force were deployed as before, waiting to chew up the Turkish units in close combat. Then fate intervened—at 2 PM, slightly more than a mile from the Russian line, Hassan el Ghazi ran aground. The Turkish ships anchored where they were at the time of Captain Pasha's grounding with the intention of regrouping.

Nassau-Siegen wanted to attack at once. Jones was reluctant to give up his advantageous position, and it turned out that his judgment was correct. The wind veered to the northwest, which made it virtually impossible for a Russian attack to be sustained. During the lull, Jones once again began reconnoitering, this time in a very small boat, rowed by a single Cossack sailor named Ivak. At one point they worked in among the Turkish ships. According to the Cossack, after having used a ruse to get the countersign for the Turkish boats moving among their own fleet, Jones chalked his calling card on the stern of one of the largest Turkish ships. At daylight it was there to be read by all within sight: "To be burned. Paul Jones." It was a dangerous and theatrical move, exactly the kind of action that could inspire confidence in a leader in a battle situation.

In the short time he spent with Jones, Ivak formed an opinion of his admiral that is instructive. Years after the battle of the Liman, Ivak described his impression of his American commander in chief: "I have never seen such a person, sweet like a vine when he wished, but when necessary, like a rock. . . . One movement of his hand you obey like a commanding voice. It seems that some people are created to command."[7]

At about 2 AM, the Turkish flagship was free, and two hours later a general melee between the two forces began. Poor Turkish intelligence and seamanship helped the Russians again, because this time both the Turkish flagship and the ship of the fleet's second in command ran aground on a small sand spit projecting from the north shore of the Liman. Nassau-Siegen and his entire flotilla pounced on the stranded ships. In the process, however, they passed up an opportunity to capture two important prizes and instead burned the grounded ships to the waterline.

Nassau-Siegen's concentration on the two grounded Turkish ships left Jones's squadron open to attack from the Turkish flotilla, and one of the Russian frigates was sunk. After failing to get the needed support from Nassau-Siegen, Jones eventually got one of the Prince's subordinates to gather enough of the Russian flotilla to join Jones's fleet and drive the Turkish fleet back to the entrance of the Liman. At that point the batteries that Jones and General Suvorov had set up began pounding the Turks, and nine of Hassan el Ghazi's ships were driven aground. On the morning of 29 June, Suvorov requested that Jones destroy the grounded ships, but Nassau-Siegen flew into a rage and insisted that was a job for his flotilla. In the end, the Prince was the one who finished off the stranded Turkish units. He burned seven and captured only the remaining two, once again rejecting an opportunity to take valuable prizes.

During the two days of the second battle of the Liman, the Turks lost ten ships and five boats; additionally,the Russians took 1,673 Turkish prisoners and approximately 3,000 Turks were killed. The Russians lost one ship and had 67 wounded and 18 killed. The second and final round went to Jones and the Russians, this time by a wide margin.

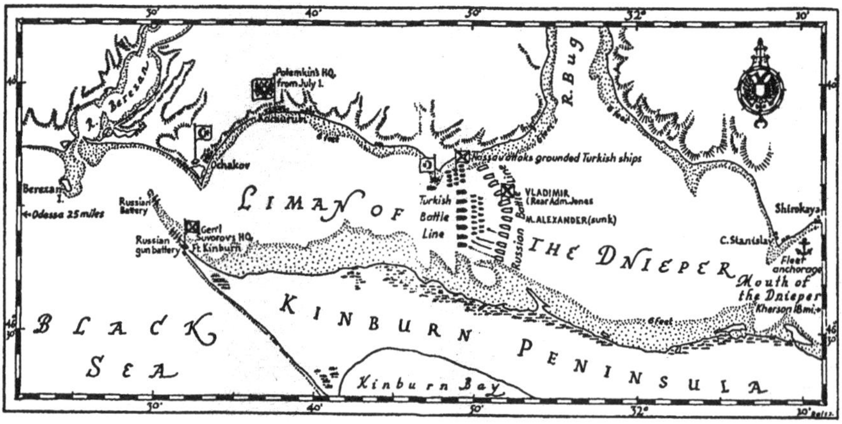

Second Battle of the Liman. This battle diagram shows the situation at four o'clock in the morning on 27 June 1788, when the Second Battle of the Liman began. Jones positioned his forces to take full tactical advantage of the restricted maneuvering room and shallow waters of the estuary. (Note: Turkish ships are solid black; Russian ships are outlined.)

From the author's collection, with special permission of Raisz Landform Maps

The two battles of the Liman would turn out to be Jones's only opportunity to command a fleet. And his leadership, under extremely difficult circumstances, can fairly be said to have been successful both tactically and strategically. The net result of Jones's leadership was that the Turkish effort to control the Liman was defeated, Potemkin was able to move his army into position to neutralize and eventually capture Fort Ochakov, and the initial strategic objectives for Jones's assignment from Catherine were met. Evidence that Jones never lost sight of the strategic basis of his assignment in the Liman is clear, not only from his actions during the two battles but from his official dispatches as well. On 24 June, for example, he wrote to Nassau-Siegen, who wanted to advance the position of the Russian flotilla after the first battle of the Liman. Jones argued from a strategic point of view: "We are in a good position here to protect the disembarkation of the Artillery destined for the siege of Ochakov, an Objective to Us more important than the benefits you seek in advancing three Versts (approximately two miles)—Benefits which We do not look upon from the same point of view."[8]

In not-so-subtle language, Jones was pointing out to his overeager colleague the importance of seeing the broad strategic picture while enveloped in the exigencies of battle. He also was demonstrating his understanding of the importance of building cooperation among combat commanders in a situation without clear lines of authority. In the latter instance, Jones's willingness to work around the flaws in his command authority demonstrated that he not only had the ability to win in single-ship combat at sea, he also had the skill and temperament to win in command of a fleet. He had passed his first and only test as a fighting admiral.

In the next battle—the one for credit for the Russian victories at the Liman—Jones did not come off well, in contrast to his military accomplishments. He was outmaneuvered by Potemkin and Nassau-Siegen, both of whom made up for their modest military skills with superior abilities in political infighting. As is often the case in military victories, the lion's share of the credit did not go to the leader who contributed the most to the victory.

In the follow-up actions to the two battles of the Liman, Potemkin laid siege to Ochakov, and Jones continued to work tirelessly and courageously, frequently involving himself with the flotilla's dangerous boat actions. Nassau-Siegen went off at the end of July for an inspection tour of the Russian base at Sevastopol and returned in early August as a vice admiral. The writing on the wall became clear to Jones when Potemkin offered him command of the

Sevastopol fleet, which was badly organized and in poor material condition. Jones declined Potemkin's offer and instead chose to carry out Potemkin's previous order for a naval attack on Fort Ochakov with the fleet he already commanded.

The initial assault on Ochakov went badly when a Greek lieutenant in the flotilla compromised the surprise that was essential for the mission's success. Jones then established a blockade of the fort, but operations in the Liman continued to be plagued by contrary weather, poorly timed orders from Potemkin, and general operational foul-ups. Potemkin increasingly micromanaged Jones's command and their correspondence reflected a steady deterioration in the relationship. Jones's dispatches began to be permeated with phrases such as: "impossible to execute my Orders," "Our enterprise of last evening did not succeed," "Luck was not with us last evening," and "it would make it difficult, perhaps impossible."

Then on 29 October, Potemkin sent a strangely vague and particularly offensive order to Jones: "I request your excellency, the captain pacha having actually a greater number of vessels, to hold yourself in readiness to receive him courageously, and drive him back. I require that this be done without the loss of time; if not, you will be made answerable for every neglect."[9]

In his vigorous response to his commander's insulting message, Jones went on the verbal offensive: "I am not here in the least as an Adventurer, nor as a Mountebank, to repair a ruined Fortune, I hope in the future to suffer no humiliation and soon to be in the Position which was promised me when I was invited to enter Her Imperial Majesty's Navy." With that unvarnished rebuke of Potemkin, his assertion that he had been promised total command in the Liman campaign, and his thinly veiled reference to the motivation of officers such as Nassau-Siegen, Jones surely had gone too far. From Potemkin's point of view, Jones would have to be discredited and eliminated, and Potemkin and Nassau-Siegen were well suited by nature and court experience to trigger the process.

In September 1788, during the period following the battles of the Liman, Jones's staunch supporter Chevalier Lewis Littlepage wrote a good-bye note to his friend. Littlepage had just resigned his commission while serving under Nassau-Siegen in the Liman. Although Littlepage was among those who had originally urged Jones to accept Catherine's invitation to serve in the Russian Navy, by the time he was writing to Jones, he was fed up with Nassau-Siegen's posturing and inept leadership. The note throws light on the professional environment in which Jones found himself at the time: "Adieu, my dear admiral, take care of yourself, and be cautious in whom you trust. Remember you have to sustain here a political as well as military character."[10]

Jones's basically mercurial personality and sense of his own professionalism were, however, no match for the opposition in this contest where subtlety and deviousness were the major weapons. And it would be impossible for him to save his "political as well as military character." Three years later, in 1791, Littlepage, who knew Russian and other European courts well, summarized the case for Jones in a letter to then-secretary of state Thomas Jefferson. He also mentioned his regret that he and Jefferson had influenced Jones to accept Catherine's offer of a commission in the Russian Navy:

> You will share my regret in reflecting that we were the principal means of engaging Admiral Sir John Paul Jones to accept the propositions made to him in 1788 by the Russian Court. Never were more brilliant prospects held forth to an individual and never an individual better calculated to attain them. The campaign upon the Liman added lustre to the arms of Russia, and ought to have established forever the reputation and the fortune of the gallant officer to whose conduct those successes were owing, but unfortunately in Russia more perhaps than elsewhere, everything is governed by intrigue. Some political motives *I have reason to think* concurred in depriving Admiral Paul Jones of the fruit of his services. He was thought to be particularly obnoxious to the English nation, and the idea of paying a servile compliment to a power whose enmity occasioned all the present embarrassments of Russia, induced some leading persons to ruin him in the opinion of the empress by an accusation too ridiculous.[11]

As Littlepage intimated in his good-bye note, Jones did indeed have much to worry about, and although he was a tough combat leader, Jones was no political match for the courtiers he was facing. Potemkin and Nassau-Siegen immediately began claiming that both of the victories should be credited to their courage and military brilliance. Catherine's conspicuously lavish military and financial rewards to Potemkin, Nassau-Siegen, and others contrasted with the lower-level military award—and lack of an immediate promotion—for Jones. Many in Saint Petersburg and other European capitals viewed Catherine's choice of who to reward as confirmation of the Potemkin version of the battles.

On the other hand, Russian captains in Jones's squadron officially authenticated Jones's *Narrative of the Campaign of the Liman* by signing a statement verifying that they had heard a Russian translation of the statements in the narrative and "found nothing in them contrary to the truth." The fact that those captains were combatants in the actual events adds weight to their testimony, and their support bolsters the conclusion that Jones exhibited superior leadership under difficult circumstances at the Liman.

When other assessments are added, including some by commentators who were presumably not biased in Jones's favor, the balance clearly tips even more in his direction. For example, in his preface to a survey of the Turkish Empire, written at the end of the eighteenth century, British historian W. Eaton assessed the official Russian record of the campaign: "The whole campaign, as it stands on [Potemkin's and Nassau-Siegen's] record, is nearly a romance."[12]

Perhaps the biggest loser in the political intrigue led by Potemkin and Nassau-Siegen was Catherine. The Turkish military hold on Ochakov had been eliminated, the use of the Dnieper and the Bug Rivers by Russia for military and commercial purposes was secured, and the sea-lane to Constantinople was open. With a strong naval force, Jones could have taken the next step south. But Catherine chose to accept the influence of her lover. When she turned her back on Jones, she missed what might well have been Russia's last best hope of getting to Constantinople and the Russian dream of direct access to the Mediterranean.

In October 1788, Potemkin relieved Jones of his Liman command, claiming that Catherine had an assignment for him in her Baltic fleet, and he replaced Jones with Rear Admiral Mordvinov. Interestingly, Mordvinov refused to accept the assignment in the Liman unless he had command of both the squadron of ships and the flotilla of boats. Jones departed from the Liman on 9 November, and after three days in an open boat, he came down with pneumonia. The aftermath of the illness would carry over to Jones's eventual return to Paris. As a result of the pneumonia, he spent the balance of November recovering in Kherson, before resuming his journey to Saint Petersburg.

Once back in Saint Petersburg in December, Jones began writing proposals for much-needed reorganization of the Russian Navy, and he even wrote a recommendation for a commercial treaty between Russia and the United States. He also wrote his *Narrative of the Campaign of the Liman.* But his effort did him little immediate good. His enemies had succeeded in distorting his accomplishments during the battles of the Liman, and he had lost favor at court. In truth, Catherine was convinced that he was of no further use to her, and she was no doubt pleased to not have to deal with ongoing tensions between Potemkin and Jones.

The most damaging attack to Jones's reputation after his return to Saint Petersburg was an accusation that he had raped a girl after he returned to that city. The situation had the clear appearance of a crude but effective frame-up. The girl's mother made the charge of rape, but subsequently admitted that she had been induced to make the charge by an unnamed, uniformed person who paid her for initiating the charge. In addition, both the accuser's husband, who claimed that his wife had deserted him for a younger man, and the churchman to whom the mother complained of the alleged event, questioned the motivation of Jones's accuser. The girl was, in all probability, a prostitute whose services Jones had employed. Jones already had a reputation as a womanizer, and his detractors very effectively used that as the weak point at which to attack his character. Once again his reputation with women was used against him.

Jones's most effective defender was French minister plenipotentiary in Saint Petersburg, Count de Ségur, who was unequivocal in his defense of Jones and who wrote effective exculpatory letters on his behalf. Among the most powerful of his letters was one written to fellow diplomats. The letter refuting the charge of rape against Jones appeared in newspapers in many of European capitals. The count was blunt:

> His Enemies and his rivals have profited by his momentary disgrace to hasten his destruction. Calumny has served their purposes, they have given credit to reports absolutely false—they have accused him of violating a girl. The empress being deceived has forbid him the court, and wished to bring him to trial. Every person has abandoned him, I alone have upheld and defended him. . . . My cares have not been in vain, I have caused his innocence to be acknowledged.[13]

De Ségur caused a condensed version of his letter to be distributed as an "Article to be inserted in the Public Prints, and particularly in the Gazette of France," and the scandal mill in Saint Petersburg ground to a halt. Clearly, however, Jones was wasting his time there. The empress continued to act as if she had been deeply offended by his alleged behavior. And she conferred the command of her Baltic fleet on, of all people, Nassau-Siegen! The political process had run its course; the innocent had been punished and the guilty rewarded. In 1789 Jones was placed on extended leave of two years from the Russian Navy and allowed to retain his rank and a modest pension for his services.

Jones left Saint Petersburg for Warsaw in September 1789. He was undoubtedly deeply wounded and angered by how the empress had treated him. In all likelihood, one of the most positive things he took away from his service in Catherine's navy was his memory of the loyalty and combat performance of his Russian captains during the combat in the Liman. That very positive memory and his own assessment of his performance as a fleet commander would have to be enough for Jones—along with his rank of rear admiral, of course.

12
Yesterday's Hero

"They bore within their breasts the grief
That fame can never heal—
The deep, unutterable woe
Which none save exiles feel."
William Edmondstoune Aytoun

On 2 November 1789, Jones left Warsaw and traveled to Alsace, where he stayed with friends for several weeks. Then, in early December he moved on to Amsterdam, and from there he traveled to London. He arrived there in April 1790, and by May, he was back in Paris. For the next several months Jones meandered through Europe, with no clear direction to his travels, either literally or figuratively.

As he traveled, he doggedly wrote to the Empress Catherine and others with influence in the Russian court, including even Potemkin, attempting to rehabilitate himself with the empress and precipitate his recall to service in the Russian Navy. His persistence in the face of the empress's clear rejection was yet another expression of the incredibly stubborn quality of his personality. Jones also communicated with various European diplomats, such as the French minister in Copenhagen, Baron de la Houze, to counter the personally damaging reports coming from Potemkin, Nassau-Siegen, and others in the Russian court. From Houze he received unequivocal support and an assurance that Count de Ségur's published letter on behalf of Jones had "destroyed all the venomous effects which calumny had employed to tarnish the distinguished reputation which you have acquired by your talents and your valor." From many others, such as the Russian minister at Copenhagen, Baron Krudiner, the reactions to Jones's letters were less reassuring.

At one point during this period, Jones toyed with the possibility of joining the Swedish Navy. But negotiating such an assignment presented a particular problem: Sweden was an enemy of Russia at the time, and Jones was still technically an officer in the Russian Navy. To skirt the problem, he insisted that the initiative would have to be perceived as coming from Sweden, rather than from him. In Warsaw, he met one of the European heroes of the American

Revolution, General Tadeusz Kosciuszko, and the general and Jones had a brief exchange of correspondence on the subject of a Swedish naval commission.

Had Jones received a commission in the Swedish Navy, it could have resulted in his leading a fleet against Russia's Baltic fleet, which by then was led by Nassau-Siegen. If there were problems involved with a Swedish commission, the prospect of such a confrontation would, no doubt, have greatly multiplied the appeal for Jones of pursuing such a commission nonetheless. The U.S. envoy in Europe, Gouverneur Morris, joined General Kosciuszko as an intermediary in the delicate process, but an actual offer of a Swedish commission for Jones never materialized.

In December 1789, Jones also wrote to his friend, then-secretary of Congress Charles Thomson, mentioning the idea of returning to America. In his letter he asked about the possibility of purchasing a small farm in Lancaster, Pennsylvania, reprising his hope of many years earlier to retire to a rural estate where he could spend his time in quiet contemplation. Writing to his business associate, John Ross, he also mentioned perhaps returning to a quiet life in retirement in the United States at the end of the coming summer.

In other samples of his correspondence he seemed to be preparing his way for that return. In late December, he wrote to Benjamin Franklin about "the danger to which I was exposed by the dark intrigues and mean subterfuges of Asiatic jealousy and malice." And the letter included three enclosures "for my justification in the eyes of my friends in America, whose good opinion is dearer to me than anything else." A week before, in a flattering letter to newly elected President George Washington, he mentioned his mission to Denmark and pointed out how his diplomatic efforts would have better prospects for success if the United States had a navy to back up all of its diplomatic negotiations in Europe.

In those letters he clearly was reminding his two politically powerful friends of his availability for an appropriate assignment, particularly if Congress saw fit to establish a U.S. Navy. His efforts bore no immediate fruit, however. Franklin died within months, and Washington was fully occupied with establishing his own position as the first president of the United States.

Jones's mood as he zigzagged away from his Russian assignment toward an uncertain future was marked by a sense of purposelessness, concerns about money, and a bit of self-mockery. All three of those qualities were reflected in a portion of a letter he wrote in December to John Parish, a merchant in Hamburg: "I am for the present the master of my time, I shall perhaps make you a visit in the spring, and pay my court to some of your kind, rich, old ladies. To be serious, I must stay in Europe till it is seen what changes the present politics will produce, and I can hear from America; and if you think I can pass my time quietly, agreeably, at a small expense at Hamburgh, I should prefer it to the fluctuating prospects of other places."[1]

Jones's last stop before returning to Paris was London, and when he landed in April, it was at Harwich, along the North Sea coast of England. It was an area that he had alarmed as a raider, and he received a rude welcome. In fact, he barely escaped being killed by an angry mob. In all likelihood, inflamed accounts of his alleged rape in Saint Petersburg had been added to the simmering resentment of his raids along the coasts of the British Isles and his victory off Flamborough Head. Although a decade had passed since his attacks against the British homeland, his image among the British as a pirate and a cutthroat had not faded. And the fact that he arrived in the Harwich customs house in his Russian admiral's uniform did not help.

Jones slipped away from the Harwich mob, once again eluding lethal danger on the coast of Britain. In London, Jones met with Gouverneur Morris on financial matters. Then, by May 1790 he was back in Paris, where he would spend the remaining days of his life in failing health and residing at a modest but pleasant apartment at 52 Rue de Tournon. It was a time when the winds of revolution were building in Paris, and the unrest complicated Jones's dealings with the French government.

For the most part, Jones appeared to keep bitterness and negative feelings in check. They did surface, however, during an attempt to secure past-due pay from the French government for the crew of *Bonhomme Richard,* including his personal claim for 7,000 livres. Jones pursued the claim with a letter to French Minister of Marine Bertrand de Moleville.

The response from de Moleville to his initiative was insulting to the extreme. The minister clearly was acting on the belief that Jones had virtually no real leverage in the situation. And based on the end of the American Revolution and the onset of the French Revolution, the minister was right. At this point, Jones's country no longer needed him and the French court had become irrelevant in diplomatic matters. Not even Jones's friendship with Jefferson or his connection with French king Louis XVI provided any bargaining leverage. As a result the minister simply deflected Jones's claim and asked for a detailed accounting of the monies that Jones had laid out on behalf of his crew. The request for an accounting was an administrative smoke screen, put forth with a high degree of bureaucratic arrogance. The minister pompously pointed out, for example, "I have the honour, Sir, of observing to you, that it is the settled custom to pay to seamen the balance of wages accruing to them, on discharging the vessel."[2] Such language from a pompous bureaucrat would have been hard for Jones to take.

Jones answered the new minister of marine in March 1792. His response was not so much a detailed accounting for his claim as an indignant defense of his honor. Early in his response, he stated that his personal and financial losses while serving his country and the interests of France amounted to "a large sum and have greatly lessened my fortune." He went on to describe the tone of the minister's letter as uncivil and having cast doubt on his past conduct. But the exchange had virtually no meaning; by this time, Jones's influence and health were in steep decline, and within months, he would die.

On a more positive note during his final years in Paris, Jones was also thinking about family matters. He wrote to his sister Janet Taylor in March 1790, expressing his regard for his sisters and saying that he was eager to know about the "talents, character, and education" of their children. He went on in the letter to provide—in some detail—his opinions about how the children should be educated, making a clear distinction between the educational requirements for boys and those for girls. He regretted that he could not offer much financially but wanted to be helpful in getting them established in their lives.

Several months later, in December, Jones wrote to his sister Janet again. This time he had a specific concern: His sisters were not on good terms with one another. His attempt at family peacemaking was gentle, pointing out that he had no intention of forcing a reconciliation, adding that it "must come free from your heart, otherwise it will not last, and therefore it will be better not to attempt it." This brotherly letter from Jones shows a side of his personality that has received little attention. In this letter Jones also alluded to his increasingly poor health.

The state of his personal finances was one of the ongoing and most troublesome problems Jones faced during the last years of his life. When he returned to Paris in the spring of 1790, his marginal finances continued to occupy a lot of his attention. To mitigate his financial stress, he attempted to take up Denmark's offer from spring 1788 to pay him a pension. Jones sought the advice of Gouverneur Morris and William Short, U.S. chargé d'affaires in Paris, both of whom advised Jones that accepting the pension would not be improper. He then queried Jefferson as to the propriety of his accepting the pension from Denmark. Jefferson never responded to Jones's question. Not surprisingly, the Danish government never made a pension payment to Jones.

Edward Bancroft, Franklin's former secretary—and a British spy—was a contact Jones tried to use to alleviate his financial difficulties. It appears that Jones, who never learned of Bancroft's covert activities as a spy during the American Revolution, had advanced money to Bancroft. The money was for a venture involving the importation of quercitron, derived from the inner bark of the black oak, for producing yellow dye for the British wool industry. Jones had received half of the money due to him from the venture when he met with Bancroft in London in 1790. At the time, he wrote to his former friend expressing his deep disappointment with his behavior: "I just take the liberty to remind you of your breach of promise . . . you can be at no loss to raise the sum now due to me."[3] Jones never received the second half of the money, which was belatedly deposited by Bancroft in a London bank at about the same time as Jones's death. Nor did Jones gain any substantial income from his bank or land investments in the United States. In net, the life Jones resumed in Paris was financially limited. He was not quite in poverty, but he was close enough to it for money to be a constant worry.

Another ongoing worry for Jones when he returned to Paris was the lingering cloud hanging over his Russian service. In order to provide his own version of that assignment, he prepared a lengthy journal, with supporting documents that recounted his version of the campaign at the Liman.[4] A copy was sent to Catherine, but apparently she never bothered to read it. What was arguably Jones's central thought, a verbal shot aimed directly at the empress, Potemkin, and Nassau-Siegen, appears toward the end of the narrative of his Russian service:

> Since I am found too frank and too sincere to make my way at the court of Russia without creating powerful enemies, I have philosophy enough to withdraw into the peaceful bosom of friendship; but, as I love virtue better than reward, and as my greatest ambition is to preserve, even in the shades of retreat, the precious favor of the empress, I may tell her majesty, that even in the midst of my persecutions, my mind was occupied by plans for the essential advancement of her service. . . . I have the satisfaction of having done my duty in Russia, and that without any views of self-interest.[5]

Notwithstanding the blunt accusation of his journal, he wrote contrastingly flattering letters to Catherine and to Potemkin, in further efforts to reestablish his reputation in their eyes. He also wrote letters proposing sweeping plans for a naval strategy to be employed by Russia in the event of a war with Great Britain. Catherine never answered a single communication from Jones after he left the Liman. In her correspondence with others, however, she referred to him dismissively, making it clear that in her eyes he was no longer worthy of her attention. For example, she wrote scornfully to Baron Grimm, the Swiss-German diplomat whom Jones had first met years earlier during his peak of celebrity in Paris: "I have nothing to say to Paul Jones . . . he should be advised to go and attend his affairs in America. . . . I gave General Zubov the book on artillery from Paul Jones; I have not the time to read all the books sent me."[6]

But as the cloud over his service in Russia lingered, another cloud was dissipating—attitudes between Jones and a few of his former countrymen were softening. For example, Jones developed a friendly relationship with Scottish Fourth Earl of Wemyss David Lord Elcho. The earl was one of the strongest advocates for Jones with Catherine, and no doubt he had a positive influence on her decision to offer Jones a Russian Navy commission. As early as February 1785, Wemyss had written to a member of the Russian court, recommending Jones to the attention of the empress in terms extremely flattering to Jones, as an officer and a gentleman. Wemyss even suggested to his contact at court that Jones was sure to be named commander in chief of the American navy in the future.

A casual encounter during Jones's last years in Paris provided another glimpse of his steady reconciliation process with the British. Jones met Lord Daer, son of the Earl of Selkirk. According to Gouverneur Morris, Daer was pleased to find that Jones had continued to show concern about the "attack on his father's house [during the] last war." Daer also remarked that he thought Jones "a sensible little fellow" and not as "dark" as he anticipated. Jones's extravagant letter-writing efforts to justify his and his crews' actions at St. Mary's Isle in 1778 suggest strongly that the incident had continued to compromise his self-image as a professional naval officer. Jones welcomed the friendly exchange with Selkirk's son as a sign that the family harbored no deep malice toward him.

As Jones's social circle drew inward, one of the pleasant connections he maintained was with a Madame Clement and three of her lady friends who lived at Trevoux, near Lyons. In contrast with Jones's earlier relationships with women, which so often were saturated with sexual tension, this situation seemed to be based on friendship and companionship. The correspondence with the group, which he addressed at one point as "Dear and Amiable Ladies," showed a more subdued side of his personality. In February 1791, he wrote, apologizing for not having visited with the ladies, one of whom gently accused Jones of preferring love in Paris to friendship in Trevoux. And in his response, Jones made an interesting distinction between those two qualities. The former he described—with one hopes a smile—as "the cordial that Providence has bestowed on mortals to help them digest the nauseous draught of life." And the latter, he claimed, has "more solid qualities than love."

While Jones's celebrity as a naval hero faded, the esteem and friendship of one important person stood in contrast. Thomas Jefferson, who had become involved in Jones's personal life by assisting Madame Townsend and who had supported Jones being offered a commission in the Russian Navy, remained a staunch supporter and friend. He was one of the few people in the new U.S. government who maintained active contact with the hero of the battle between *Bonhomme Richard* and *Serapis,* and he reassured Jones, "No proof was necessary to satisfy us of your good conduct everywhere." Part of the glue for the relationship was that Jones and Jefferson were both concerned about the attacks on U.S. merchant ships by the Barbary states of North Africa, including Algiers, Morocco, Tripoli, and Tunis, and particularly troubled about the fate of U.S. merchant seamen imprisoned by the Dey of Algiers.

During the American Revolution, Jones continuously showed concern for the sailors of the Continental Navy held prisoner by the British. When he returned from his deployment in 1779 and his victory over *Serapis,* one of his primary efforts was to exchange the hundreds of British prisoners he had taken for Americans held by the British. It was totally consistent then that he would show concern for the U.S. merchant sailors who had been captured by the commerce raiders of the Muslim states of North Africa.

When the U.S. Congress disbanded the American navy after the Treaty of Paris of 1783, it was an open invitation for the Barbary raiders to prey on the unarmed U.S. merchant ships that were increasingly found in the Mediterranean. In its shortsightedness, Congress looked to other nations, including Portugal, to hold the Barbary raiders in check. There also were efforts to bribe potentates such as the Dey of Algiers, an imitation of a strategy employed by some European nations, including even Great Britain. Congress mistakenly thought that paying tribute would be cheaper than building and maintaining a navy. Congress did eventually fund the building of six frigates and the establishment of a U.S. Navy in March 1794. A short but violent naval war after Jones's death finally convinced the Barbary states that attacking U.S. merchant ships was not economically or politically profitable.

As the American Revolution drew to a close, Jones had proposed that a squadron be formed around the Continental ship *America* to show the flag in the Mediterranean and discourage depredations against American merchant ships.

The proposal was another reflection of his ongoing ability to see beyond his immediate career circumstances to larger issues of maritime power. Later, in a letter in July 1787 to John Jay, then–U.S. secretary of foreign affairs, he proposed a pragmatic, short-term solution to the problem of rescuing American prisoners held in Algeria. The letter dealt mostly with the issue of prize money, but in the last paragraph, Jones wrote eloquently about the plight of the prisoners, a significant number of whom had already died in captivity:

> I should act inconsistently if I omitted to mention the dreadful situation of our fellow-citizens in slavery at Algiers. Their almost hopeless fate is a deep reflection of our national character in Europe. I beg leave to influence the humanity of Congress in their behalf, and to propose that some expedient may be adopted for their redemption. A fund might be raised for that purpose, by a duty of a shilling per month from seamen's wages throughout the continent, and I am persuaded that no difficulty would be made to that requisition.[7]

Early in 1791, the prisoners of the Dey of Algiers were still on his mind. In a letter to William Carmichael, a U.S. diplomat in Madrid, Jones wrote, "Pray can you inform me if any thing efficacious is in agitation, for the relief of our unhappy countrymen at Algiers? Nothing provokes me so much, as the shameful neglect they have so long experienced."[8] By the time Jones was writing to Carmichael, only thirteen of the original twenty-one prisoners captured seven years earlier and held in Algiers were still alive.

Then in June 1792, President Washington took action, naming Jones as a special U.S. commissioner to negotiate the release of the Americans held in Algiers. In a parallel action, Jefferson also signed the executive order, authorizing Jones to ransom—for up to $27,000—the captives and arrange for a treaty in exchange for monetary payment of up to $25,000. Jones was also to be paid $2,000 for his services. It would have been a daunting assignment, particularly in light of the lack of any real negotiating leverage for Jones in the situation. It is unlikely that his inherent stubbornness and reputation as a warfighter would have carried the day. In any event, the timing of the message to Jones about his important new diplomatic assignment coincided with his death.

The most limiting factor of all during Jones's remaining years was clearly his physical health. The pneumonia he suffered immediately after the battles of the Liman broke his naturally tough constitution. The subject of deteriorating health emerges frequently in his correspondence. In late December 1790, he responded to an invitation from a lady friend in Avignon that he did not have "an hour of health" since his arrival in Paris and that his health was "an invincible obstacle" to his visiting her. Also in December, he wrote to his sister, Mrs. Taylor, apologizing for not responding to her letter and talking of "having been for the most part obliged to keep my bed." In December 1791 he wrote to the Marquis de Lafayette in a similar vein, complaining of being unable to write to him because of poor health.

Jones was suffering from both liver and kidney diseases, illnesses that are reflected in jaundice, headaches, low-grade fever, and high blood pressure. And all of those symptoms would have accelerated as the diseases progressed. He also had lesions on his lungs that made him susceptible to colds and bronchitis and no doubt added considerably to his discomfort and general weakness. In simple terms, Jones's deteriorating health was working symbiotically with his troublesome departure from Russia and descent from celebrity status. There were no life-and-death battles to be fought, and there was no companion in arms to share the long days of remembering. There also was no lover to ease the ache of old injuries, and worst of all, there were no great challenges to drive out the profound sadness of being found uninteresting by the world around oneself.

A message that Jones was dying brought Gouverneur Morris to Jones's apartment on the afternoon of 18 July 1792. It was only a few days after Jones's forty-fifth birthday. His estate was left to his two sisters, and Morris witnessed his last will and testament. There was very little cash on hand, but when all of the assets were accounted for, the estate amounted to something more than $30,000. The commemorative sword that had been presented to Jones by the King of France was bequeathed to his immediate heirs, and it then took on a storied life of its own.

Jones's heirs gave the sword to Robert Morris in appreciation of all that he had done for Jones. Morris, who sank into financial distress and debt, passed it to Commodore John Barry, and Barry passed it to then–Commodore Richard Dale. In 1938, Dale's family gave the sword to the Naval Academy. The Naval Academy, in turn, placed it in the crypt with Jones. The sword returned, after nearly a century and a half and five different owners, to its original owner.

After witnessing the will, Gouverneur Morris then left for a dinner engagement. A former aide to Lafayette, Jean-Baptiste Beaupoil, and a retired colonel from North Carolina, Samuel Blackden, were also there during the afternoon, along with the attending physician, who had no particular attachment to his patient.

Jones was reportedly aware and coherent that afternoon, although obviously weak and having difficulty with his breathing. At some point, after he was left with only a servant in his apartment, Jones got up from the chair in his sitting room and walked into the adjacent bedroom. He was found later, face down on the bed with his feet still on the floor. During his last moments, he was alone.

At about 8 PM, Morris returned to the apartment with his mistress and a well-known physician who lived in the neighborhood. But it was too late—Jones was gone. Morris gave instructions to Jones's former landlord to arrange an inexpensive and private burial. Morris's instructions were a sad sign of the nation's official indifference to Jones's death.

But the final chapter of Jones's last days took one more turn, a turn for the better. Colonel Blackden and the local official for the section of Paris where Jones had resided intervened. The funeral arrangements were taken over by the French Legislative Assembly, then in session. Jones's body was placed in alcohol in a sealed lead coffin, an action that turned out to be an important part of the discovery and identification of Jones's body a century later. Because Jones had been raised in the Church of Scotland, it was determined that his burial ceremony would—at least nominally—be a Protestant service, and a minister was recruited for the ceremony. The clergyman, the Reverend Paul-Henri Marron, was also designated to deliver the graveside remarks. Jones had shown no inclination toward formal religion during his life, and despite the participation of a Protestant minister, there was absolutely nothing religious about his burial.

Jones was buried on 20 July 1792. The modest funeral cortège moved solemnly for about four miles through the streets of Paris. It was led by units of French grenadiers and Paris gendarmerie, accompanied by drummers beating a halting funeral cadence. The hearse bearing Jones's body rolled slowly behind the drummers, followed by the carriages of a special committee of twelve from the Assembly. The clatter of the horses' hoofs on the cobblestones would have echoed off the buildings along the way, as traffic and bystanders stopped momentarily and fell silent as the slowly moving column passed. Parisians perhaps wondered for a few seconds who the deceased was. The procession ended with a handful of people made up of some of the Protestants of Paris, Jones's few servants, neighborhood shopkeepers with whom he did business, and a few sailors who had served with Jones on less mournful days. Gouverneur Morris did not attend the funeral because of a dinner appointment.

Just before the cemetery, the cortège passed through the Port St.-Martin, which marked the city limit, and onto a country road. That final passing out from the city Jones had chosen for his last years, above even the cities of his adopted country, had its own simple symbolism. It marked both the end of Jones's short but danger-filled journey through life and the beginning of his long journey toward lasting fame and gratitude from his country. The former journey encompassed only forty-five years and the latter would cover more than a century.

The procession finally reached the end of its winding way at a small plot, the St. Louis graveyard, which was set aside for Protestant burials. There was nothing especially moving about the graveside ceremony. Revered Marron delivered a politically correct exhortation that began with: "Legislators! Citizens! Soldiers! Friends! Brethren! And Frenchmen! We have just returned to the earth the remains of an illustrious stranger, one of the first champions of the liberty of America; of that liberty which so gloriously ushered in our own." The Reverend then went on to warn the assemblage, "The country is in danger." And then he asked, "Who amongst us would not shed the last drop of their blood to save it?"[9] Not only was there no mention of God in the Reverend's remarks, there was no solace for the bereaved. Yet—in fact, no deeply bereaved were in attendance at the grave. The only military honor rendered to Jones was a musket volley fired over his remains by some of the soldiers who had been part of the cortège.

Since Jones was known to disapprove of the excesses of Republican France that were surfacing and the impact those excesses were having on his benefactors, particularly the king, it can be assumed that he would have been taken aback by the final words the minister spoke over his coffin. On the other hand, there would have been at least a flicker of a smile of satisfaction at the Reverend's reference to his being a champion of American liberty.

Within weeks of Jones's funeral, a Paris mob attacked the royal palace at the Tuileries, killing the Swiss Guards who were protecting the King and Queen. The bodies of the guards, who were mostly Protestants, were hastily buried in a common grave next to Jones's, thus providing a macabre honor guard for the mostly forgotten naval hero. The cemetery was closed shortly after that ignominious act.

In a footnote to the funeral, Catherine dispelled any possible doubt about her lasting opinion of Jones and revealed much of her own character in her reaction to his death. On 15 August 1792, she proposed an epitaph for Jones in a letter to Baron Grimm. Her words, triggered by Jones's funeral, would have been unworthy of even those who honestly believed Jones to be a pirate: "That Paul Jones was a very hard rogue, and it was quite fitting that he should be celebrated by a rabble of detestable creatures."[10]

Fortunately, a different and lasting epitaph was to be written eventually for Jones, one that would be more than a hundred years in the making. Embedded in marble at the head of Jones's sarcophagus, the epitaph would be burned into the consciousness of generations of sailors in the United States Navy.

John Paul Jones 1747–1792 United States Navy
He Gave Our Navy its Earliest Traditions of
Heroism and Victory

On 27 March 1794 Congress approved the construction or purchase of six frigates to protect United States shipping in the Mediterranean against the Barbary raiders. With that resolution, the United States Navy was born. Six U.S. Navy captains were appointed in June of the same year. One was Richard Dale, the man who fought alongside John Paul Jones at the battle off Flamborough Head. Jones was dead and the Continental Navy had been disbanded. But the foundation for the most powerful navy of modern history had been laid, and John Paul Jones had played a dramatic role in the process.

13
The Coffin without a Nameplate

"Time discovers truth."
Seneca

The crypt where the remains of John Paul Jones finally came to rest reflects a simple and profound restraint. Visitors must actually seek it out below the main level of the Naval Academy Chapel. Jones's accomplishments are not trumpeted; it is left to the visitor to seek the meaning of the unlikely events of his life.

The room is capped with a domed ceiling eighteen feet high, centered precisely under the skyline-dominating main dome of the chapel. The chapel's original architect, Ernest Flagg, intended the crypt for multiple U.S. Navy heroes, but as it turned out, it is the final resting place for one.

Visitors move around the circular outer perimeter of the crypt, a space designed by Whitney Warren. Along that perimeter selected items associated with Jones's career are on display; one wonders why there is not more in the way of memorabilia. Among the select items is the commemorative sword presented to Jones by King Louis XVI of France, a Houdon bust of Jones, a few paintings, and ship models—and Jones's original commission in the Continental Navy.

At the center of the area and supported by large bronze dolphins is the raised sarcophagus that was created by sculptor Sylvain Salaries. The compact mass of the black-and-white Royal Pyrenees marble vessel that holds John Paul Jones's remains is a metaphor for the conviction that drove him to his victories.

The pervading mood in the crypt during public visiting hours is one of quiet but intense interest. A stationary U.S. Marine guard and the subdued lighting reinforce that mood. The expressions of the visitors who circle slowly around the room, alternately looking at the display items and then back at the sarcophagus, seem to question who was this man, how did he find his way to this place? Perhaps some are beginning to realize that they are about to learn more about themselves than about a naval hero of the American Revolution.

How Jones finally arrived at his final port of call in 1913 is a story as unlikely as the events of his life.

Between Jones's death in Paris in 1792 and the return of his remains to the United States in 1905, the United States fought the Quasi War against France, the Barbary War against the North African states, the War of 1812 against Great Britain, the U.S.-Mexican War, the American Civil War, and the Spanish-American War. All but two of those conflicts were predominantly naval wars, and even the U.S.-Mexican War and the Civil War had crucial naval components.

In those violent struggles, the elements of combat doctrine established by John Paul Jones became deeply ingrained in the sailors of the U.S. Navy. In a broader, strategic perspective, Jones's commitment to the proactive, forward employment of naval forces as an essential part of a national maritime strategy was validated.

During that same time frame, the United States evolved from the original thirteen colonies into forty-six states, the east and west coasts were connected by railroad, and the Wright brothers demonstrated the feasibility of manned flight. In addition, American leadership in mass production was accelerating the Industrial Revolution exponentially and propelling the United States into a role as a major geopolitical factor. As a corollary to those developments, the U.S. Navy had transitioned from wind-driven wooden sailing craft to steam-driven steel ships, and new classes of sleek fighters called destroyers and cruisers were performing the assignments that had been carried out by square-rigged frigates like *Bonhomme Richard.*

During that more than one-hundred-year period, the United States went from a nation with no navy in 1792 to one of the world's leading maritime powers by 1905. And with its arrival as a global maritime power, a circumstance Jones had predicted, it was time for him to be brought back to the United States. And it was appropriate that he be returned home with recognition of the part he played in the birth and early survival of American liberty. The man Thomas Jefferson called "the principal hope" of American fortunes at sea deserved a place—literally and figuratively—in his adopted homeland.

There was a problem, however, with returning Jones to the United States—no one knew exactly where his body was. The small cemetery where he was buried in 1792 had disappeared under the steadily expanding construction of Paris. It was a retired U.S. Army general, Horace Porter, at the time serving as ambassador to France, who took up the search-and-rescue mission on behalf of his country. Porter had served as aide to General Ulysses S. Grant during the American Civil War, as assistant secretary of war when Grant was secretary of war, and he was an author prior to becoming ambassador to France.

With poorly drawn maps, fragmentary records, and his own funding, Porter struck out on the search phase of his self-assigned mission in June 1899. Akin to many of Jones's career assignments, things did not go well for Porter at first. He retained a number of researchers who produced little in the way of results for the first few years. His target was challenging to locate, since the original St. Louis cemetery was tiny, only 120 by 130 feet. Then in 1904 the site of the old graveyard was narrowed down to a small area of one- and two-story buildings, yards, and small gardens. Convinced that he had located the site of the old cemetery, Porter requested funding for the excavation, which would have to be conducted around and under existing structures. President Theodore Roosevelt responded quickly with a request to Congress for the money. Roosevelt's strong patriotism was evident in his request:

> The great interest which our people feel in the story of Paul Jones's life, the national sense of gratitude for the great service done by him toward the achievement of independence, and the sentiment of mingled distress and regret felt because the body of one of our greatest heroes lies forgotten and unmarked in foreign soil, lead me to approve the ambassador's suggestion that Congress should take advantage of this unexpected opportunity to do proper honor to the memory of Paul Jones, and appropriate the sum of $35,000 . . . for the purposes above described, to be expended under the direction of the Secretary of State.[1]

The money was appropriated and the final phase of the search begun. Four coffins of lead were revealed, and three were identified with nameplates. In all probability the nameplate of the fourth had been dislodged from its outer wood casing when another grave was dug immediately on top of it. On 7 April 1905, the coffin without a nameplate was opened, and it was determined that the remains within fit the general description of Jones, as well as the circumstances of his burial. Two anthropologists at L'école de Médecine in Paris conducted a detailed examination that involved comparisons with the Houdon bust, matching of hair color, establishment of the cause of death, and other specific details. Because the remains had been preserved in alcohol and a lead coffin, the anthropologists were able to determine that without a doubt the body was that of John Paul Jones. Porter wired the secretary of state, "My six years' search for remains of Paul Jones has resulted in success."[2]

Jones's remains were preserved and replaced in the original lead casket, along with some remnants of the original gravesite. The original casket was then placed in a new oak coffin with eight silver handles, and the lid was secured with sixteen silver screws. Jones's body was then moved to the American

Church of the Holy Trinity on Avenue de l'Alma in Paris, where it was covered with an American flag and, after a prayer offered by the rector of the church, the Reverend Dr. Morgan, the body was placed in a receiving vault.

On 6 July, Jones's birthday, a ceremony took place at Holy Trinity Church to mark the beginning of Jones's final journey back to the United States. Ambassador Porter reported that the ceremony was not intended to be funereal but celebratory and patriotic. The ceremony also marked the official turning over of the body to the U.S. government. To sum up his remarks, Porter alluded to a comment reportedly made by Jones that he and the new American flag were inseparable and "born of the same womb of destiny."

At the end of the service, eight U.S. Navy sailors, each more than six feet tall, bore the coffin to a French artillery caisson. By then it was 5 PM, and in the lowering light of a soft summer day, the procession set out from the church. This procession was quite different from that associated with Jones's burial a century before. This one began with a platoon of police, followed by a regiment of French cuirassiers; five hundred U.S. Navy sailors; Rear Admiral Charles D. Sigsbee, who commanded the squadron that was to transport Jones to America; French and U.S. government officials; delegations from the U.S. Navy League, the American Chamber of Commerce, the Society of the Cincinnati, Sons of the American Revolution, and other groups; two batteries of French horse artillery; two companies of U.S. Marines; and two battalions of French infantry with their bands. With that assemblage, it would be difficult to imagine Jones feeling underappreciated by his country any longer.

The column moved through the streets that were lined by Parisians standing in respectful silence. It advanced slowly down the Champs-Elysées, over the Seine bridge of Alexander III, and eventually to the Esplanade des Invalides. At the Esplanade des Invalides the coffin was removed from the caisson and placed on an elaborate catafalque, and then covered by a purple velvet tent. At the catafalque, the military units passed in review. From Paris, the coffin was transported by a special railroad car to Cherbourg where it was taken aboard the cruiser USS *Brooklyn,* the flagship of the squadron of cruisers that were sent to Cherbourg to return Jones's remains. The squadron also included the cruisers USS *Tacoma,* USS *Chattanooga,* and USS *Galveston.*

In a one-sailor-to-another salute, Rear Admiral Sigsbee identified his force as it approached Cherbourg as the John Paul Jones Squadron. The squadron was a command Jones would have relished. Upon arrival the next day, the John Paul Jones Squadron rendered a twenty-one-gun salute, which was promptly returned by the senior French officer present. Again, Jones would have been pleased at the appropriate recognition of United States sovereignty. Beyond the formalities, Sigsbee would later report to the secretary of the navy about the exceptional "tact and consideration" demonstrated by the French military officers and diplomats during the official events associated with the transfer of Jones's remains to U.S. custody.

On 8 July, *Brooklyn,* accompanied by the cruisers, sailed from Cherbourg for America. Jones was making his final voyage home, and he was making the transit with shipmates who honored his achievements. As Jones's squadron approached Nantucket Shoals, it was joined by no less than seven U.S. Navy battleships: USS *Maine* with Commander in Chief, North Atlantic Fleet, Rear Admiral Robley D. Evans embarked; USS *Missouri;* USS *Kentucky;* USS *Kearsage;* USS *Alabama;* USS *Illinois;* and USS *Massachusetts.*

What had now become a truly impressive fleet by any standards sailed southwest, and on 22 July, it cleared the open sea and passed the historic Virginia Capes—where the critical Revolutionary War battle of the Chesapeake was fought in 1781—into Chesapeake Bay. Once into the Chesapeake, four of the battleships left the formation, and the remaining fleet of four cruisers and three battleships steamed up the Chesapeake and anchored off the U.S. Naval Academy. Then, on 24 July, the remains were brought ashore from *Brooklyn.*

The solemn and strictly naval ceremony ashore began promptly at 10 AM. The morning was clear and fresh, following a heavy rain during the previous night. The Naval Academy superintendent and chaplain met the landing party. Commanding officers from the naval squadron plus one French naval officer acted as pallbearers. Jones's body was placed in a hearse, and the naval cortège proceeded quietly through the Naval Academy campus in the softness of the summer morning.

Near the chapel at a small, red brick mausoleum—where the body would await Congress's determination of Jones's final resting place—the cortège stopped. Jones's body was taken through the entrance, which was draped with simple funeral bunting, and placed inside. Hundreds of white uniformed midshipmen stood at parade rest in perfectly formed ranks behind the building. A small cluster of Naval Academy civilian family members and faculty stood quietly, and a few women in the group shaded themselves from the rapidly strengthening Maryland sun with umbrellas.

A squad of U.S. Marines fired a volley that ripped through the silence that had settled around the small tomb, and the heartaching sound of a bugler's taps followed quickly as the volley reverberated.

Following the naval ceremony of July 1905, the official public commemoration of the return of Jones's remains to the United States was conducted at the Naval Academy in Annapolis on 24 April 1906. It was the 128th anniversary, to the day, of the capture of HMS *Drake* in the Irish Sea by Jones and the men of *Ranger.* President Theodore Roosevelt was the main speaker. The principal guests were French Ambassador to the United States J. J. Jusserand, U.S. Ambassador to France General Horace Porter, Secretary of the Navy Charles J. Bonaparte, and Governor of the State of Maryland Edwin Warfield.

It is difficult to imagine a more appropriate U.S. president to be the centerpiece of an event recognizing the accomplishments of Jones. President Teddy Roosevelt had several of the same important personality traits that drove Jones. He was patriotic to the extreme, and he was very action oriented in his approach to international problem solving. In addition, he was the U.S. president most responsible for making real Jones's predictions about the United States becoming a great maritime nation on the world stage. All of those Roosevelt qualities would be translated into action with his decision to send the "Great White Fleet" in its around-the-world cruise from December 1907 to February 1909.

Arguably the most striking aspect of Roosevelt's relatively brief remarks was their relevance to today's world. The president quickly got to the essential lesson of Jones's life for the sailors of the U.S. Navy when he spoke of the need "to emulate the energy, the professional capacity, the indomitable determination and dauntless scorn of death which marked John Paul Jones above all his fellows." The president also emphasized the importance of learning "the lessons that history teaches," and then he followed with a blunt political sally: "The courage which never yields can not take the place of the possession of good ships and good weapons."

But Roosevelt, with the instincts of a brilliant political persuader, saved his most enduring and most provocative admonition for the latter part of his speech. "To applaud patriotic sentiments and to turn out to do honor to the dead heroes who by land or by sea won honor for our flag is only worthwhile if we are prepared to show that our energies do not exhaust themselves in words."

Appropriately, French Ambassador Jusserand emphasized the close relationship between the United States and France. Jusserand spoke of Jones finding "not only ships and supplies, but friendship and admiration" in France—a comment that can't help but bring to mind the present alienation between the United States and France. The contrast becomes even more vivid with the ambassador's reference to "the shores of that Chesapeake Bay at the entrance of which the combined action of Washington, Rochambeau, and de Grasse ended the war." The tenor and the specific content of Jusserand's speech provoke questions about the divergence of geopolitical interests that currently splits the United States and France.

Following the remarks of the French ambassador, the secretary of the navy introduced Ambassador Porter as the person who found the remains of "our first great sailor" who had been "lost to his country and the world."

Porter's remarks were by far the longest of the day. He focused extensively on Jones's persona, and although he was guilty of periodic floridness, his observations often hit the mark with verbal economy. At one point, for example, Porter put Jones's difficult ongoing battle to get command of good ships in proper perspective when he said simply, "His battles were won, not by his ships, but by his genius."[3] Porter also struck a profoundly disturbing note when he described the shocking site at which Jones's body was discovered. The site was, in his words, "an abandoned cemetery which had been covered later by a dump pile to a height of 15 feet, where dogs and horses had been buried, and the soil was soaked with polluted waters from undrained laundries."

Ambassador Porter must also be credited with providing the day's best example of unintended humor when he attempted to burnish Jones's character: "He had no fondness for revelry, jolly coffee-house dinners, or drinking bouts, which formed the principal amusements in foreign ports. While others were carousing ashore he was studying in his cabin, perfecting himself in history and languages, pondering upon the maneuvering of ships and the great strategy of naval warfare."

While Jones unarguably studied, perfected himself, and pondered in his ships' cabins, just as unarguably, he could never be accused of failing to seek—and find—"amusements" ashore. Sometimes he even managed to combine his studying and amusements as when Jones used a "sleeping dictionary" to improve his French language skills soon after his first stay in Paris began.

Governor Warfield of Maryland ended the speeches. Following Teddy Roosevelt on a speakers' platform was a difficult assignment, but in his brief remarks, the Governor delivered the perfect final thought for the historic return of John Paul Jones to America and for the events of 24 April 1906 at the U.S. Naval Academy. Warfield said, "Whatever else may be said of him, there can be no doubt that the love of liberty was the master passion of his soul, and that he longed to have his name and fame associated with his adopted country, America."

For seven years after the April 1906 ceremony, Congress failed to come to a decision about the permanent location of Jones's remains. Many cities lobbied for the privilege of being Jones's final resting place. In the meantime, Jones's body was placed at the bottom of the grand staircase of Bancroft Hall, the core building of the Naval Academy, and the place where all of the midshipmen live. Finally Congress decided. Jones's body was moved on 26 January 1913 to the special crypt at the U.S. Naval Academy Chapel, where it has remained for a century.

Epilogue

> "No treasures the earth contains or the sea conceals can be compared to it. For liberty one can rightfully risk one's life."
>
> Cervantes

More than thirty biographies and hundreds of articles about John Paul Jones have appeared over the past two centuries. Almost all were extreme in their praise, and many even fictionalized events in order to enlarge Jones's image as an American hero. In contrast, other than then–Lieutenant Richard Dale, who went on to a distinguished career in the United States Navy, we know very little about the hundreds of other individuals who gave life to *Bonhomme Richard,* watch by watch and day by day.

Those unknowns of one of the best-known ships of U.S. naval history deserve far greater recognition than has been accorded them to date. And they are as much a part of what can be learned from the naval history of the American Revolution as is their commander.

The battle off Flamborough Head was a vision of hell. With a few notable exceptions, it was fought and won by anonymous men. Those rank-and-file warfighters who endured the more than three hours of horrendous combat—soaked in sweat, choking on gunpowder smoke, and splattered with blood—deserve more than a passing reference in our nation's history. Scores of them died during the fight, and as far as we know, all the dead were buried at sea. Scores more were wounded and would live with the marks of their fight to stay alive on 23 September 1779. By Jones's own account, about half of *Bonhomme Richard*'s crew of three hundred plus were either killed or wounded.

Bonhomme Richard's crew members endured the unspeakable to preserve the priceless. They were not sophisticated men; many, no doubt, could not even read. But there is no doubt that the sum of their strength was as essential to winning the battle off Flamborough Head as was the leadership of John Paul Jones. Their incredible ability to continue doing their duty—and more—under the most appalling combat conditions was as important as a force multiplier as was the astonishing mental and physical toughness of their captain.

If the Americans among the crew had been asked what they were fighting for, some would have said, "liberty." Others would have said simply, "to win." But throughout the internationally mixed crew, all would have agreed that they fought to see another day.

Today, Jones is rightly credited with "giving our Navy its earliest traditions of heroism and victory," and the Americans in the crew who fought with him in *Bonhomme Richard* must be credited with helping to give our country its earliest traditions of military service. They laid down an example that has been followed by military draftees and volunteers who, for more than two centuries, have acted on their personal answer to the question, "If not me, then who?" The American sailors of *Bonhomme Richard* weren't bred to be warriors, but they believed instinctively that at certain times, warriors are required. They would have had difficulty articulating the concept of political liberty, but their performance in *Bonhomme Richard* had to be based on something more than discipline and fear of death. Someplace in the mix of culture and instinct there must have been an awareness that, at times, only warriors can deal with deadly threats to our nation, and at those times only warriors can preserve a future with hope.

There is no public monument or burial ground for the men of *Bonhomme Richard.* Their bodies were entombed off Flamborough Head at the bottom of the North Sea. But their monument is something more impressive, and, one hopes, more durable than marble or bronze. Their monument is a nation that believed in a new kind of political structure, was willing to fight for it, and remains the world's most promising national embodiment of limited and liberal governance. For what the men of *Bonhomme Richard* did in their deadly struggle with *Serapis,* they deserve more than our respect. They deserve our continuing recognition.

We need to better understand the unique quality of their willingness to serve in deadly danger; we need to understand the unique American military culture they helped initiate. Generation after generation of Americans has taken up the burden of fighting our country's wars. Many lost their lives in the process. The vast majority of those who fought were not professional soldiers, sailors, marines, or airmen.

Undeniably, there is a special quality to the Marines who faced a wall of deadly fire to gain the shore at Tarawa. There also was something special about the airmen who faced long survival odds in the early days of the air war over Europe during World War II, as well as the sailors who beat back fanatical suicide bombers from the decks of their ships and in the cockpits of their aircraft off Okinawa during the latter stage of that same war. That same willingness to accept the risks of combat on behalf of their country was present in the soldiers who fought their way yard by yard into Baghdad on what has been nicknamed the "Thunder Run."

Technology, strategy, doctrine, and tactics alone did not win any of those battles or wars. When all is said and done, people who are willing to overcome fear and endure physical danger that is incomprehensible to those who have not experienced it are what win wars. America's military is a unique institution. And, as we continue to reassess its role in our society and its performance, we need to better understand its roots, relevance to our individual lives, and role in sustaining our national ideals in the face of external threats.

Winston Churchill said, "The empires of the future are the empires of the mind."[1] Although he was thinking of the twenty-first century when he spoke those words, the idea he expressed is also startlingly appropriate for the American Revolution. That war was not a defense against a foreign invader, and it was not a war for territory. It was a war fought for a concept, an idea that had its origins with the very nation that had become America's mortal enemy in 1776. No matter what other factors contributing to America's first victory in war are analyzed by historians, the belief in the overriding importance of fighting for one's liberty should be the starting point.

It was the idea of liberty—made palpable by people like Thomas Paine and Patrick Henry and made politically practical by people like George Washington, John Adams, Thomas Jefferson, and Benjamin Franklin—that motivated John Paul Jones to fight his way to a most unlikely victory off the coast of England in 1779. It was the idea of preserving liberty that sustained the United States through a civil war and two world wars. It was the realization that Americans'—indeed the world's—concept of liberty was under attack that fueled America's reaction to 11 September 2001.

Many political scientists claim that it was the pamphlet *Common Sense,* written by Thomas Paine (appropriately, an immigrant from England) that actually triggered the American Revolution.[2] At one point in that very brief work, Paine wrote, "The cause of America is in a great measure the cause of all mankind." John Paul Jones's brief career should be remembered as a significant part of that cause.

Appendixes

The following items include three different views of the battle between the men of the Continental ship *Bonhomme Richard* and the men of HMS *Serapis,* and each version was provided by a participant. The descriptions by Jones and Pearson were provided a short time after the event. Dale's account of the battle, in contrast, was related many years after the battle. The three different viewpoints, taken together, provide a unique and no doubt basically accurate view of what happened off Flamborough Head on 23 September 1779.

Also included in this section is the Congressional report on the promotion of officers that caused such deep resentment in Jones, plus a long letter from him to Congress that catalogues the injustices he believed, with considerable justification, had been done to him during his career in the Continental Navy.

John Paul Jones's Report of His Deployment in *Bonhomme Richard*

John Paul Jones's report of his deployment in *Bonhomme Richard.* As published in *The Life and Character of John Paul Jones,* John Henry Sherburne, 1851, pp. 108–20.

On board the Ship Serapis, at anchor without
The Texel in Holland, October 3, 1779

His Excellency Benjamin Franklin,
Honored and Dear Sir,

When I had the honor of writing to you on the 11th of August, previous to my departure from the Road of Groaix, I had before me the most flattering prospect of rendering essential service to the common cause of France and America. I had a full confidence in the voluntary inclination and ability of every captain under my command to assist and support me in my duty with cheerful emulation; and I was persuaded that every one of them would pursue glory in preference to interest.

Whether I was or was not deceived will best appear by a relation of circumstances.

The little squadron under my orders consisting of the Bon homme Richard of 40 guns, the Alliance of 36 guns, the Pallas of 32 guns, the Cerf of 18 guns, and the Vengeance of 12 guns, joined by two privateers, the Monsieur and the Granville, sailed from the Road of Groaix at daybreak on the 14th of August; the same day we spoke with a large convoy bound from the southward to Breast.

On the 18th we retook a large ship belonging to Holland, laden chiefly with brandy and wine that had been destined from Barcelona to Dunkirk, and taken eight days before by an English privateer. The captain of the Monsieur, however, took out of this prize such articles as he pleased in the night, and the next day being astern of the squadron and to windward, he actually wrote orders *in his proper name,* and sent away the prize under one of his own officers. This, however, I superseded by sending her for L'Orient under my orders in the character of commander-in-chief. The evening of the day following the Monsieur separated from the squadron.

On the 20th we saw and chased a large ship, but could not overtake her, she being to windward.

On the 21st we saw and chased another ship that was also to windward, and thereby eluded our pursuit. The same afternoon we took a brigantine called the Mayflower, laden with butter and salt provisions, bound from Limerick in Ireland for London; this vessel I immediately expedited for L'Orient.

On the 23rd we saw Cape Clear and the S.W. part of Ireland. That afternoon, it being calm, I sent some armed boats to take a brigantine that appeared in the N.W. quarter. Soon after in the evening it became necessary to have a boat ahead of the ship to tow, as the helm could not prevent her from laying across the tide of flood, which would have driven us into a deep and dangerous bay, situated between the rocks on the south called the Skallocks, and on the north called the Blaskets. The ship's boats being absent, I sent my own barge ahead to tow the ship. The boats took the brigantine, she was called the Fortune, and bound with a cargo of oil, blubber, and staves, from Newfoundland to Bristol; this vessel I ordered to proceed immediately for Nantes or St. Malo. Soon after sunset the villains who towed the ship, cut the tow rope and decamped with my barge. Sundry shots were fired to bring them to without effect; in the meantime the master of the Bon homme Richard, without orders, manned one of the ship's boats, and with four soldiers pursued the barge in order to stop the deserters. The evening was clear and serene, but the zeal of that officer, Mr. Cutting Lunt, induced him to pursue too far, and a fog which came on soon afterwards prevented the boats from rejoining the ship, although I caused signal guns to be frequently fired. The fog and calm continued the next day till towards evening. In the afternoon Capt. Landais came on board the Bon homme Richard and behaved towards me with great disrespect, affirming in the most indelicate manner and language, that I had lost my boats and people through my imprudence in sending boats to take a prize! He persisted in his reproaches, though he was assured by Messrs. De Weibert and De Chamillard that the barge was towing the ship at the time of elopement, and that she had not been sent in pursuit of the prize. He was affronted, because I would not the day before suffer him to chase without my orders, and to approach the dangerous shore I have already mentioned, where he was an entire stranger, and when there was not sufficient wind to govern a ship. He told me he was the only American in the squadron, and was determined to follow his own opinion in chasing when and where he thought proper, and in every other matter that concerned the service, and that, if I continued in that situation three days longer, the squadron would be taken, &c. By the advice of Capt. De Cottineau, and with the free consent and approbation of M. De Varage, I sent the Cerf in to reconnoiter the coast, and endeavor(ed) to take the boats and people the next day, while the squadron stood off and on in the S.W. quarter, in the best possible situation to intercept the enemy's merchant ships, whether outward or homeward bound. The Cerf had on board a pilot well acquainted with the coast, and was ordered to join me again before night. I approached the shore in the afternoon, but the Cerf did not appear; this induced me to stand off again in the night in order to return and be rejoined by the Cerf the next day; but to my great concern and disappointment, though I ranged the coast along, and hoisted our private signals, neither the boats nor the Cerf joined me. The evening of that day, the 26th, brought with it stormy weather, with the appearance of a gale from the S.W, yet I must declare I did not follow my own judgment, but was led by the assertion which had fallen from Captain Landais, when I in the evening made a signal to steer to the northward and leave that station, which I wished to have occupied at least a week longer. The gale increased in the night with thick weather; to prevent separation, I carried a top light and fired a gun every quarter of an hour. I carried also a very moderate sail, and the course had been clearly pointed out by a signal before night; yet, with all this precaution, I found myself accompanied only by the brigantine Vengeance in the morning, the Granville having remained astern with a prize; as I have since understood the tiller of the Pallas broke after midnight, which disabled her from keeping up, but no apology has yet been made in behalf of the Alliance.

On the 31st, we saw the Flamie Islands situated near the Lewis on the N.W. coast of Scotland; and the next morning, off Cape Wrath, we gave chase to a ship to windward, at the same time two ships appearing in the N.W. quarter, which proved to be the Alliance and a prize ship which she had taken, bound, as I understood, from Liverpool to Jamaica. The ship which I chased brought to at noon; she proved to be the Union letter of Marque, bound from London for Quebec, with a cargo of naval stores on account of government, adapted for the services of British armed vessels on the lakes. The public dispatches were lost, as the Alliance very imprudently hoisted American colors, though English colors were then flying on board the Bon homme Richard. Capt. Landais sent a small boat to ask whether I would man the ship, or he should, as in the latter case he would suffer no boat nor person from the Bon homme Richard to go near the prize. Ridiculous as this appeared to me, I yielded to it for the sake of peace, and received the prisoners on board the Bon homme Richard, while the prize was manned from the Alliance. In the afternoon another sail appeared, and I immediately made the signal for the Alliance to chase; but, instead of obeying he wore and laid the ship's head the other way. The next morning I made a signal to speak with the Alliance, to which no attention was shown; I then made sail with the ships in company for the second rendezvous which was not far distant, and where I fully expected to be joined by the Pallas and the Cerf.

The second of September we saw a sail at daybreak, and gave chase; that ship proved to be the Pallas, and had met with no success while separated from the Bon homme Richard.

On the 3rd the Vengeance brought to a small Irish brigantine, bound homeward from Norway. The same evening I sent the Vengeance in the N.E. quarter to bring up the two prize ships that appeared to me to be too near the islands of Shetland. While with the Alliance and Pallas, I endeavored to weather Fair Isle, and to get into my second rendezvous, where I directed the Vengeance to join me with the three prizes. The next morning, having weathered Fair Isle, and not seeing the Vengeance nor the prizes, I spoke the Alliance and ordered her to steer to the northward and bring them up to the rendezvous.

On the morning of the 4th the Alliance appeared again, and had brought to two very small coasting sloops in ballast, but without having attended properly to my orders of yesterday. The Vengeance joined me soon after, and informed me that in consequence of Captain Landais' orders to the commanders of the two prize ships, they had refused to follow him to the rendezvous. I am to this moment ignorant of what orders these men received from Captain Landais, nor know I by virtue of what authority he ventured to give his orders to prizes in my presence, and without either my knowledge or approbation. Captain Ricot further informed me that he had burnt the prize brigantine, because that vessel proved leaky; and I was sorry to understand afterward that though the vessel was Irish property, the cargo was the property of the subjects of Norway.

In the evening I sent for all the captains to come aboard the Bon homme Richard, to consult on future plans of operations. Captains Cottineau and Ricot obeyed me, but Captain Landais obstinately refused, and after sending me various uncivil messages, wrote me a very extraordinary letter in answer to a written order which I had sent him, on finding that he had trifled with my verbal orders. The next day a pilot boat came on board from Shetland, by which means I received such advices as induced me to change a plan which I otherwise meant to have pursued; and as the Cerf did not appear at my second rendezvous, I determined to steer towards the third in hopes of meeting her there.

In the afternoon a gale of wind came on, which continued four days without intermission. In the second night of that gale the Alliance, with her two little prizes, again separated from the Bon homme Richard. I had now with me only the Pallas and the Vengeance, yet I did not abandon the hopes of performing some essential service. The winds continued contrary, so that we did not see the land till the evening of the 13th, when the hills of the Cheviot in the S.E. of Scotland appeared. The next day we chased sundry vessels, and took a ship and a brigantine, both from the Firth of Edinburgh, laden with coal. Knowing that there lay at anchor in Leith road an armed ship of 20 guns, with two or three fine cutters, I formed an expedition against Leith, which I proposed to lay under a large contribution, or otherwise to reduce it to ashes. Had I been alone, the wind being favorable, I would have proceeded directly up the Firth, and must have succeeded, as they lay there in a state of perfect indolence and security, which would have proved their ruin. Unfortunately for me, the Pallas and the Vengeance were both at a considerable distance in the offing, they having chased to the southward; this obliged us to steer out of the Firth again to meet them. The captains of the Pallas and Vengeance being come on board the Bon homme Richard, I communicated to them my project, to which many difficulties and objections were made by them; at last, however, they appeared to think better of the design after I had assured them that I hoped to raise a contribution of 200,000 pounds sterling on Leith, and that there was no battery of cannon there to oppose our landing. So much time, however, was unavoidably spent in pointed remarks and sage deliberation that night, that the wind became contrary in the morning.

We continued to work to windward up the Firth without being able to reach the road of Leith, till, on the morning of the 17th, when, being almost within cannon shot of the town, having everything in readiness for a descent, a very severe gale of wind came on, and being directly contrary, obliged us to bear away, after having in vain endeavored for some time to withstand its violence. The gale was so severe, that one of the prizes that had been taken on the 14th sank to the bottom, the crew being with difficulty saved. As the alarm at this time had reached Leith by means of a cutter that had watched our motions that morning, and as the wind continued contrary (though more moderate in the evening), I thought it impossible to pursue the enterprise with a good prospect of success: especially as Edinburgh, where there is always a number of troops, is only a mile distant from Leith, therefore I gave up the project.

On the 19th, having taken a sloop and a brigantine in ballast, with a sloop laden with building timber, I proposed another project to M. Cottineau, which would have been highly honorable though not profitable; many difficulties were made, and our situation was represented as being the most perilous. The enemy, he said, would send against us a superior force, and that if I obstinately continued on the coast of England two days longer, we should all be taken. The Vengeance having chased along the shore to the southward, Captain Cottineau said he would follow her with the prizes, as I was unable to make much sail, having that day been obliged to strike the main-top-mast to repair damages;

and as I afterward understood, he told M. De Chamillard that unless I joined them the next day, both the Pallas and the Vengeance would leave that coast. I had thoughts of attempting the enterprise alone after the Pallas had made sail to join the Vengeance. I am persuaded even now, that I would have succeeded, and to the honor of my young officers, I found them as ardently disposed to the business as I could desire; nothing prevented me from pursuing my design but the reproach that would have been cast upon my character, as a man of prudence, had the enterprise miscarried. It would have been said, was he not forewarned by Captain Cottineau and others?

I made sail along the shore to the southward, and next morning took a coasting sloop in ballast, which, with another that I had taken the night before, I ordered to be sunk. In the evening, I again met with the Pallas and Vengeance off Whitby. Captain Cottineau told me he had sunk the brigantine, and ransomed the sloop, laden with building timber, that had been taken the day before. I had told Captain Cottineau the day before, that I had no authority to ransom prizes.

On the 21st we saw and chased two sail, off Flamborough Head, the Pallas in the N.E. quarter, while the Bon homme Richard followed by the Vengeance in the S.W. The one I chased, a brigantine collier in ballast, belonging to Scarborough, was soon taken, and sunk immediately afterward, as a fleet then appeared to the southward: it was so late in the day that I could not come up with the fleet before night; at length, however, I got so near one of them as to force her to run ashore, between Flamborough Head and the Spurn. Soon after I took another, a brigantine from Holland, belonging to Sunderland; and at daylight the next morning, seeing a fleet steering towards me from the Spurn, I imagined them to be a convoy, bound from London for Leith, which had been for some time expected, one of them had a pendant hoisted, and appeared to be a ship of force. They had not, however, courage to come on, but kept back all except the one which seemed to be armed, and that one also kept to windward very near the land, and on the edge of dangerous shoals where I could not with safety approach. This induced me to make a signal for a pilot, and soon afterward two pilot boats came off; they informed me that the ship that wore a pendant was an armed merchant ship, and that a king's frigate lay there in sight, at anchor within the Humber, waiting to take under convoy a number of merchant ships bound to the northward. The pilots imagined the Bon homme Richard to be an English ship of war, and consequently, communicated to me the private signal which they had been required to make. I endeavored by this means to decoy the ships out of the port, but the wind then changing, and with the tide becoming unfavorable for them, the deception had not the desired effect, and they wisely put back. The entrance of the Humber is exceedingly difficult and dangerous, and as the Pallas was not in sight, I thought it not prudent to remain off the entrance; I therefore steered out again to join the Pallas off Flamborough Head. In the night we saw and chased two ships, until three o'clock in the morning, when being at a very small distance from them, I made the private signal of recognizance, which I had given to each captain before I sailed from Groaix, one half of the answer only was returned. In this position both sides lay until daylight, when the ships proved to be the Alliance and the Pallas.

On the morning of that day, the 23rd, the brig from Holland not being in sight, we chased a brigantine that appeared laying to windward. About noon we saw and chased a large ship that appeared coming round Flamborough Head, from the northward, and at the same time I manned and armed one of the pilot boats to sail in pursuit of the brigantine, which now appeared to be the vessel that I had forced ashore. Soon after this a fleet of forty-one sail appeared off Flamborough Head, bearing N.N.E.; this induced me to abandon the single ship which had then anchored in Burlington Bay; I also called back the pilot boat and hoisted a signal for a general chase. When the fleet discovered us bearing down, all the merchant ships crowded sail towards the shore. The two ships of war that protected the fleet, at the same time steered from the land, and made the disposition for the battle: in approaching the enemy I crowded every possible sail, and made the signal for the line of battle, to which the Alliance showed no attention. Earnest as I was for the action, I could not reach the commodore's ship until seven in the evening, being then within pistol shot, when he hailed the Bon homme Richard, we answered him by firing a whole broadside.

The battle being thus begun, was continued with unremitting fury. Every method was practised on both sides to gain an advantage, and rake each other; and I must confess that the enemy's ship being much more manageable than the Bon homme Richard, gained thereby, several times an advantageous situation, in spite of my best endeavors to prevent it. As I had to deal with an enemy of *greatly superior force,* I was under the necessity of closing with him, to prevent the advantage he had over me in point of manoeuvre. It was my intention to lay the Bonhomme Richard athwart the enemy's bow, but as that operation required great dexterity in the management of both sails and helm, and some of our braces being shot away, it did not exactly succeed to my wishes; the enemy's bowsprit, however, came over the Bon homme Richard's poop by the mizzen mast, and I made both ships fast together in that situation, which by the action of the wind on the enemy's sails, forced her stern close to the Bon homme Richard's bow, so that the ships lay square alongside of each other, the yards being all entangled, and the cannon of each ship touching the opponent's side. When this position took place it was eight o'clock, previous to which the Bon homme Richard had received sundry eighteen pounds shot below the water, and leaked very much. My battery of 12-pounders, on which I had placed my chief dependance, being commanded by Lieut. Dale and Col. Weibert, and manned principally with American seamen and French volunteers, were entirely silenced and abandoned. As to the six old 18-pounders that formed the battery of the lower gun-deck, they did no service whatever; two out of three of them burst at the first fire, and killed almost all the men who were stationed to manage them. Before this time, too, Col. De Chamillard, who commanded a party of twenty soldiers on the poop, had abandoned that station, after having lost some of his men. These men deserted their quarters. I had only two pieces of cannon, 9-pounders, on the quarter deck that were not silenced, and not one of the heavier cannon was fired during the rest of the action. The purser, Mr. Mease, who commanded the guns on the quarterdeck, being dangerously wounded in the head, I was obliged to fill his place, and with great difficulty rallied a few men, and shifted over one of the lee quarter-deck guns, so that we afterwards played three pieces of 9 pounders upon the enemy. The tops alone seconded the fire of this little battery, and held out bravely during the whole of the action; especially the main top where Lieut. Stack commanded. I directed the fire of one of the three cannon against the main-mast with double-headed shot, while the other two were exceedingly well served with grape and canister-shot to silence the enemy's musketry, and clear her decks, which was at last effected. The enemy were, as I have since understood, on the instant of calling for quarters, when the cowardice or treachery of three of my under officers induced them to call to the enemy. The English commodore asked me if I demanded quarters, and I having answered him in the most determined negative, they renewed the battle with double fury; they were unable to stand the deck, but the fire of their cannon, especially the lower battery, which was entirely formed of 18 pounders, was incessant. Both ships were set on fire in various places, and the scene was dreadful beyond the reach of language. To account for the timidity of my three under officers, I mean the gunner, the carpenter, and the master-at-arms, I must observe that the two first were slightly wounded, and as the ship had received various shots under the water, and one of the pumps being shot away, the carpenter expressed his fear that she would sink, and the other two concluded that she was sinking, which occasioned the gunner to run off on the poop, without my knowledge, to strike the colors; fortunately for me, a cannon ball had done that before, by carrying away the ensign staff; he was, therefore, reduced to the necessity of sinking,—as he supposed,—or of calling for quarter, and he preferred the latter.

All this time the Bon homme Richard had sustained the action alone, and the enemy, though much superior in force, would have been very glad to have got clear, as appears by their own acknowledgments, and their having let go an anchor the instant that I laid them on board, by which means they would have escaped, had I not made them well fast to the Bon homme Richard.

At last, at half past nine o'clock, the Alliance appeared. And I now thought the battle at an end; but to my utter astonishment, he discharged a broadside full into the stern of Bon homme Richard. We called to him for God's sake to forbear firing into the Bon homme Richard; yet he passed along the off side of the ship and continued firing. There was no possibility of his mistaking the enemy's ship for the Bon homme Richard, there being the most essential difference in their appearance and construction; besides it was then full moonlight, and the sides of the Bon homme Richard were all black, while the sides of the prizes were yellow; yet, for the greater security, I showed the signal of our reconnaissance, by putting out three lanthorns, one at the head (bow), another at the stern (quarter), and the third in the middle, in a horizontal line. Every tongue cried that he was firing into the wrong ship, but nothing availed, he passed round, firing into the Bon homme Richard's head, stern, and broadside and by one of his vollies killed several of my best men, and mortally wounded a good officer on the forecastle. My situation was really deplorable. The Bon homme Richard received various shots under water from the Alliance; the leak gained on the pumps; and the fire increased much on board both ships. Some officers persuaded me to strike, of whose courage and good sense, I entertain a high opinion. My treacherous master-at-arms let loose all my prisoners without my knowledge, and my prospect became gloomy indeed. I would not, however, give up the point. The enemy's main-mast began to shake, their firing decreased, ours rather increased, and the British colors were struck at half an hour past ten o'clock.

This prize proved to be the British ship-of-war the Serapis, a new ship of 44 guns, built on their most approved construction, with two complete batteries, one of them of 18 pounders, and commanded by the brave Commodore Richard Pearson. I had yet two enemies to encounter far more formidable than the Britons:—I mean fire and water. The Serapis was attacked only by the first, but the Bon homme Richard was assailed by both: there were five feet water in the hold, and although it was moderate from the explosion of so much gunpowder, yet the three pumps that remained could with difficulty only keep the water from gaining. The fire broke out in various parts of the ship, in spite of all the water that could be thrown to quench it, and at length broke out as low as the powder magazine, and within a few inches of the powder. In that dilemma, I took out the powder upon deck, ready to be thrown overboard at the last extremity, and it was 10 o'clock the next day, the 24th, before the fire was entirely extinguished. With respect to the situation of the Bon homme Richard, the rudder was cut entirely off the stern frame, and the transoms were almost entirely cut away; the timbers, by the lower deck especially, from the main-mast to the stern, being greatly decayed with age, were mangled beyond my power of description; and a person must have been an eyewitness to form a just idea of the tremendous scene of carnage, wreck, and ruin that everywhere appeared. Humanity cannot but recoil from the prospect of such finished horror, and lament that war should produce such fatal consequences.

After the carpenters, as well as Capt. De Cottineau, and other men of sense had well examined and surveyed the ship (which was not finished before five in the evening), I found every person to be convinced that it was impossible to keep the Bon homme Richard afloat so as to reach a port if the wind should increase, it being then only a very moderate breeze. I had but little time to remove my wounded, which now became unavoidable, and which was affected in the course of the night and next morning. I was determined to keep the Bon homme Richard afloat, and, if possible, to bring her into port. For that purpose, the first lieutenant of the Pallas continued on board with a party of men to attend the pumps, with boats in waiting, ready to take them on board, in case the water should gain on them too fast. The wind augmented in the night and the next day, on the 25th, so that it was impossible to prevent the good old ship from sinking. They did not abandon her till after 9 o'clock; the water was then up to the lower deck, and a little after ten, I saw with inexpressible grief the last glimpse of the Bon homme Richard. No lives were lost with the ship, but it was impossible to save the stores of any sort whatever. I lost even the best part of my clothes, books, and papers; and several of my officers lost all their clothes and effects.

Having thus endeavored to give a clear and simple relation of the circumstances and events that have attended the little armament under my command, I shall freely submit my conduct therein to the censure of my superiors and the impartial public. I beg leave, however, to observe, that the force that was put under my command was far from being well composed; and as the great majority of the actors in it have appeared bent on the pursuit of interest only, I am exceedingly sorry that they and I have been at all concerned. I am in the highest degree sensible of the singular attentions which I have experienced from the court of France, which I shall remember with perfect gratitude until the end of my life, and will always endeavor to merit, while I can, consistent with my honor, continue in the public service. I must speak plainly. As I have been always honored with the full confidence of Congress, and as I also flattered myself with enjoying in some measure the confidence of the Court of France, I could not but be astonished at the conduct of M. de Chaumont. When, in the moment of my departure from Groaix, he produced a paper, a concordat, for me to sign, in common with the officers whom I had commissioned but a few days before. Had that paper, or even a less dishonorable one, been proposed to me at the beginning, I would have rejected it with just contempt, and the word *deplacement,* among others, should have been necessary. I cannot, however, even now suppose that he was authorized by the Court to make such a bargain with me; nor can I suppose that the minister of the marine meant that M. de Chaumont should consider me merely as a colleague with the commanders of the other ships, and communicate to them not only all he knew, but all he thought, respecting our destination and operations. M. de Chaumont has made me various reproaches on account of the expenses of the Bon homme Richard, wherewith I cannot think I have been justly chargeable. M. de Chamillard can attest that the Bon homme Richard was at last far from being well fitted or armed for war. If any person or persons who have been charged with the expense of that armament have acted wrong, the fault must not be laid to my charge. I had no authority to superintend that armament, and the persons who had authority were so far from giving me what I thought necessary, that M. de Chaumont even refused, among other things, to allow me irons for securing the prisoners of war.

In short, while my life remains, if I have any capacity to render good and acceptable services to the common cause, no man will step forth with greater cheerfulness and alacrity than myself, but I am not made to be dishonored nor can I accept of the *half confidence* of any man living; of course I cannot, consistent with my honor and a prospect of success, undertake future expeditions, unless when the object and destination is communicated to me alone, and to no other person in the marine line. In cases where troops are embarked, a like confidence is due alone to their commander-in-chief. On no other condition will I ever undertake the chief command of a private expedition; and when I do not command in chief, I have no desire to be in the secret.

Captain Cottineau engaged the Countess of Scarborough, and took her after an hour's action, while the Bon homme Richard engaged the Serapis. The Countess of Scarborough is an armed ship of 20 six-pounders, and was commanded by a king's officer. In the action, the Countess of Scarborough and the Serapis were at a considerable distance asunder; and the Alliance, as I am informed, fired into the Pallas and killed some men. If it should be asked why the convoy was suffered to escape, I must answer, that I was myself in no condition to pursue, and that none of the rest showed any inclination, not even Mr. Ricot, who had held off at a distance to windward during the whole action, and withheld by force the pilot boat with my lieutenant and 15 men. The Alliance, too, was in a state to pursue the fleet, not having had a single man wounded, or a single shot fired at her from the Serapis, and only three that did execution from the Countess of Scarborough, at such a distance that one stuck in the side, and the other two just touched and then dropped into the water. The Alliance killed one man only on board the Serapis. As Captain de Cottineau charged himself with manning and securing the prisoners of the Countess of Scarborough, I think the escape of the Baltic fleet cannot so well be charged to his account.

I should have mentioned that the mainmast and mizentopmast of the Serapis fell overboard soon after the captain had come on board the Bon homme Richard.

Upon the whole, the captain of the Alliance has behaved so very ill in every respect, that I must complain loudly of his conduct. He pretends that he is authorized to act independent of my command: I have been taught the contrary; but supposing it to be so, his conduct has been base and unpardonable. M. de Chamillard will explain the particulars. Either Captain Landais or myself is highly criminal, and one or the other must be punished. I forbear to take any steps with him until I have the advice and approbation of your excellency. I have been advised by all the officers of the squadron to put M. Landais under arrest; but as I have postponed it so long, I will bear with him a little longer, until the return of my express.

We this day anchored here, having since the action been tossed to and fro by contrary winds. I wished to have gained the Road of Dunkirk on account of our prisoners, but was overruled by the majority of *my colleagues*. I shall hasten up to Amsterdam, and there if I meet with no orders from my government, I will take the advice of the French ambassador. It is my present intention to have the Countess of Scarborough ready to transport the prisoners from hence to Dunkirk, unless it should be found more expedient to deliver them to the

English ambassador, taking his obligation to send to Dunkirk, &c. immediately an equal number of American prisoners. I am under strong apprehensions that our object here will fail, and that through the imprudence of M. de Chaumont, who has communicated everything he knew or thought on the matter to persons who cannot help talking of it at a full table. This is the way he keeps state secrets, though he never mentioned the affair to me.

I am ever, &c.
John P. Jones

Commodore Richard Dale's Account of the Battle off Flamborough Head

Description by Commodore Richard Dale of the battle off Flamborough Head, during which he was first lieutenant in *Bonhomme Richard.* This written account of the action was provided directly to John Henry Sherburne for his work, *The Life and Character of John Paul Jones,* 1851, pp. 120–23.

On the 23d of September, 1779, being below, was aroused by an unusual noise upon deck. This induced me to go upon deck, when I found the men were swaying up the royal yards, preparatory to making sail for a large fleet under our lee. I asked the coasting pilot what fleet it as? He answered: 'The Baltic fleet, under convoy of the Serapis of 44 guns, and the Countess of Scarborough of 20 guns.' A general chase then commenced of the Bon homme Richard, the Vengeance, the Pallas, and the Alliance. The latter ship being then in sight after a separation from the squadron of nearly three weeks, but which ship, as usual, disregarded the private signals of the commodore. At this time our fleet headed to the northward, with a light breeze, Flamborough head being about two leagues distant. At 7 P.M. it was evident the Baltic fleet perceived we were in chase, from the signal of the Serapis and Countess of Scarborough, tacked ship, and stood off shore, with the intention of drawing off our attention from the convoy. When these ships had separated from the convoy about two miles, they again tacked and stood in shore after the merchantmen. At about eight, being within hail, the Serapis demanded, 'what ship is that?' He was answered, 'I can't hear what you say.' Immediately after the Serapis hailed again, 'what ship is that? Answer immediately, or I shall be under the necessity of firing into you.' At this moment I received orders from Commodore Jones to commence the action with a broadside, which indeed appeared to be simultaneous on board both ships. Our position being to windward of the Serapis, we passed ahead of her, and the Serapis coming up on our larboard quarter, the action commenced abreast of each other. The Serapis soon passed ahead of the Bon homme Richard, and when he thought he had gained a distance sufficient to go down athwart the fore foot to rake us, found he had not enough distance, and that the Bon homme Richard would be aboard him, put his helm a-lee, which brought the two ships on a line, and the Bon homme Richard, having headway, ran her bows into the stern of the Serapis. We had remained in this situation but a few minutes when we were again hailed by the Serapis, 'Has your ship struck?' To which Captain Jones answered, 'I have not yet begun to fight.'

As we were unable to bring a single gun to bear upon the Serapis, our topsails were backed, while those of the Serapis being filled, the ships separated. The Serapis wore short round upon her heel, and her jibboom ran into the mizzen rigging of the Bon homme Richard; in this situation the ships were made fast together with a hawser, the bowsprit of the Serapis to the mizzenmast of the Bon homme Richard, and the action recommenced from the starboard sides of the two ships. With a view of separating the ships, the Serapis let go her anchor, which manoeuvre brought her head, and the stern of the Bon homme Richard to the wind, while the ships lay closely pressed against each other. A novelty in naval combats was now presented to many witnesses, but to few admirers. The rammers were run into the respective ships to enable the men to load after the lower ports of the Serapis had been blown away, to make room for running out their guns, and in this situation the ships remained until between 10 and 11 o'clock P.M., when the engagement terminated by the surrender of the Serapis.

From the commencement to the termination of the action, there was not a man on board the Bon homme Richard ignorant of the superiority of the Serapis, both in weight of metal, and in the qualities of the crews. The crew of that ship was picked seamen, and the ship itself had been only a few months off the stocks; whereas the crew of the Bon homme Richard consisted of part American, English and French, and part of Maltese, Portuguese, and Malays, these latter contributing, by their want of naval skill and knowledge of the English language, to depress rather than elevate a just hope of success in a combat under such circumstances. Neither the consideration of the relative force of the ships, the fact of the blowing up of the gun-deck above them by the bursting of two of the 18 pounders, nor the alarm that the ship was sinking, could depress the ardor or change the determination of the brave Captain Jones, his officers and men. Neither the repeated broadsides of the Alliance, given with the view of sinking or disabling the Bon homme Richard, the frequent necessity of suspending the combat to extinguish the flames, which several times were within a few inches of the magazines, not the liberation of the master-at-arms of nearly 500 prisoners, could change or weaken the purpose of the American commander. At the moment of the liberation of the prisoners, one of them, a commander of a 20 gun ship taken a few days before, passed through the ports on board the Serapis, and informed Captain Pearson that if he would hold out only a little while longer, the ship alongside would either strike or sink, and that all the prisoners had been released to save their lives. The combat was accordingly continued with renewed ardor by the Serapis.

The fire from the tops of the Bon homme Richard was conducted with so much skill and effect as to destroy ultimately every man who appeared on the quarter-deck of the Serapis, and induced her commander to order the survivors to go below. Nor even under the shelter of the decks were they more secure. The powder-monkeys of the Serapis finding no officer to receive the 18 pound cartridges brought from the magazines, threw them on the main-deck, and went for more. These cartridges being scattered along the deck, and numbers of them broken, it so happened that some of the hand-grenades thrown from the main-yard of the Bon homme Richard, which was directly over the main-hatch of the Serapis, fell upon this powder, and produced a most awful explosion. The effect was tremendous; more than twenty of the enemy were blown to pieces, and many stood with only the collars of their shirts upon their bodies. In less than an hour afterward, the flag of England, which had been nailed to the mast of the Serapis, was struck by Captain Pearson's *own hand,* as none of his people would venture aloft on this duty; and this too, when more than 1500 persons were witnessing the conflict, and the humiliating termination of it, from Scarborough and Flamborough head.

Upon finding that the flag of the Serapis had been struck, I went to Captain Jones and asked whether I might board the Serapis? To which he consented; and jumping upon the gunwale, seized the main-brace pennant, and swung myself upon her quarter-deck. Midshipman Mayrant followed with a party of men, and was immediately run through the thigh with a boarding-pike by some of the enemy stationed in the waist, who were not informed of the surrender of their ship. I found Captain Pearson standing on the leeward side of the quarter-deck, and, addressing myself to him, said—'Sir, I have orders to send you on board the ship alongside.' The first lieutenant of Serapis coming up at this moment, inquired of Captain Pearson whether the ship alongside had struck to him? To which I replied, 'No, sir, to the contrary; he has struck to us.' The lieutenant renewing his inquiry, have you struck sir? was answered, 'Yes, I have.' The lieutenant replied, 'I have nothing more to say;' and was about to return below, when I informed him he must accompany Captain Pearson on board the ship alongside. He said, 'If you will permit me to go below, I will silence the firing of the lower-deck guns.' This request was refused, and with Captain Pearson (he) was passed over to the deck of the Bon homme Richard. Orders being sent below to cease firing, the engagement terminated, after a most obstinate contest of three hours and a half.

After receiving Captain Pearson on board the Bon homme Richard, Captain Jones gave orders to cut loose the lashings, and directed me to follow him with the Serapis. Perceiving the Bon homme Richard leaving the Serapis, I sent one of the quarter-masters to ascertain whether the wheel-ropes were cut away, supposing something extraordinary must be the matter, as the ship would not pay off, although the head sails were aback, and no after sail; the quarter-master returning, reported that the wheel-ropes were all well, and the helm hard a-port. Excited by this extraordinary circumstance, I jumped off the binnacle, where I had been sitting, and falling upon the deck, found to my astonishment I had the use of only one of my legs: a splinter of one of the guns had struck and badly wounded my leg, without my perceiving my injury until this moment. I was replaced upon the binnacle, when the sailing-master of the Serapis coming up to me, observed that from my orders he judged I must be ignorant of the ship being *at anchor.* Noticing the second lieutenant of the Bon homme Richard, I directed him to go below and cut away the cable, and follow the Bon homme Richard with the Serapis. I was then carried on board the Bon homme Richard to have my wound dressed.

Captain Richard Pearson's Report of the Battle off Flamborough Head

Report by Captain Richard Pearson of the battle off Flamborogh Head. As published in *The Life and Character of John Paul Jones*, by John Henry Sherburne, 1851, pp. 123–26.

ADMIRALTY OFFICE,
OCTOBER 12, 1779.
A LETTER FROM CAPT. RICHARD PEARSON, OF HIS MAJESTY'S SHIP SERAPIS TO MR. STEPHENS, OF WHICH THE FOLLOWING IS A COPY, WAS YESTERDAY RECEIVED AT THIS OFFICE

Pallas, French Frigate, in Congress service, Texel, October 6, 1779

Sir,

You will be pleased to inform the Lords Commissioners of the Admiralty, that on the 23rd ult, being close in with Scarborough, about 4 o'clock, a boat came on board with a letter from the bailiff's of that corporation, giving information of a flying squadron of the enemy's ships being on the coast, and a part of the said squadron having been seen from thence the day before, standing to the southward. As soon as I received this intelligence I made the signal for the convoy to bear down under my lee, and repeated it with two guns; notwithstanding which the van of the convoy kept their wind, with all sail stretching out to the southward from under Flamborough Head, till between twelve and one, when the headmost of them got sight of the enemy's ships, which were then in chase of them; they then tacked, and made the best of their way under the shore for Scarborough, &c. letting fly their top-gallant sheets, and firing guns; upon which I made all the sail I could to windward, to get between the enemy's ships and the convoy, which I soon effected. At 1 o'clock we got sight of the enemy's ships from the masthead, and about 4 we made them plain from the deck to be three large ships and a brig, upon which I made the Countess of Scarborough a signal to join me, she being in shore with the convoy. At the same time I made the signal for the convoy to make the best of their way, and repeated the signal with two guns: I then brought to, to let the Countess of Scarborough come up, and cleared ship for action. At half past 5 the Countess of Scarborough joined me, the enemy's ships bearing down upon us with a light breeze at S.S.W., at 6 tacked, in order to keep our ground the better between the enemy's ships and the convoy: soon after which we perceived the ships bearing down upon us to be a two-decked ship and two frigates, but from keeping their end on, and bearing upon us, we could not discern what colors they were under; at about 20 minutes past 7 the largest ship of the three brought to on our larboard bow, within musket-shot. I hailed him and asked what ship it was; they answered in English, "The Princess Royal." I then asked where they belonged to, they answered evasively; on which I told them, if they did not answer directly I would fire into them; they then answered with a shot which was instantly returned with a broadside; and, after exchanging two or three broadsides, he backed his topsails, and dropped upon our quarter within pistol shot, then filled gain, put his helm-a-weather, and run us on board upon our weather quarter, and attempted to board us, but being repulsed, he sheered off; upon which I backed our topsails, in order to get square with him again, which, as soon as he observed, he then filled, put his helm a-weather, and laid us athwart hause; his mizzen shrouds took our jib-boom, which hung him for some time until it last gave way, and we dropt alongside of each other, head and stern, when the fluke of our spare anchor hooking his quarter, we became so close fore and aft that the muzzles of our guns touched each other's sides. In this position we engaged from half past 8 till half past 10, during which time, from the great quantity and variety of combustible matters which they threw in upon our decks, chains, and in short, into every part of the ship, we were on fire no less than ten or twelve times in different parts of the ship, and it was with the greatest difficulty and exertion imaginable at times that we were able to get it extinguished. At the same time the largest of the two frigates kept sailing round us the whole action and raking us fore and aft, by which means she killed or wounded almost every man on the quarter and main decks. About half past 9, either from a hand-grenade being thrown in one of our lower-deck ports, or from some other accident, a cartridge of powder was set on fire, the flames of which running from cartridge to cartridge all the way aft, blew up the whole of the people and officers that were quartered abaft the main-mast; from which unfortunate circumstance all those guns were rendered useless for the remainder of the action and, I fear, the greatest part of the people will lose their lives. At 10 o'clock they called for quarters from the ship alongside, and said they had struck; hearing this I called upon the captain to know if he had struck, or if he asked for quarters; but no answer being made, after repeating my words two or three times, I called for the boarders and ordered them to board, which they did; but the moment they were on board her, they discovered a superior number laying under cover with pikes in their hands, ready to receive them, on which our people retreated instantly to their guns again till past 10, when the frigate coming across our stern, and pouring her broadside into us again, without our being able to bring a gun to bear on her, I found it in vain, and indeed impracticable from the situation we were in, to stand out any longer with the least prospect of success. I therefore struck (our mainmast at the same time went by the board). The first lieutenant and myself were immediately escorted into the ship alongside, when we found her to be an American ship-of-war, called the Bon homme Richard of 40 guns and 375 men, commanded by Capt. Paul Jones, the other frigate which engaged us to be the Alliance of 40 guns and 300 men, and the third frigate which engaged and took the Countess of Scarborough, after two hour's action, to be the Pallas, a French frigate of 32 guns and 275 men, the Vengeance an armed brig of 12 guns and 70 men, all in Congress service and under the command of Paul Jones. They fitted out and sailed from Port L'Orient the latter end of July, and came north about; they have on board 300 English prisoners which they have taken in different vessels in their way round since they left France, and have ransomed some others. On my going on board the Bon homme Richard I found her to be in the greatest distress; her counters and quarter on the lower deck entirely drove in, and the whole of her lower deck guns dismounted; she also was on fire in two places, and six or seven feet water in her hold, which kept increasing on them all night and the next day, til they were obliged to quit her, and she sunk with a great number of her wounded people on board her. She had 306 men killed and wounded in the action; our loss in the Serapis was also very great. My officers and people in general behaved well, and I should be very remiss in my attention to their merit, were I to omit recommending the remains of them to their Lordship's favor.

Herewith I enclose you the most exact list of the killed and wounded I have as yet been able to procure, from my people being dispersed among the different ships, and having been refused permission to muster them; there are, I find, many more both killed and wounded than appears in the enclosed list, but their names I find as yet impossible to ascertain; as soon as I possibly can, I shall give their Lordships a full account of the whole.

I am, Sir, &c.
R. Pearson.

Congressional Committee Report on the Promotion of Officers

Congressional Committee Report on the Promotion of Officers. As published in *The Life and Correspondence of John Paul Jones, Including his Narrative of the Campaign of the Liman* by Robert C. Sands, 1830. pp. 309–10.

COPY OF CONGRESSIONAL COMMITTEE REPORT ON JONES'S LETTER CONCERNING HIS RANK (ENDORSED "AUGUST 24, 1781, NOT TO BE ACTED UPON")

The committee to whom were referred the application of Captain John Paul Jones; and also the applications of Captain James Nicholson and Captain Thomas Reed [sic], beg to report,

That by an arrangement of the captains of the navy which was adopted by Congress on the tenth day of October, A.D. 1776, Captain James Nicholson was placed first in rank, Captain Thomas Reed [sic] eighth, and Captain John Paul Jones the eighteenth.

The committee cannot fully ascertain the rule by which the arrangement was made, as the relative rank was not comformable to the times of appointment or dates of commission, and seems repugnant to a resolution of Congress, of the 22d of December, 1775. It appears that Captains Whipple, Barry, Hollock, and Alexander, were appointed captains previous to either of the applicants; Captain Nicholson was later than either, excepting Reed [sic]; but Captain Nicholson had a command of armed vessels under the authority of the state of Maryland, prior to his being adopted in the continental navy. It is, therefore, to be presumed that preference was given to him on that account. Upon the whole, the committee submit to Congress whether it will be advisable to alter that arrangement? If they should, Captain Jones will now stand the fifth captain, if respect be had only to time of appointment in that grade; but if regard be had to Captain Jones' being a lieutenant in the navy prior to the appointment of many of the other gentlemen, he would then stand second in the rank of captains, and Whipple first.

The committee also recommends to Congress the expediency of appointing a commander in chief of the navy, in the place of the late Ezek [sic] Hopkins, Esq. Dismissed.

John Paul Jones's Complaints to Congress

Letter from John Paul Jones to Robert Morris, Head of the Marine Committee of Congress, listing his complaints about his ranking in the navy and other matters. As published in *The Life and Correspondence of John Paul Jones, Including his Narrative of the Campaign of the Liman* by Robert C. Sands, 1830. pp. 304–9.

Philadelphia, October 10, 1783

Sir,

It is the custom of nations, on the return of peace, to honor, promote, and reward, such officers as have served through the war with the greatest *"zeal, prudence, and intrepidity."* And since my country has, after an eight years' war, attained the inestimable blessing of peace and the sovereignty of an extensive empire; I presume that, (as I have constantly and faithfully served through the Revolution, and at the same time supported it, in a degree, with my purse,) I may be allowed to lay my grievances before you, as the head of the marine. I will hope, sir, through you, to meet with redress from Congress. *Rank,* which opens the door to glory, is too near the heart of every officer of true *military feeling,* to be given up in favor of any other man who has not, by the achievement of some brilliant action, or by known and superior abilities, merited such preference. *If this* be so, how must I have felt, since by the second table of captains in the navy, adopted by Congress, on the 10th of October 1776, I was superseded in favor of thirteen persons, two of whom were my junior lieutenants at the beginning; the rest were only commissioned into the continental navy on that day; and, if they had any superior abilities, these were not then known, nor have since been proved! I am the oldest sea officer (except Captain Whipple) on the Journal, and under the commission of Congress, remaining in the service. In the year, 1775, when the navy was established, some of the gentlemen by whom I was superseded, were applied to, to embark in the first expedition; but they declined. Captain Whipple has often and lately told me they said to him, "they did not choose to be hanged." It is certain the hazard at the first was very great; and some respectable gentlemen, by whom I am superseded, accepted the appointments of captain and of lieutenant of a provincial vessel for the protection of the river, after our fleet had sailed from it; and on board of which *they had refused to embark,* though I pretend not to know their reason. But the face of affairs having changed, as we ripened into the declaration of independence in 1776, their apprehensions subsided; and in a letter I received from the late Mr. Joseph Hewes, of Congress, and of the marine committee, dated at Philadelphia, May the 26th, 1776, and directed to me *as captain of the Providence of New York,* he says, "You would be surprised to hear what a vast number of applications, are continually making for officers of the new frigates, especially for the command. The strong *recommendations* from those provinces where any frigates are building, have great weight."

He adds, "My utmost endeavours shall be exerted to serve you; from a conviction that your merit entitles you the promotion, and that you ought to command some who were placed higher than yourself." I ask, sir, did these "recommendations" plead more successful than the merit of all the gallant men who first braved the ocean in the cause of America? Your candor must answer, Yes. What hapless prospect then have those, who can only claim from past, though applauded services? Credit, it is alleged, has been, however, taken in this Revolution for "unparalleled heroism." I am sorry for it; for great as our pretensions to heroism may be, yet modesty becomes young nations as well as young men. But the first beginning of our navy was, as navies now rank, so singularly small, that I am of opinion, it has no precedent in history. Was it a proof of madness in the first corps of sea officers to have, at so critical a period, launched out on the ocean, with only two armed merchant ships, two armed brigantines, and one armed sloop, to make war against such a power as Great Britain? They had, perhaps, in proportion to their number, as much sense as the present table of officers can boast of; and it has not yet been proved, that they did not understand, at least *as well* their duty.

Their first expedition was far more glorious than any other that has been since attempted *from our coast.* Every officer on that service merited promotion, who was capable of receiving it. And, if there was an improper man placed over them as commander in chief, was that a reason to sleight or disgrace the whole corps? Has the subsequent military conduct of those officers, by whom the first corps of sea officers were superseded, justified the preference they had to command the new frigates? If it has not, what shall we say in favor of the precedence, which, "Repugnant to an Act of Congress, of the 22d of December, 1775," and contrary to all rule or example, was given them in the second table of naval rank, adopted the 10th of October, 1776? Could anything be more humiliating than this to sea officers appointed and commissioned in 1775? Would it not have been more kind to have dismissed them from the service, even without assigning a reason for so doing? Before any second arrangement of naval rank had been made, perhaps it would have been good policy, to have commissioned, five or seven old mariners, who had seen war, to have examined the qualifications of the candidates, especially, those who made their *conditions* and sought so earnestly after the *command* of the new frigates. Those commissioners might also have examined the qualifications of the first corps of sea officers, promoted such as were capable of it, and struck from the list such as were unequal to the commission they bore, &c. Thus, by giving precedence in rank to all the captains who had served and were thought worthy of being continued; and also to all lieutenants promoted to the rank of captains, for their meritorious services and fit qualifications, justice might have been done both to individuals and the public. It has been said, with a degree of contempt, by some of the gentlemen who came into the continental navy, the second year of the war, that "I was *only a lieutenant* at the beginning;" and pray, what were they when I was out on the ocean in that character? They pay me a compliment. To be diffident, is not always a proof of ignorance, but sometimes the contrary. I was offered a captain's commission at the first, to command the Providence, but declined it. Let it, however, be remembered that there were three grades of sea lieutenants established by the Act of Congress of the 22d of December, 1775; and as I had the honor to be placed at the head of the first of those grades, it is not quite fair in those gentlemen to confound me with the last; yet when I came to try my skill, I am not ashamed to own, I did not find myself perfect in the duties of a first lieutenant. However, I by no means admit that any one of the gentlemen who so earnestly sought after *rank* and the *command* of the new frigates the next year, was at the beginning able to teach me any part of the duty of a sea officer. Since that time it is well known, there has been no comparison between their *means* of acquiring military marine knowledge and mine.

If midnight study, and the instruction of the greatest and most learned sea officers, can have given me *advantages,* I am not without them. I confess, however, I am yet to learn. It is the work of many years' study and experience, to acquire the high degree of science necessary for a great sea officer. Cruising after merchant ships, the service on which our frigates have generally been employed, affords, I may say, no part of the knowledge necessary for conducting fleets and their operation. There is *now,* perhaps, as much difference between a single battle between two ships, and an engagement between two fleets, as there is between a single duel and a *ranged* battle between two armies. I became captain, by right of service and succession, and by order and commission of his excellency Ezek Hopkins, Esq. Commander in chief, the 10th day of May, 1776, at which time the captain of the Providence was broke and dismissed from the navy, by a court martial. Having arrived at Philadelphia, with a little convoy from Boston, soon after the declaration of independence, President Hancock gave me a captain's commission *under the United States,* dated the 8th day of August, 1776. I did not, at the time, think that this was doing me justice; as it did not correspond with my appointment by the commander in chief. It was, however, I presumed *the first naval commission* granted under the United States. And as a resolution of Congress had been passed the 17th day of April, 1776, "that the *nomination* of captains should not determine rank, which was to be settled *before* commissions were granted." My commission of the 8th of August, 1776 must, by that resolution, take rank of every commission dated the 10th of October, 1776. My duty brought me again to Philadelphia in April, 1776; and President Hancock then told me that new naval commissions were ordered to be distributed to the officers.

He requested me to show him the captain's commission he had given me the year before. I did so. He then desired me to leave it with him a day or two, till he could find a leisure moment to fill up a new commission. I made no difficulty. When I waited on him the day before my departure, to my great surprise, he put into my hands a commission, dated the 10th day of October, 1776, and numbered eighteen on the margin! I told him that was not what I expected, and requested my former commission. He turned over various papers on the table, and at last told me he was sorry to have lost or mislaid it. He paid me many compliments on the services I had performed in vessels of little force, and assured me no officer stood higher in the opinion of Congress than myself; a proof of which, he said, was my late appointment to the command of secret expeditions, with five sail and men proportioned, against St. Kitts, Pensacola, Augustine, &c. That the table of naval rank that had been adopted the 10th of October, 1776, had been drawn up in a hurry, and without well knowing the different merits and qualifications of the officers; but it was the intention of Congress to render impartial justice, and always to honour, promote, and reward merit. And, as to myself, that I might depend on receiving a very agreeable appointment soon after my return to Boston; and, until I was perfectly satisfied respecting my rank, I should have a separate command. See Paper No. 1. I retired to Boston, and it was not long before I received orders to proceed to Europe to command the great frigate building at Amsterdam, for the United States; then called the Indien, and since the South Carolina. It was proposed that I should proceed to France in a ship belonging to that kingdom; but, some difficulties arising, the sloop of war Ranger of eighteen guns, was put under my command for that service, and to serve afterwards as a tender to the Indien. Political reasons defeated the plan, after I had met our commissioners at Paris, agreeable to their order, to consult on the ways and means of carrying it into execution. I returned in consequence to Nantes, and resumed the command of the Ranger. When I returned from Europe and my sovereign told the world that some of my military conduct on the coast of England had been *"attended with circumstances so brilliant as to excite general applause and admiration;"* when the honours conferred on me by his most Christian majesty; to whit, a gold sword, on which is impressed the highly flattering words, *"Vindicati Maris Ludovicus XVI. Remunerator Strenuo Vindici,"* and emblems of the alliance between the United States and France, accompanied with the *order and patent* of military merit, and a very strong and *particular letter* of recommendation to Congress in my behlf, No. 2, were declared *by them* to be "highly acceptable;" when I was thought worthy of a vote of thanks and general approbation so strong and comprehensive, as that hereto subjoined, in Paper No. 3, I was far from thinking that such *pleasing expressions* were all the gratification I had to expect. The committee of Congress to whom was referred my general examination by the board of admiralty, with the report of that board thereon, were of opinion that I had merited a gold medal, with devices declarative of the vote of thanks, which I had received from the United States in Congress assembled. And I was persuaded that I should also be promoted, or at least restored to the place I held in the naval line of rank in the year 1775. I waited patiently for some time; but nothing was done on either of these subjects. Being informed by some members of Congress, that it was necessary I should present my claim respecting rank in writing, I did so, in a letter of which No. 4 is a copy, addressed to his excellency the president of Congress, the 28th of May 1781. My application was referred to a special committee who, as I have been informed by one of its members, made a report in my favour, and gave as their opinion, that I had merited to be promoted to the rank of rear admiral. Before Congress had taken up the report an application in opposition to me, was made by two of the captains who had superseded me. Upon this the report was recommitted. The committee once more reported in my favour; but without giving a direct opinion respecting my promotion; and recommended the appointment of a commander in chief of the navy, as may be seen by the annexed copy, No. 5, of that report; which, on account of the thinness of Congress was on the 24th of August, 1781, endorsed *"Not to be acted upon."* It is, however, plain, it was intended to be taken up again, when a proper opportunity presented itself; otherwise it would not have been retained on the files of Congress. This appears also by the extract of a letter, No. 6, which I wrote from Portsmouth in New Hampshire, and the answer, No. 7, that I received from the honourable John Mathews, Esq. who was chairman of the committee respecting the honorary medal, and a member of the committee on my rank. While my claim for rank stood recommitted before the committee, I was unanimously elected by ballot in Congress, the 26th of June, 1781, to command the America of 74 guns; (and, as I was erroneously informed, ready to launch at Portsmouth;) on which occasion several of the members of Congress had resolved that captains of ships of 40 guns and upwards should rank as colonels, and captains of ships between 20 and 40 guns as lieutenant colonels. There appeared so much reason and justice in that opinion, that I was then and am still inclined to believe it was not without good foundation; for certainly there is no comparison between the trust reposed in a captain of the line and a captain of a frigate; and, except in England, where avarice is the ruling principle of the corps, there is no equality between their distinct ranks. A captain of the line *must* at this day be a tactician. A captain of a cruising frigate *may make shift* without having ever heard of the naval tactic. Until I arrived in France, and became acquainted with that great tactician Count D'Orvilliers and his judicious assistant the Chevalier Du Pavillion, who each of them honoured me with instructions respecting the science of governing the operations and police of a fleet, I confess I was *not* sensible how ignorant I had been of naval tactics.

I have many things to offer respecting the formation of our navy, but shall reserve my observations upon that head until you shall have leisure to attend to them, and require them of me. I have the honour to be presented with copies of the signals, tactics, and police, that have been adopted under the different admirals of France and Spain during the war; and I have in my last campaign seen them put in practice. While I was at Brest, as well as while I was inspecting the building of America, as I had furnished myself with good authors, I applied much of my leisure time to the study of naval architecture and other matters, that relate to the establishment and police of dock-yards, &c. (I, however, feel myself bound to say again, I have yet much need to be instructed.) But if, such as I am, it is thought I can be useful in the formation of the future marine of America, *make whole my honour,* and I am so truly a citizen of the United States, that I will cheerfully do my best to effect that great object. It was my fortune, as the senior of the first lieutenants, to hoist the flag of America the first time it was displayed. Though this was but a light circumstance, yet I feel for its honour more than I think I should have done if it had not happened. See Paper No. 8. I drew my sword at the beginning, not after having made *sinister conditions* but purely from principle in the glorious cause of freedom; which I hope has been amply evinced by my conduct during the Revolution. I hope I shall be pardoned in saying, it will not be expected, after having fought and bled for the purpose of contributing to make millions happy and free, that I should remain miserable and dishonoured by being superseded, *without any just cause assigned.* Permit me now, sir, to draw your particular attention to the following points: 1st, By virtue of my commission as the senior of the first lieutenants of the American navy, I stand the next in rank to Captain Abraham Whipple, who is the only one of my senior officers now remaining in the service. 2ndly, By the commission as captain *under the United States,* which I received from the hands of President Hancock at the door of the chamber of Congress, dated the 8th day of August, 1776, I am entitled to precede all the captains whose commissions *under the United States* are dated the 10th day of October, following. 3dly, My right of precedence is confirmed by the Act of Congress of the 26th of June, 1781, appointing me to the command of the America of 74 guns, Congress having previously resolved, that captains of ships of 40 guns and upwards should rank as colonels, and that captains of ships from 40 down to 20 guns should only rank as lieutenant colonels. I will at present say nothing of those pretensions which the favourable notice and recommendation of his most Christian majesty might encourage me to form, and which have hitherto proved so fruitless to me, though similar recommendations from Congress to that monarch have proved so efficacious in favour of those who were honoured with them. Though I have only mentioned two things that afflict me, i.e. the delay of a decision respecting my rank, and the honorary medal, yet I have met with many other humiliations in the service, that I have borne in silence. I will just mention one of them. When the America was presented to his most Christian majesty, I presume it would not have been inconsistent with that act of my sovereign, if it had mentioned my name. Such little attentions to the military pride of officers are always of use to a state, and *cost nothing.* In the present instance, it could have been no displeasing circumstance, but the contrary, to a monarch who condescends to honour me with his attention. I appeal to yourself, sir, whether, after being unanimously elected to command the first and only American ship of the line, my conduct, for more than sixteen months while inspecting her building and launching, had merited only such cold neglect? When the America was taken from me, I was deprived of my tenth command.

Will posterity believe, that out of this number the *sloop* of war *Ranger* was the best I was ever enabled *by my country* to bring into actual service? If I have been instrumental in giving the American flag some reputation and making it respectable among European nations, will you permit me to say, that, it is not because I have been honoured, *by my country,* either with proper *means* or proper *encouragement.* I cannot conclude this letter without reminding you of the insult offered to the flag of America, by the court of Denmark; in giving up to England, towards the end of the year, 1779, two large letter of marque ships (the one the Union, from London, the other the Betsy, from Liverpool,) that had entered the port of Bergen, in Norway, *as my prizes.* Those two ships mounted 22 guns each, and were valued, as I have been told, at sixteen hundred thousand livres Tournois. I acquit myself of my duty by giving you this information, now when the sovereignty and independence of America is acknowledged by Great Britain; and I trust that Congress will now demand and obtain proper acknowledgement and full restitution from the court of Denmark.

I have the honour to be, with the greatest respect, sir, your most obedient and most humble servant,

J. Paul Jones.

Notes

Introduction

1. Internet, http://www.quotationspage.com/quotes/Lord_Acton/. The Quotations Page, Quotations by Author, accessed 13 July 2005.
2. U.S. Naval History Division, *Naval Documents of the American Revolution* (Washington, D.C.: Government Printing Office, 1964), 6: 1303; John Paul Jones Papers, reel 1, document 53.
3. Declaration of Independence, paragraphs 20, 21.
4. Ibid., final paragraph.
5. "Introduction of President Theodore Roosevelt by Secretary of the Navy Charles J. Bonaparte," *John Paul Jones: Commemoration at Annapolis, April 24, 1906,* compiled by Charles W. Stewart (Washington, D.C.: Government Printing Office, 1907), 15.

1. Beginnings

1. See description of the triangle trade in the Glossary.
2. Mrs. Reginald de Koven, *The Life and Letters of John Paul Jones* (New York: Charles Scribner's Sons, 1913), 2: 440, appendix B.
3. Ibid.
4. John Paul became a Mason at Kirkcudbright, Scotland, probably in 1770.
5. See definition of mercantilism in the Glossary.
6. John Ferling, *A Leap in the Dark: The Struggle to Create the American Republic* (Oxford: Oxford University Press, 2003), 25.
7. Niall Ferguson, *Empire: The Rise and Demise of the British World Order and the Lessons for Global Power* (London: Allen Lane, 2002), 93.
8. Peter Padfield, *Maritime Supremacy and the Opening of the Western Mind* (Woodstock, N.Y.: Overlook Press, 1999), 222.
9. Internet, http://libertyonline.hypermail.com/henry-liberty.html. "Give Me Liberty or Give Me Death," accessed 1 July 2005. Also "Patrick Henry" in *The New Encyclopædia Britannica* (Chicago: 2002), 5: 854.
10. Ibid.

2. The Miracle Birth of a Navy

1. *Journal of the Continental Congress,* 1775.
2. George Modeleski and William R. Thompson, *Seapower in Global Politics, 1494–1993* (London: Macmillan, 1988), 223.
3. Vice Admiral P. H. Calomb, *Naval Warfare: Its Ruling Principles and Practice Historically Treated* (London: W. H. Allen & Co., 1891; Annapolis, Md.: Naval Institute Press, 1990), 417. Also, *The Sandwich Papers,* edited by G. R. Barnes and J. H. Owen (London: The Navy Records Society and William Clowes & Sons, 1932–38), 3: 328.
4. Piers Mackesy, *The War for America* (Cambridge, Mass.: Harvard University Press, 1964), xiv.

5. *Congressional Journal,* December 22, 1775.
6. Mrs. Reginald de Koven, *The Life and Letters of John Paul Jones* (New York: Charles Scribner's Sons, 1913), 1: 103.
7. Ibid., 104.
8. John Henry Sherburne, *The Life and Character of John Paul Jones,* 2nd ed. (New York: Adriance, Sherman & Co., 1851), 19.
9. Two helpful sources for definitions and more information on navy ranks are *A Sea of Words: A Lexicon and Companion for Patrick O'Brian's Seafaring Tales* by Dean King (New York: Henry Holt, 1995), and *Jane's Dictionary of Naval Terms,* compiled by Joseph Palmer (London: Macdonald and Jane's, 1975).
10. U.S. Naval History Division, *Naval Documents of the American Revolution* (Washington: Government Printing Office, 1964), 6: 1303; John Paul Jones Papers, reel I, document 46.
11. Ibid.
12. U.S. Naval History Division, *Naval Documents,* 7: 1303; Jones Papers, reel I, document 104.
13. U.S. Naval History Division, *Naval Documents,* 7: 1155; Jones Papers, reel I, document 104.
14. *The Dispatches and Letters of Vice Admiral Lord Viscount Nelson,* edited by Sir Nicholas Harris Nicolas (London: Henry Colburn, 1845), 4: 446.
15. See *The Command of the Howe Brothers During the American Revolution* by Troyer S. Anderson (New York: Oxford University Press, 1936) for an analysis of the British military leadership of Admiral Richard Howe and General William Howe during the American Revolution.

3. The Cutting Edge of Strategy

1. Internet, www.seacoast.nh.com/jpj/handbill.html. *The Freeman's Journal,* Portsmouth, N.H., July 26, 1777. Accessed 12 October 2004.
2. U.S. Naval History Division, *Naval Documents of the American Revolution* (Washington, D.C.: Government Printing Office, 1964), 10: 352; John Paul Jones Papers, reel I, document 205.
3. Mrs. Reginald de Koven, *The Life and Letters of John Paul Jones* (New York: Charles Scribner's Sons, 1913), 1: 247.
4. The present-day use of asymmetrical warfare techniques by terrorist groups and tyrannical national regimes involves no moral equivalency between those groups and the government or leaders of the American Revolution. Fundamental differences exist; most obvious is the use of deliberate killing of civilians for political purposes by modern terrorists and tyrannical regimes, tactics that were not employed by the American revolutionary government or its military forces.
5. Samuel Eliot Morison, *John Paul Jones: A Sailor's Biography* (Boston: Little, Brown, 1959), 142.
6. Don C. Seitz, *Paul Jones: His Exploits in English Seas During 1778–1780—Contemporary Accounts Collected from English Newspapers* (New York: E. P. Dutton, 1917), 11.
7. Ibid., 14, 15.

8. M. Mac Dermot Crawford, *The Sailor Whom England Feared* (London: Eveleigh Nash, 1913), 136.
9. *The Papers of John Paul Jones,* edited by James C. Bradford, nine microfilm reels (Alexandria, Va.: Chadwyck-Healey, 1986), 2: 287.
10. Ibid., 335.
11. Seitz, *Paul Jones,* 21, 22.
12. de Koven, *Life and Letters,* 1: 333, 334.

4. Beached

1. John Henry Sherburne, *The Life and Character of John Paul Jones,* 2nd ed. (New York: Adriance, Sherman & Co., 1851), 61.
2. Mrs. Reginald de Koven, *The Life and Letters of John Paul Jones* (New York: Charles Scribner's Sons, 1913), 1: 339, 340.
3. Ibid., 225.
4. Samuel Eliot Morison, *John Paul Jones: A Sailor's Biography* (Boston: Little, Brown, 1959), 169.
5. Sherburne, *Life and Character,* 51.
6. de Koven, *Life and Letters,* 1: 341.
7. Ibid., 202.
8. *The Papers of John Paul Jones,* edited by James C. Bradford, nine microfilm reels (Alexandria, Va.: Chadwyck-Healey, 1986), 2: 404.
9. Sherburne, *Life and Character,* 77, 78.
10. *Papers of John Paul Jones,* microfilm reels, 2: 433.
11. Sherburne, *Life and Character,* 81.
12. *Papers of John Paul Jones,* microfilm reels, 3: 459.
13. Letter from John Paul Jones to Le Ray de Chaumont, 16 November 1778, found on Internet, http://www.history.navy.mil/trivia/trivia102.htm. "Famous Navy Quotes." Accessed 9 July 2005.
14. See "frigate" in the Glossary; also see *A Sea of Words,* edited by Dean King with John B. Hattendorf and J. Worth Estes (New York: Henry Holt, 1995), 14, 15, 16.
15. *The Dispatches and Letters of Vice Admiral Lord Viscount Nelson,* edited by Sir Nicholas Harris Nicolas (London: Henry Colburn, 1845; republished by Chatham Publishing, London, 1998), 3: 98.
16. From John Adams's diary entry written on board the Continental ship *Alliance* quoted in Morison, *John Paul Jones,* 201.

5. A Hard Beginning

1. Troyer S. Anderson, *The Command of the Howe Brothers During the American Revolution* (New York: Oxford University Press, 1936), 159. Also David McCullough, *John Adams* (New York: Simon & Schuster, 2001), 154–57.
2. *The Papers of John Paul Jones,* edited by James C. Bradford, nine microfilm reels (Alexandria, Va.: Chadwyck-Healey, 1986), 4: 661.
3. Ibid., 96.
4. *Papers of John Paul Jones,* microfilm reels, 3: 646.
5. Ibid., 659.
6. John Henry Sherburne, *The Life and Character of John Paul Jones,* 2nd ed. (New York: Adriance, Sherman & Co., 1851), 97.

7. *Papers of John Paul Jones,* microfilm reels, 4: 723.
8. Sherburne, *Life and Character,* 102.
9. Don C. Seitz, *Paul Jones: His Exploits in English Seas During 1778–1780—Contemporary Accounts Collected from English Newspapers* (New York: E. P. Dutton, 1917), 35, 36.
10. Ibid., 61.
11. Ibid., 36, 37.
12. *Papers of John Paul Jones,* microfilm reels, 4: 749.
13. Seitz, *Paul Jones,* 42.

6. A Pivot Point of History

1. Serapis, also spelled Sarapis, began as an ancient Egyptian god of the underworld and evolved into a sun god and other religious conceptualizations in ancient Egyptian, Greek, and Roman cultures.
2. See John Ferling, *A Leap in the Dark: The Struggle to Create the American Republic* (Oxford: Oxford University Press, 2003).
3. Don C. Seitz, *Paul Jones: His Exploits in English Seas During 1778–1780—Contemporary Accounts Collected from English Newspapers* (New York: E. P. Dutton, 1917), 44.
4. See Appendix, Report by Captain Richard Pearson of the Battle off Flamborough Head.
5. Round shot was intended to smash hulls and masts. Double-headed shot was intended to tear up sails and rigging. Grapeshot was an antipersonnel munition, and langrage was used both to tear up rigging and for its antipersonnel effects. See the Glossary for definitions of these terms.
6. See Appendix, Description by Commodore Richard Dale of the Battle off Flamborough Head, 213.
7. In a memorandum to his captains before the battle of Trafalgar in October 1805, Vice Admiral Lord Nelson expressed a combat doctrine for his "Band of Brothers": "But, in case Signals can neither be seen or perfectly understood, no Captain can do very wrong if he places his Ship alongside that of an Enemy." See *The Dispatches and Letters of Admiral Lord Viscount Nelson,* edited by Sir Nicholas Harris Nicolas (London: Henry Colburn, 1845; republished by Chatham Publishing, London, 1998), 7: 91.
8. See Appendix, John Paul Jones's Report of His Deployment in *Bonhomme Richard,* 195.
9. Ibid., 206.
10. See Appendix, Report by Captain Richard Pearson, 214.
11. See Appendix, John Paul Jones's Report, 201–2.
12. *The Greenhill Dictionary of Military Quotations,* edited by Peter G. Tsouras (London: Greenhill Books, 2000), 311 (Moral Ascendancy/Moral Force—"Napoleon, 14 June 1817, on St. Helena, quoted in R. M. Johnston, ed., *The Corsican,* 1910").
13. Seitz, *Paul Jones,* 51, 52.
14. *The Dispatches and Letters of Vice Admiral Lord Viscount Nelson,* edited by Sir Nicholas Harris Nicolas (London: Henry Colburn, 1845; republished by Chatham Publishing, London, 1998), 6: 133.

7. Victory's Aftermath

1. *The Papers of Benjamin Franklin,* edited by Leonard W. Labaree et al. (New Haven, Conn.: Yale University Press, 1996), 32: 90–91.
2. Samuel Eliot Morison, *John Paul Jones: A Sailor's Biography* (Boston: Little, Brown, 1959), 258.
3. John Henry Sherburne, *The Life and Character of John Paul Jones,* 2nd ed. (New York: Adriance, Sherman & Co., 1851), 128.
4. *The Papers of John Paul Jones,* edited by James C. Bradford, nine microfilm reels (Alexandria, Va.: Chadwyck-Healey, 1986), 5: 906.
5. Ibid., 936.
6. Morison, *John Paul Jones,* 271, 272.
7. U.S. Naval History Division, *Naval Documents of the American Revolution* (Washington, D.C.: Government Printing Office, 1964), 4: 818; John Paul Jones Papers, reel I, document 17.
8. Mrs. Reginald de Koven, *The Life and Letters of John Paul Jones* (New York: Charles Scribner's Sons, 1913), 2: 61.
9. Ibid., 64.

8. Paris and Celebrity's Cost

1. John Henry Sherburne, *The Life and Character of John Paul Jones,* 2nd ed. (New York: Adriance, Sherman & Co., 1851), 195.
2. Ibid., 193.
3. Don C. Seitz, *Paul Jones: His Exploits in English Seas During 1778–1780—Contemporary Accounts Collected from English Newspapers* (New York: E. P. Dutton, 1917), 51, 52.
4. Ibid., 159.
5. Mrs. Reginald de Koven, *The Life and Letters of John Paul Jones* (New York: Charles Scribner's Sons, 1913), 2: 153.
6. Ibid., 161.
7. Samuel Eliot Morison, *John Paul Jones: A Sailor's Biography* (Boston: Little, Brown, 1959), 293, 294.
8. de Koven, *Life and Letters,* 2: 125.
9. Ibid., 130, 131.
10. *The Papers of John Paul Jones,* edited by James C. Bradford, nine microfilm reels (Alexandria, Va.: Chadwyck-Healey, 1986), 6: 1235.

9. Homecoming

1. Mrs. Reginald de Koven, *The Life and Letters of John Paul Jones* (New York: Charles Scribner's Sons, 1913), 2: 196.
2. John Henry Sherburne, *The Life and Character of John Paul Jones,* 2nd ed. (New York: Adriance, Sherman & Co., 1851), 225.
3. Ibid., 226.
4. *The Papers of John Paul Jones,* edited by James C. Bradford, nine microfilm reels (Alexandria, Va.: Chadwyck-Healey, 1986), 7: 1419.
5. Harold A. Larrabee, *Decision at the Chesapeake* (New York: Clarkson N. Potter, 1964), xiv.
6. See Appendix, Congressional Committee Report on the Promotion of Officers, 217.

7. The Portsmouth boardinghouse in which Jones lived was owned by the widow of Captain Gregory Purcell and is now the headquarters of the Portsmouth Historical Society.
8. Sherburne, *Life and Character,* 229.
9. Ibid., 230–33.
10. Ibid., 234, 235.
11. Ibid., 230.
12. Mahan's *The Influence of Sea Power Upon History* was published initially in 1890 by Little, Brown in Boston and subsequently republished in many editions.
13. Sherburne, *Life and Character,* 23.
14. "Letter to Robert Morris from John Paul Jones," in *John Paul Jones: Commemoration at Annapolis, April 24, 1906,* compiled by Charles W. Stewart (Washington, D.C.: Government Printing Office, 1907), 162.

10. Peace and Paris

1. Internet, http://www.earlyamerica.com/. Milestone Historic Documents, The Paris Peace Treaty of 1783, from Johnson's *Oxford Journal,* England, October 4, 1783. Accessed 5 July 2005.
2. The official "Navy Birthday" is celebrated on 13 October, marking the date in 1775 when the Continental Congress authorized the purchase of two armed ships to attack British commerce and established a Naval Committee to deal with matters related to the Continental Navy.
3. *Joshua Barney, A Biographical Memoir,* edited by Mary Barney (Boston: Gray and Bowen, 1832), 143, 144.
4. Don C. Seitz, *Paul Jones: His Exploits in English Seas During 1778–1780—Contemporary Accounts Collected from English Newspapers* (New York: E. P. Dutton, 1917), 164.
5. Peter Padfield, *Maritime Supremacy and the Opening of the Western Mind* (Woodstock, N.Y.: Overlook Press, 1999), 288.
6. John Ferling, *A Leap in the Dark: The Struggle to Create the American Republic* (Oxford: Oxford University Press, 2003), 293.
7. Mrs. Reginald de Koven, *The Life and Letters of John Paul Jones* (New York: Charles Scribner's Sons, 1913), 2: 176.
8. Samuel Eliot Morison, *John Paul Jones: A Sailor's Biography* (Boston: Little, Brown, 1959), 345.
9. John Henry Sherburne, *The Life and Character of John Paul Jones,* 2nd ed. (New York: Adriance, Sherman & Co., 1851), 284.

11. In Command of a Fleet

1. F. A. Golder, *John Paul Jones in Russia* (New York: Doubleday, Page & Company, 1927), 38.
2. *The Papers of John Paul Jones,* edited by James C. Bradford, nine microfilm reels (Alexandria, Va.: Chadwyck-Healey, 1986), 8: 1724.
3. Prince de Ligne, *Memoirs, Letters, and Miscellaneous Papers,* translated by Katherine P. Wormeley (Boston: Hardy, Pratt & Co., 1899), 70.

4. *The Dispatches and Letters of Vice Admiral Lord Viscount Nelson,* edited by Sir Nicholas Harris Nicolas (London: Henry Colburn, 1846; republished by Chatham Publishing, London, 1998), 7: 55.
5. Golder, *Jones in Russia,* 155.
6. Ibid., 162, 163.
7. Morison, *John Paul Jones,* 377.
8. Golder, *Jones in Russia,* 167.
9. From the original letters of John Paul Jones in the collection of his niece Janette Taylor. See *The Life and Correspondence of John Paul Jones, Including His Narrative of the Campaign of the Liman,* edited by Robert C. Sands (New York: A. Chandler, 1830), 451.
10. Morison, *John Paul Jones,* 381, 382.
11. John Henry Sherburne, *The Life and Character of John Paul Jones,* 2nd ed. (New York: Adriance, Sherman & Co., 1851), 319.
12. Ibid., 300.
13. Ibid., 308.

12. Yesterday's Hero

1. From the original letters of John Paul Jones in the collection of his niece Janette Taylor. See *The Life and Correspondence of John Paul Jones, Including His Narrative of the Campaign of the Liman,* edited by Robert C. Sands (New York: A. Chandler, 1830), 506.
2. Ibid., 533.
3. Correspondence with Edward Bancroft, Library of the Massachusetts Grand Lodge, Masonic Temple of Boston.
4. Sands, *Life and Correspondence,* 401–72.
5. Ibid., 469, 470.
6. F. A. Golder, *John Paul Jones in Russia* (New York: Doubleday, Page & Company, 1927), 217.
7. *The Papers of John Paul Jones,* edited by James C. Bradford, nine microfilm reels (Alexandria, Va.: Chadwyck-Healey, 1986), 8: 1635.
8. Sands, *Life and Correspondence,* 525.
9. Ibid., 545.
10. Golder, *Jones in Russia,* 220.

13. The Coffin without a Nameplate

1. Roosevelt's remarks are printed in *John Paul Jones: Commemoration at Annapolis, April 24, 1906,* compiled by Charles W. Stewart (Washington, D.C.: Government Printing Office, 1907), 44.
2. "Ambassador Porter to the Secretary of State—Telegram," in *John Paul Jones: Commemoration at Annapolis, April 24, 1906,* 44.
3. Porter's remarks are printed in *John Paul Jones: Commemoration at Annapolis, April 24, 1906,* 29.

Epilogue

1. Winston Churchill, speech at Harvard University, 6 September 1943.
2. Thomas Paine, *Common Sense, Addressed to the Inhabitants of America* (Philadelphia: W. and T. Bradford, 1791).

Glossary

abaft: Farther aft (toward the rear), as in "abaft the mainmast."

abeam: In a direction 90 degrees away from the center point on the fore and aft axis line of a ship, as in "the lighthouse was abeam at noon."

admiral: The most senior group of officers in a navy generally referred to as "flag officers" and usually divided into rear admirals, vice admirals, and admirals. During World War II, the United States established a rank of admiral of the fleet, which was senior to the rank of admiral. *See also* commodore.

alee: Toward the lee side (the side of the ship sheltered from the wind).

astern: Directly behind a ship. Also, in the direction of the ship's stern (the rear end of the ship).

asymmetrical warfare: Armed conflict between two nations or opposing forces that are widely separated in their military capabilities.

athwart: Across, meaning in a port to starboard direction in a boat or ship (from side to side).

a-weather: In a direction toward the wind.

backed: A backed sail is set so the wind pressure is on the backside of the sail. Backing sail is a means of slowing or stopping a sailing ship or boat.

barge: In navies in the age of sail, an oared ship's boat of approximately 32 feet that could also be rigged with a sail; was the captain's personal boat. Sometimes used in amphibious and other boat actions. Smaller than the ship's launch and larger than a cutter or pinnace.

beam-ends: The end of the ship's beams. When a ship is "on her beam-ends," she is lying on her side in the water, having tipped over (heeled) approximately 90 degrees. A ship "on her beam-ends" is at or very close to the point of capsizing.

bearing: The direction of an object in relation to a ship. True bearings are indicated by degrees of the compass, as in "the lighthouse bears 190." Relative bearings are indicated in relation to the ship, as in "the lighthouse bears ten degrees off the starboard bow."

beat: Sailing close-hauled on alternate tacks to travel in a cumulative direction directly into the wind.

binnacle: The box near the helm that contains the ship's compass.

boom: A long spar (made of wood during the age of sail) usually used at the bottom of a fore-and-aft sail but also used to position the foot of other sails.

bow: The most forward part of a ship.

bowsprit: In square-rigged ships, the long fore-and-aft pole extending from the ship's bow. Anchors the forestays and the tack (lower forward corner) of the jibs. Also used on fore-and-aft rigged ships and boats to anchor the jibs' tacks.

brig: A two-masted ship (larger mainmast aft and smaller foremast forward), with square sails on both masts and a gaff-rigged fore-and-aft sail on the mainmast. Also the term for a naval prison.

brigantine: A two-masted ship with square sails on the foremast and a large fore-and-aft sail on the mainmast. Usually somewhat smaller than a brig.

bring to: To take turns around a capstan with a line. Also to bring a ship to a stop by heaving to or backing sails.

broadside: The simultaneous or near simultaneous firing of the cannons on one side of a ship.

by the board: Over the side, as in "the foremast went by the board during the storm."

cable: In the age of sail, anchor chain or heavy line used for anchoring or towing. Also a measure of distance equal to about 200 yards.

canister: In the age of sail, a tin can filled with many small iron balls and fired from a cannon, used primarily as an antipersonnel munition.

capstan: A cylinder-shaped device around which a line is wrapped several times, so the line can be hauled in by turning the capstan. In the age of sail, the capstan was turned by several sailors pushing on the capstan bars that were inserted at the top of the device. Usually used for hauling heavy lines, such as the anchor cable.

careening: To beach a ship and force her over on her side in order to repair, clean, or paint the bottom.

carronade: A short barrel, large caliber cannon that was used at short range primarily for smashing the hulls of enemy ships.

chain pump: A manually operated mechanical device consisting of chains and buckets that is used to bail water out of a ship.

chains: In the age of sail, the small built-out sections on the ship where the bottoms of the shrouds were secured.

close-hauled: Sailing with the sails trimmed to allow the ship to sail as close as possible to the direction from which the wind is coming.

cockpit: In a square-rigged warship, the after section of the orlop deck, invariably a dark and unventilated below-decks section. During combat it was the area where the wounded were treated.

come about: To change the direction of sailing by bringing the wind across the ship's bow.

commission pennant: A long thin pennant (also called a "pendant") flown to indicate that the ship is a commissioned navy ship.

commodore: In some navies, the lowest flag officer rank, ranking below rear admiral and above captain. In many navies, the term is used for a captain in charge of a squadron of ships; commodore in those navies is not an official rank.

convoy: A group of merchant ships organized to avoid attack.

coppering: Covering the hull of a ship below the waterline with copper sheeting. Prevented the attack of marine worms and the growth of barnacles and seaweed on the bottom of the hull. A major advance in ship design during the age of sail that increased speed and maneuverability.

corvette: A small warship with a single bank of guns on its exposed main deck.

counter: Overhang of the stern.

crank: Top heavy, making a ship less maneuverable and less seaworthy.

cutter: In the age of sail, an oared ship's boat of approximately 18 feet that could also be rigged with a sail. Used for ship-to-shore transportation of people and light cargo, and sometimes used in amphibious and other boat actions. Smaller than the ship's launch, barge, and pinnace.

double-headed shot: Two cannonballs connected and fired together.

double-shotted: A round of cannon fire with two cannonballs rather than one.

East Indiaman: In the age of sail, a merchant ship that sailed in the regular trade between Europe and the East Indies. Usually relatively large and heavily armed for a merchant ship. Owned by the British, French, or Dutch commercial companies organized to carry out that trade (as in "French East Indiaman"). Usually had gilded sterns with ornate carving.

fathom: Equal to six feet; a nautical term used to indicate the depth of water.

fetch: To reach or arrive at by traveling over the water. Also, the distance over water that the wind blows (the size of waves correlates with the strength of the wind and the wind's fetch).

fid: A pointed wooden hand tool used to separate ("unlay") the strands of a line in order to splice the line.

firth: Scottish term for a long and narrow sea inlet.

fitting out: The process of preparing a ship to go to sea. In a warship of the age of sail the process would have included making needed repairs and adjustments to the hull, rigging, sails, and boats, as well as loading powder, shot, other munitions, small arms, food (possibly including livestock). Recruiting the officers and crew would have been a simultaneous activity.

forecastle: The section of exposed deck that is farthest forward on a ship. Generally where the anchors were handled and secured. Often this is a raised section on a square-rigged ship.

forefoot: The lowest part of the ship's stem.

foremast: On a ship with more than one mast, the mast closest to the bow.

frigate: A three-masted warship that usually mounted between twenty and forty-four guns. Used for such naval tasks as convoy duty, scouting for a fleet, commerce raiding, and a wide variety of other assignments. Frequently operated independently and considered a desirable command for aggressive captains. In the British classification of warships during Jones's day, frigates usually were either fifth-rate (32–44 guns) or sixth-rate (20–28 guns) ships. *See also* heavy frigate.

gaff: A diagonal spar at the top of a four-sided fore-and-aft sail. Full-rigged ships and brigs carried a fore-and-aft "spanker" sail on the mizzenmast, the top of which was attached to a gaff.

galley: Area in a ship where food is prepared. Also, a large low-profile oared boat, generally capable of traveling in the open sea.

grapeshot: Clusters of small iron balls usually wrapped in canvass and fired from cannon for antipersonnel effect.

gunwale: The upper edge of a ship's side; usually extends from the bow to the stern of a ship.

halyard: A line used to hoist a sail, yard, or flag.

hatch (or **hatchway**): An opening in the deck through which cargo can be loaded or a person can move from one deck level to another in a ship.

haul the wind: To trim the sails in order to sail closer to the direction from which the wind is blowing.

"hause": An alternative spelling of "hawse."

hawse: The small deck area between the bow of the ship and the anchor line when the anchor is in the water.

hawser: A heavy line used for towing, warping, or for securing a ship to a pier. Usually more than five inches in circumference.

heave to: To stop a ship by letting it head into the wind and remain in that position. A ship in that position was "hove to."

heavy frigate: During the War of 1812, a term generally used to describe the frigates of the United States Navy designed by Joshua Humphreys. Usually armed with at least forty-four guns (a mixture of 24-pounders and carronades), with thicker, longer, and wider hulls than even the large frigates in other navies. They could outfight other frigates and outrun ships of the line.

heel: The lean of a ship to port or starboard, caused by wind pressure on the sails. Also, the bottom end of a mast or the lower end of a boom.

helm: The long narrow pole (tiller) or the wheel used to control the angle of the rudder and steer a ship.

hold: Large below-decks section where ship's cargo is carried.

hulling: Firing into the hull of a ship with cannons.

in ballast: When a merchant ship is sailing without any cargo.

inshore: Close to the shore; sometimes defined as inside the five-fathom (thirty feet) curve along a coastline.

inside the enemy's decision cycle: Forcing an enemy in war to plan on the basis of your initiatives, rather than vice versa.

jack: *See* union jack.

jib: A triangular sail. On a square-rigged ship, the head is secured at the foremast, the forward lower corner secured at the jib boom, and the lower aft corner is controlled by a line used to adjust the sail depending on the direction of the wind. The line used to adjust (set) the sail is secured on deck. Most square-rigged ships have more than one jib.

jury: In a nautical context, temporary and generally improvised, as in a "jury-rigged mast."

keel: The first timber of a ship to be laid down in construction. The ship is then built out and up from the keel, which forms a kind of "backbone" of the ship. The stem is attached to the forward end, the sternpost is attached to the aft end, and the ribs are built out and up.

keelson: A line of timbers fastened to the top of a ship's keel. The bases of the ship's masts are normally anchored into the keelson, and the lowest deck of the ship rests on the keelson.

langrage: Jagged pieces of iron fired to cut up an enemy's rigging. Also used as an antipersonnel munition.

larboard: In the age of sail, the left (as in "the larboard side") or to the left (as in "to larboard" or "on the larboard hand"). To avoid confusion with the word "starboard," "larboard" was replaced by "port."

launch: In the age of sail, an oared ship's boat of approximately 34 feet that could also be rigged with a sail. Used for ship-to-shore transportation of people and light cargo; sometimes used in amphibious and other boat actions. Larger than the ship's barge, pinnace, and cutter.

lee shore: Any shore downwind of a ship.

lee side: The side farthest away from the direction of the wind.

leeward: In a direction away from the wind, as in "the enemy ship was to leeward," or "we were drifting to leeward."

leeway: The sideways drift of a ship under sail, caused by the wind and always driving the ship downwind.

letter of marque: Written authorization provided by a government to a privateer for the privateer to attack and seize enemy ships.

lie to: To bring a sailing ship to a stop by heading directly into the wind, or, in a square-rigged ship, to come to a stop by backing (trimming the sail in the opposite direction than normal, so the wind pressure on the sail stops forward motion). By trimming some sails to provide potential forward motion and balancing them with some sails backed, a ship could effectively lie to for an extended period.

line of battle: In the seventeenth and eighteenth centuries, naval battles between fleets were generally begun by two opposing single lines of ships of the line (generally ships of fifty guns of more). Prior to the battle, one of the initial tactical maneuvers of a commodore or an admiral was to assemble his ships in a line of battle.

lower decks: Decks below the main deck. The ordinary seamen were quartered here, hence the term was also used to refer to crew members who were not officers.

luff: The leading edge of a fore-and-aft sail. "To luff" means to bring the bow into the wind or to slack off a sheet to cause the sails to flutter.

main brace: Lines attached to the ends of the yardarm from which the mainsail is hung. Used to control ("set") the sail.

mainmast: In the age of sail, the center and largest mast in a ship with three masts. The farthest aft and largest mast in a ship with two masts.

mainsail: The lowest and largest sail on the mainmast.
marlinspike: A pointed wood or metal hand tool used to separate (unlay) the strands of a line in order to splice the line.
mast: A vertical pole extending from the ship's keelson upward over the open decks of the ship. Yards and booms were attached to masts.
mercantilism: Economic theory practiced by European powers from the sixteenth to eighteenth centuries and based on trade. Among the principles were (1) a nation's wealth is based on precious metals, (2) the value of exported goods should exceed that of imports, (3) colonies should provide markets for a nation's finished products as well as raw materials for the industry of the mother country. This theory was articulated by Adam Smith in *Wealth of Nations* (1776).
mizzenmast: The shortest mast on a ship with two or more masts.

offing: In a ship, the distance maintained off an area of land. Also, the distant part of the sea visible from an anchorage or a point on shore.
orlop deck: The lowest deck of a ship. Also called simply "orlop."

packet: A passenger, mail, and light cargo ship that sailed over a regular route.
pay off: To move to leeward.
pendant: A special signal flag; a particularly long variation flown at the masthead signified that the ship was a commissioned naval ship, and a conventionally sized, rectangular version ("broad pendant") was flown to indicate the ship had a commodore or admiral aboard (thus the term "flagship").
pennant: Same as "pendant."
pinnace: An oared ship's boat of approximately 28 feet that could also be rigged with a sail. Used for ship-to-shore transportation of people and light cargo; sometimes used in amphibious and other boat actions. Larger than the ship's cutter and smaller than the ship's launch and barge.
point: The end of a narrow piece of land jutting into the sea. Also one of thirty-two equal segments used to identify a relative direction, as in "two points off the starboard bow."
poop deck: The short exposed deck at the stern of the ship, located aft and somewhat higher than the quarterdeck. Because of its height, it was an advantageous position and frequently used as a position for sharpshooters firing into an enemy ship that was close aboard.
port: In nautical context, the left (as in "the port side") or to the left (as in "to port" or "on the port hand").

powder monkey: Young seamen designated to carry the prepared bags of powder from the ship's magazine to the individual guns during battle.

press-gang: A small group of seamen, led by an officer or petty officer, dedicated to forcibly "enlisting" men into the crew of a ship, often from waterfront taverns and other sites along the waterfront.

privateer: A privately owned warship that was usually provided with letters of marque by the country for which she fought. Also, those who fought in privateers. Commissioned naval officers generally held privateers in low esteem.

prize: In the age of sail, any warship or merchant ship captured at sea and sold to the benefit of her captors.

prize crew: In the age of sail, a small crew put on board a prize ship by her captor to sail her to a port where she could be sold for prize money.

prize money: In the age of sail, the money received for the sale of a prize ship. The money was distributed in fixed percentages to the captain, officers, and crew of the captor. Under certain circumstances, a percentage of the prize money was also distributed to the admiral in whose squadron or fleet the captor was assigned.

quarter: The ship's side close to the stern.

quarterdeck: In the age of sail, the area of the upper deck between the mainmast and the poop deck. While under way, the officer on watch in command of the ship and others involved with his duties (and at times the captain) operated from this area. The windward half of the quarterdeck was the exclusive domain of the captain and others entered this area only if invited by the captain or if their duties required it.

reach: To sail with the wind coming over the ship's port or starboard quarter.

reef (to): To shorten (reduce) sail in heavy weather by using horizontal rows of short ties sewn into the sails.

roadstead or road: An anchorage. Frequently used in combination with another word, such as "Roadtown" or "Hampton Roads."

royal: In a square-rigged ship, the sail or mast above the topgallant. From the main deck up: mainsail, topsail, topgallant, royal.

run: To sail with the wind coming directly over the ship's stern.

schooner: Generally a working sailing ship, initially with two masts but later with three or more. Schooners carried fore-and-aft sails and sometimes one or more small square topsails. They were fast and could sail closer to the wind and were more maneuverable than square-rigged ships. Used for fishing, carrying small cargo loads, and, at times, armed and used for military purposes.

sheet: A line secured to a sail that is used to adjust the sail.

ship (also **full-rigged ship**): In the age of sail, a ship with three masts (foremast, mainmast, mizzenmast), with square sails on all masts, plus a fore-and-aft gaff-rigged sail on the mizzenmast.

ship of the line: A warship in the age of sail large enough to fight in the line of battle; usually carried between fifty and one hundred or more guns. In the British system of rating warships at the time, ships of the line were fourth-, third-, second-, and first-rate (the largest) ships.

shrouds: Heavy ropes extending from the top or upper part of a mast to the port and starboard sides of a ship. The shrouds prevent the masts from falling to one side or the other of a ship, in contrast to stays, which prevent the mast from falling forward or aft. The shrouds were used to form ratlines on which sailors climbed or descended from aloft.

sloop of war: In the age of sail, any small ship that did not fit into other categories of warships at the time. Later came to mean a relatively small sailing ship with one mainsail and smaller triangular headsails.

slops: Clothing and other utilitarian items that were carried aboard ship for sale to the crew members.

spar: A generic term for the long pieces that are used to support the sails and rigging of a ship (wooden pieces, in the age of sail). Include but not limited to yards and booms.

spritsail: On a square-rigged ship, a relatively small four-sided sail rigged with a diagonal spar.

squadron: A group of ships assigned to a specific mission. Also, separate portions of a fleet, as in the three squadrons comprising the van, center, and rear of a fleet formed into a line of battle.

stand off: For a ship to remain at a distance from a point or object.

stand off and on: To alternately steer away from a point of land and then toward the same point in order to remain in approximately the same position over a period of time.

starboard: The right (as in "the starboard side") or to the right (as in "to starboard" or "on the starboard hand").

stays: Heavy ropes extending from the top or a high point on a mast to prevent the mast from falling forward or aft. Triangular fore-and-aft headsails were attached to forestays. *See also* shrouds.

steerageway: To have sufficient speed through the water to steer with the rudder.

stem: In a nautical context, the curved upright timber that forms the most forward part of the ship—the leading edge of the bow.

stern: In a nautical context, the rear (aft) end of a ship.

sternpost: A vertical or nearly vertical beam attached to the aft end of the keel. In the latter stages of ship construction in the age of sail, the rudder would have been attached to the sternpost.

supercargo: A person aboard a ship who was in charge of selling and buying cargo.

tack: Direction of sailing when the wind is coming from a point forward of midships, thus "port tack" or "starboard tack." Can also refer to the act of changing direction (coming about) with the wind moving across the ship's bow.

tackle: An arrangement of ropes and pulleys (blocks). Also "ground tackle," the combination of anchor, line, and equipment used in anchoring.

top: A horizontal platform at the head of each lower mast of a ship.

top (fighting): A top manned by sharpshooters, sailors with hand grenades, and sailors manning small swivel cannons used for firing grapeshot into enemy personnel.

topmast: A mast that stands on top of the foremast, mainmast, or mizzenmast, as in foretopmast, maintopmast, mizzentopmast.

topsail: On a square-rigged ship, the sail above the lowest sail on the mast, as in foretopsail, maintopsail, and mizzentopsail.

transom: The flat, vertical stern of a ship that meets the sides at an approximately 90-degree angle.

triangle trade: In the eighteenth century, trade involving ships sailing in a triangle pattern that included these three routes: England-West Indies-Colonial America-England; England-West Africa-West Indies-England; New England-West Africa-West Indies-New England. Trade that included West Africa involved slaves. Trade items included sugar, molasses, rum, tobacco, and other products. Variations in the pattern included England-West Africa-West Indies-American Colonies-England, for example.

union jack: A small flag, usually flown in addition to the national ensign. Modern U.S. Navy practice is to fly the union jack on a staff at a ship's bow while anchored or moored alongside a pier; it is not flown while under way.

The modern union jack is the blue rectangular portion of the national ensign with fifty stars. During particular periods, such as the first Gulf War, a special union jack with a rattlesnake and the words "Don't Tread on Me" was used. A similar union jack with a rattlesnake and the words "Don't Tread on Me" was used by the Continental Navy's first ship, *Alfred.*

van: The front, as in "the van of the line of battle."

waist: In a nautical context, the middle section of the main deck of a ship (between the quarterdeck and the forecastle).

wardroom: The dining area in a ship for commissioned and warrant officers. Also an area at a naval base used for the same purpose.

warp: The most common usage: a line attached to a fixed point and used to pull a ship toward that point; when a sailing vessel was becalmed it could be moved ahead slowly by repeatedly rowing the anchor ahead, dropping it and then hauling the ship up to the anchor.

wear: To change the course of a ship by steering to bring the wind across the ship's stern.

weather gage: To be upwind of an enemy ship.

weather side: The side of a ship closest to the direction of the wind.

weigh: To lift the anchor, as in "prepare to weigh anchor."

weight of metal: The sum of the number of guns, plus the weight of each cannonball (32-pound, 12-pound, etc.) a ship can fire from its armament; thus, a measure of the firepower of a ship, squadron, or fleet.

windward: The side of a ship closest to the direction of the wind (same as "weather side"). Also, toward the direction of the wind, as in "going to windward."

yard: A spar that runs athwartship and supports a square sail.

yardarm: Either end of a yard. Sometimes used to mean the entire yard.

Bibliography

Abbot, Willis J. *The Naval History of the United States,* two volumes. New York: Peter Fenelon Collier, 1886.

Anderson, Troyer Steele. *The Command of the Howe Brothers During the American Revolution.* New York: Oxford University Press, 1936.

Barnes, G. R. and J. H. Owen, editors. *The Sandwich Papers,* four volumes. The Navy (of Great Britain) Records Society. London: William Clowes & Sons, 1932–38.

Boudriot, Jean, translated by David H. Roberts. *Bonhomme Richard 1779* (monograph and 26 plans of *Bonhomme Richard*). Paris: self-published by Jean Boudriot, 1987.

———. *John Paul Jones and the Bonhomme Richard.* Annapolis, Md.: Naval Institute Press, 1987.

Bradford, James C. *The Reincarnation of John Paul Jones: The Navy Discovers Its Professional Roots.* Washington, D.C.: Naval Historical Foundation, 1986.

Calomb, P. H., Vice Admiral, Royal Navy. *Naval Warfare: Its Ruling Principles and Practice Historically Treated,* two volumes. London: W. H. Allen & Co., 1891. (Reprinted by Naval Institute Press, Annapolis, 1990.)

Canney, Donald L. *Sailing Warships of the US Navy.* Annapolis, Md.: Naval Institute Press, 2001.

Chapelle, Howard I. *The History of the American Sailing Navy: The Ships and Their Development.* New York: W. W. Norton, 1949.

Clowes, William Laird. *The Royal Navy: A History from the Earliest Times to 1900,* volumes three and four. London: Sampson Low, Marston and Company, 1898. (Republished by Chatham Publishing, Rochester, England, 1996.)

Corbett, Julian S. *Some Principles of Maritime Strategy.* London: Longmans, Green and Co., 1911. (Republished by Naval Institute Press, Annapolis, 1988.)

de Koven, Mrs. Reginald. *The Life and Letters of John Paul Jones,* two volumes. New York: Charles Scribner's Sons, 1913.

Engle, Eloise and Arnold S. Lott. *American Military Heritage.* Annapolis, Md.: Naval Institute Press, 1975.

Ferguson, Niall. *Empire: The Rise and Demise of the British World Order and the Lessons for Global Power.* London: Allen Lane, 2002.

Ferling, John. *A Leap in the Dark: The Struggle to Create the American Republic.* Oxford: Oxford University Press, 2003.

Frost, John. *The Book of the Navy; Comprising a General History of the American Marine.* New York: D. Appleton & Company, 1842.

Gilkerson, William. *The Ships of John Paul Jones.* Annapolis, Md.: The United States Naval Academy Museum and Naval Institute Press, 1987.

Golder, F. A. *John Paul Jones in Russia.* Garden City, N.Y.: Doubleday, Page & Company, 1927.

Gray, Colin S. *The Leverage of Sea Power: The Strategic Advantage of Navies in War.* New York: The Free Press, 1992.

Hagen, Kenneth J. *This People's Navy: The Making of American Sea Power.* New York: The Free Press, 1991.

Hearn, Chester G. *George Washington's Schooners: The First American Navy.* Annapolis, Md.: Naval Institute Press, 1995.

———. *An Illustrated History of the United States Navy.* London: Salamander Books, 2002.

Henderson, James. *The Frigates: An Account of the Lesser Warships of the Great French Wars, 1793–1815.* London: Adlard Coles, 1970.

Hill, J. R., ed. *The Oxford Illustrated History of the Royal Navy.* Oxford: Oxford University Press, 1995.

Hill, Richard. *The Prizes of War: The Naval Prize System in the Napoleonic Wars, 1793–1815.* Gloucestershire: Sutton Publishing in association with the Royal Naval Museum, 1998.

Holland, W. J., Jr., Rear Admiral, USN (Ret.), editor. *The Navy.* Washington, D.C.: Naval Historical Foundation/Hugh Lauter Levin Associates, 2000.

Kennedy, Paul M., *The Rise and Fall of British Naval Mastery.* London: Allen Lane, 1976.

King, Dean. *A Sea of Words: A Lexicon and Companion for Patrick O'Brian's Seafaring Tales.* New York: Henry Holt, 1995.

Knox, Dudley W. *The Naval Genius of George Washington.* Boston: Houghton Mifflin, 1932.

Labaree, Benjamin W., William M. Fowler, Jr.; Edward W. Sloan, John B. Hattendorf, Jeffrey J. Safford, and Andrew W. German. *America and the Sea: A Maritime History.* Mystic, Conn.: Mystic Seaport Museum, 1998.

Larrabee, Harold A. *Decision at the Chesapeake.* New York: Clarkson N. Potter, 1964.

Lehman, John. *On Seas of Glory: Heroic Men, Great Ships, and Epic Battles of the American Navy.* New York: The Free Press, 2001.

Lorenz, Lincoln. *John Paul Jones: Fighter for Freedom and Glory.* Annapolis, Md.: Naval Institute Press, 1943.

Mackesy, Piers. *The War for America.* Cambridge, Mass.: Harvard University Press, 1964.

Mahan, A. T. *The Influence of Sea Power upon History.* Boston: Little, Brown, 1890.

Marion, H. *John Paul Jones' Last Cruise and Final Resting Place.* Washington, D.C.: George E. Howard, 1906.

McCullough, David. *John Adams.* New York: Simon & Schuster, 2001.

Millar, John Fitzhugh. *Early American Ships.* Williamsburg, Va.: Thirteen Colonies Press, 1986.

Miller, Nathan. *Sea of Glory.* Annapolis, Md.: Naval Institute Press, 1992.

———. *The U.S. Navy: An Illustrated History.* New York: American Heritage Publishing Co., and Annapolis, Md.: Naval Institute Press, 1977.

Modelski, George and William R. Thompson. *Seapower in Global Politics, 1494–1993.* London: Macmillan Press, 1988.

Morison, Samuel Eliot. *John Paul Jones: A Sailor's Biography.* Boston: Little, Brown, 1959.

The Naval Battles of the United States in the Different Wars With Foreign Nations, from the Commencement of the Revolution to the Present Time: Including Privateering. Boston: Higgins, Bradley, and Dayton, 1858.

Nicolas, Sir Nicholas Harris, editor. *The Dispatches and Letters of Vice Admiral Lord Viscount Nelson,* seven volumes. London: Henry Colburn, 1844–46. (Republished by Chatham Publishing, Rochester, England, 1997.)

O'Brian, Patrick. *Men-of-War: Life in Nelson's Navy,* first American edition. New York: W. W. Norton, 1995.

Otis, James, editor and compiler. *The Life of John Paul Jones.* New York: The Perkins Book Company, 1900.

Owen, John B. *The Eighteenth Century 1714–1815.* New York: W. W. Norton, 1974.

Padfield, Peter. *Maritime Supremacy and the Opening of the Western Mind.* Woodstock, N.Y.: Overlook Press, 1999.

Palmer, Joseph, compiler. *Jane's Dictionary of Naval Terms.* London: Macdonald and Jane's, 1975.

Potter, E. B. and Chester W. Nimitz, editors. *Sea Power: A Naval History.* Englewood Cliffs, N.J.: Prentice-Hall, 1960.

Reynolds, Clark G. *Famous American Admirals.* New York: Van Nostrand Reinhold, 1978. (Republished by Naval Institute Press, Annapolis, 2002.)

Robinson, William. *Jack Nastyface: Memoirs of an English Seaman.* London: self-published by William Robinson, 1836. (Republished by Wayland, London, and Naval Institute Press, Annapolis, 1973.)

Sands, Robert C., editor. *The Life and Correspondence of John Paul Jones, Including His Narrative of the Campaign of the Liman.* New York: A. Chandler, 1830.

Sawtelle, Joseph G., editor. *John Paul Jones and the* Ranger. Portsmouth, N.H.: Portsmouth Marine Society, 2002.

Seitz, Don C. *Paul Jones: His Exploits in English Seas During 1778–1780.* New York: E. P. Dutton, 1917.

Sherburne, John Henry. *The Life and Character of John Paul Jones,* 2nd ed. New York: Adriance, Sherman & Co., 1851.

Silverstone, Paul H. *The Sailing Navy, 1775–1854.* Annapolis, Md.: Naval Institute Press, 2001.

Spears, John R. *History of the United States Navy: From Its Origin to the Present Day, 1775–1897,* four volumes. London: Bickers & Son, 1898.

Spiller. Roger J., editor. *Dictionary of American Military Biography,* three volumes. Westport, Conn.: Greenwood Press, 1984.

Stewart, Charles W., compiler. *John Paul Jones: Commemoration at Annapolis, April 24, 1906.* Washington, D.C.: Government Printing Office, 1907.

Sweetman, Jack. *American Naval History: An Illustrated Chronology of the U.S. Navy and Marine Corps, 1775–Present,* third edition. Annapolis, Md.: Naval Institute Press, 2002.

Thomas, Evan. *John Paul Jones: Sailor, Hero, Father of the American Navy.* New York: Simon & Schuster, 2003.

Westcott, Allan, editor. *Mahan on Naval Warfare: Selections from the Writings of Rear Admiral Alfred T. Mahan.* London: Sampson Low, Marston and Company, 1919.

Woodman, Richard. *The Sea Warriors: Fighting Captains and Frigate Warfare in the Age of Nelson.* London: Constable, 2001.

Index

Note: Page numbers followed by the letter *f* in italics signify a figure on that page.

About the Author

Joseph F. Callo was commissioned from the Yale Naval Reserve Officers Training Corps and served two years of sea duty with the U.S. Navy's Atlantic Amphibious Forces. After thirty-plus years of duty as a naval reservist, he retired as a rear admiral. Before writing full time, Callo was a senior executive with major advertising agencies and an award-winning freelance television producer and writer. Callo, who learned to sail at age thirteen, skippers sailboats up to fifty feet in length in the Caribbean and has crewed in the full-scale reproduction of Captain Cook's square-rigged *Endeavour.*

Callo, *Naval History* magazine's 1998 Author of the Year, contributed to *The Trafalgar Companion* (Osprey Publishing, 2005) and is the U.S. editor/author for *Who's Who in Naval History* (Routledge, 2004). The Naval Institute Press published Callo's *Nelson in the Caribbean: The Hero Emerges, 1785–1787* (2002) and *Nelson Speaks: Admiral Lord Nelson in His Own Words* (2001). He has also published *Legacy of Leadership: Lessons from Admiral Lord Nelson* (Hellgate Press, 1999), along with articles in a variety of magazines and newspapers.

The Naval Institute Press is the book-publishing arm of the U.S. Naval Institute, a private, nonprofit, membership society for sea service professionals and others who share an interest in naval and maritime affairs. Established in 1873 at the U.S. Naval Academy in Annapolis, Maryland, where its offices remain today, the Naval Institute has members worldwide.

Members of the Naval Institute support the education programs of the society and receive the influential monthly magazine *Proceedings* and discounts on fine nautical prints and on ship and aircraft photos. They also have access to the transcripts of the Institute's Oral History Program and get discounted admission to any of the Institute-sponsored seminars offered around the country.

The Naval Institute also publishes *Naval History* magazine. This colorful bimonthly is filled with entertaining and thought-provoking articles, first-person reminiscences, and dramatic art and photography. Members receive a discount on *Naval History* subscriptions.

The Naval Institute's book-publishing program, begun in 1898 with basic guides to naval practices, has broadened its scope to include books of more general interest. Now the Naval Institute Press publishes about one hundred titles each year, ranging from how-to books on boating and navigation to battle histories, biographies, ship and aircraft guides, and novels. Institute members receive significant discounts on the Press's more than eight hundred books in print.

Full-time students are eligible for special half-price membership rates. Life memberships are also available.

For a free catalog describing Naval Institute Press books currently available, and for further information about subscribing to *Naval History* magazine or about joining the U.S. Naval Institute, please write to: